GUERRILLA ECONOMY

GUERRILLA ECONOMY

The Development of
the Shensi-Kansu-Ninghsia
Border Region, 1937-1945

Peter Schran

State University of New York Press
Albany, 1976

First published in 1976 by
State University of New York Press
99 Washington Avenue, Albany, New York 12210

Library of Congress Cataloging in Publication Data
Schran, Peter.
Guerrilla economy : the development of the Shensi-
Kansu-Ninghsia border region, 1937-1945.

Bibliography: p.
1. Sino-Japanese Conflict, 1937-1945—Economic
aspects. 2. China—Economic conditions—1912-1949.
3. China—Statistics. I. Title.
HC427.8.S3   1976   330.9'51'43042   75-45052
ISBN 0-87395-344-4

To Tina, Mary-Ann, and Steven

Contents

Preface

From the fall of the Ch'ing Dynasty till the rise of the People's Republic, China passed through an interregnum, a modern "warring kingdoms" period. This study considers the economic problems which one of the contenders for a new order, the Chinese communist movement, had to solve during those years in order to persevere against the others and emerge victorious in the end. It relates for this purpose an outline of what might be termed the "economics of insurgency" to the area and era of Yenan, i.e., the Shensi-Kansu-Ninghsia Border Region 1937-1945. The history of this base during the Sino-Japanese War appears in such a perspective as a special case of economic development, made unusual by the circumstances of the war as well as by extreme economic backwardness.

The study's principal conclusion is that the communists developed a particular strategy and related tactics which were quite effective in meeting the basic needs not only of the communist movement but also of the base-area people. Their ability to generate both popular political support and logistic supplies helps first of all explain the Chinese communists' rise to power. More generally, of course, their strategy suggests interpretations for similar wars of "national liberation" elsewhere in the world.

In addition, the study's findings contribute to an understanding of Chinese communist economic policies since the formation of the People's Republic. For my view of the relationship between guerrilla experiences and events such as the Great Leap Forward, the interested reader is referred to my essay "On the Yenan Origins of Current Economic Policies" in *China's Mod-*

ern Economy in Historical Perspective, edited by Dwight H. Perkins, Stanford: Stanford University Press, 1975.

From beginning to end, the study has been aided greatly by many people. I am deeply indebted to the Center for International Comparative Studies and the Research Board of the University of Illinois at Urbana-Champaign for repeated financial support. Librarians everywhere and notably Ernst Wolff of the University of Illinois Library have gone out of their way to provide me with materials. Several colleagues and especially my friend Fred Gottheil have spent a good deal of time discussing with me earlier interpretations of my findings. Preliminary drafts of chapters 3 and 4 have benefitted from the comments of seminar audiences. And Robert Crawford, Lloyd Eastman, Charles Hoffman, Mark Selden, John Service, Koji Taira, plus the anonymous readers of the Press have read the next-to-final draft and suggested numerous improvements. I am profoundly grateful to all of them. The remaining errors and omissions are mine.

Peter Schran

WEIGHTS AND MEASURES

One bolt (p'i) of cloth	=35.8m × 0.86m	Customs norm
	=32.3m × 0.78m	SKN standard
One cask (t'ung) of oil	=5 gallons	SKN standard
	=18.9265 liters	
One catty (chin)	=0.500 kg	SKN standard
	=0.457 kg	Tingpien, 1930
	=0.597 kg	Hsunyi, 1931
One hectare (ha)	=2.471 acres	
One kilogram (kg)	=2.205 pounds	
One kilometer (km)	=2 li	
	=0.621 miles	
One sq. kilometer (km²)	=0.386 sq. miles	
One load of salt	=150 big catties	SKN standard
	=225 regular catties	
	=112.5 kg	
One meter (m)	=39.37 inches	
One mou of land	=0.0614 ha	Buck's standard
	=0.06067 ha	Tingpien, 1930
	=0.06574 ha	Hsunyi, 1931
	=0.0667 ha	SKN standard?
One picul (tan) of grain	=300 catties	SKN standard
	=150 kg	

ABBREVIATIONS

CCP: Chinese Communist Party
KMT: Kuomintang (Chinese Nationalist Party)
SKN: Shensi-Kansu-Ninghsia (Border Region)

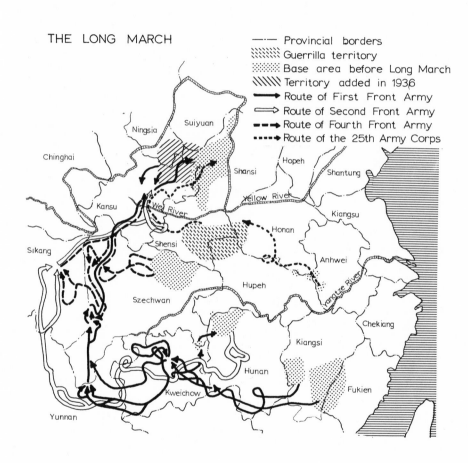

THE LONG MARCH

—·— Provincial borders
Guerrilla territory
Base area before Long March
Territory added in 1936
Route of First Front Army
Route of Second Front Army
Route of Fourth Front Army
Route of the 25th Army Corps

Chinghai

Ningsia

Suiyuan

Shansi

Hopeh

Shantung

Kansu

Wei River

Yellow River

Kiangsu

Shensi

Honan

Sikang

Anhwei

Hupeh

Yangtze River

Szechwan

Chekiang

Kiangsi

Hunan

Fukien

Kweichow

Yunnan

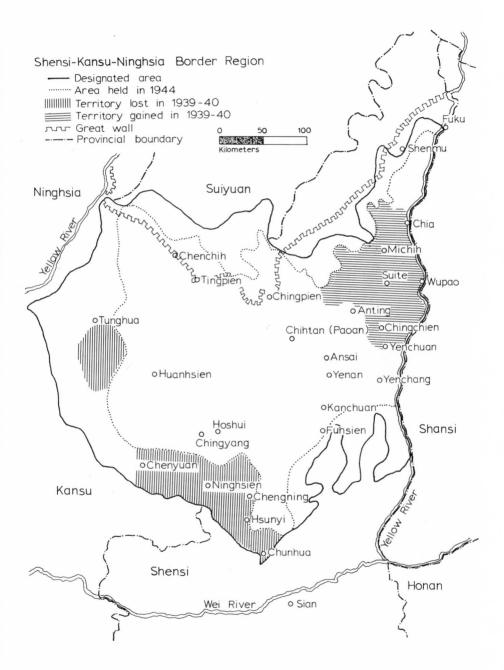

Shensi-Kansu-Ninghsia Border Region
—— Designated area
········· Area held in 1944
||||||||| Territory lost in 1939-40
≡≡≡≡ Territory gained in 1939-40
ᴵⁿⁿⁿ Great wall
—·—·— Provincial boundary

0   50   100
Kilometers

Ninghsia

Suiyuan

Yellow River

Chenchih
Tingpien
Chingpien
Anting
Tunghua
Chihtan (Paoan)
Chingchien
Yenchuan
Ansai
Huanhsien
Yenan
Yenchang
Kanchuan
Hoshui
Fuhsien
Chingyang
Shansi
Chenyuan
Ninghsien
Chengning
Kansu
Hsunyi
Chunhua
Shensi
Yellow River
Wei River
Sian
Honan

Fuku
Shenmu
Chia
Michih
Suite
Wupao

Tables

I

Introduction

The Chinese communists' rise to power on the Chinese mainland has focussed much attention on two acknowledged causes of this extraordinary event: agrarian revolution and national liberation. It also has evoked substantial interest in their political-military *modus operandi*: mass mobilization for armed struggle in the form of guerrilla warfare. In contrast, their success has generated little interest in the protraction of the struggle and its principal consequence: the need to solve economic problems in order to sustain and advance the process of gradual conquest.

The Guerrilla Period

The struggle in the countryside lasted for more than twenty years, and it had its most fantastic ups as well as downs. When it started, in 1927, the Chinese communist movement was in extreme difficulties. Most of its urban strongholds had been destroyed or severely impaired, many of its members had been liquidated or driven underground, and its former revolutionary strategy had become impracticable. It was in such desperate circumstances that the movement had to reorient itself toward a strategic alternative which some of its members — in particular Mao Tse-tung — had been exploring for some time. Mao himself described the revolutionary climate in the countryside and the prospects for a rural revolutionary strategy in his "Report on an Investigation of the Peasant Movement in Hunan" of March 1927. His report stated the principal finding of this investigation in powerful words:

> All talk directed against the peasant movement must be speedily set right. All the wrong measures taken by the

revolutionary authorities concerning the peasant movement must be speedily changed. Only thus can the future
of the revolution be benefited. For the present-upsurge
of the peasant movement is a colossal event. In a very
short time, in China's central, southern and northern
provinces, several hundred million peasants will rise like
a mighty storm, like a hurricane, a force so swift and
violent that no power, however great, will be able to hold
it back. They will smash all the trammels that bind them
and rush forward along the road to liberation. They will
sweep all the imperialists, warlords, corrupt officials,
local tyrants and evil gentry into their graves. Every
revolutionary party and every revolutionary comrade
will be put to the test, to be accepted or rejected as they
decide. There are three alternatives. To march at their
head and lead them? To trail behind them, gesticulating
and criticizing? Or to stand in their way and oppose
them? Every Chinese is free to choose, but events will
force you to make the choice quickly.[1]

Those who chose with Mao the first alternative soon took to
the countryside in order to foment the "autumn harvest uprising" of the same year. The remaining activists of this campaign
persevered through the following winter in the Chingkang Mountains and other remote areas, where they established the first
regular base areas in the form of soviets. From such small
beginnings, the rural revolutionary activities spread like "prairie
fire" in South-Central China, against numerous obstacles within
and without. As a consequence, the base areas multiplied and
expanded rapidly in spite of severe difficulties. After merely six
years, when the process of expansion reached a maximum, the
six South-Central soviets incorporated territories inhabited by
nine million persons according to Mao Tse-tung[2] and were said
to field a Red Army of 350,000 fighters plus 600,000 militia.[3]

Needless to say, this development had not been thought out
fully in advance, and it also did not occur in a vacuum. Rather,
many particulars of the agrarian revolution, soviet organization,
military strategy, and economic policy had to be solved as they
emerged by trial and error. Such problems tended to pit the
"generalist" or "dogmatist" advisors of the COMINTERN

against the "specialist" or "pragmatist" practitioners in the base areas, apparently to the increasing detriment of the latter. The extent of the conflict and the related question of Mao's originality as a Marxist theorist, which have been researched repeatedly,[4] need not be explored once more. But it should be noted that the differences were sufficiently real for Mao to be able to dissociate himself from the debacle of 1934 and to attribute it to mistaken policies of the COMINTERN-sponsored CCP leadership of "Russian-returned students" who had taken over command in the base areas since 1931.

In 1934, after six years of escalating military efforts, the Kuomintang government of the host state made extraordinary headway in its fifth "encirclement and suppression" campaign against the communist base areas. The campaign failed to achieve its principal objective, the annihilation of the communist movement in the countryside, because the Red Army managed to break out of the encirclement. But it made the situation of the communists in the Central South untenable and forced them to embark on their famous Long March to a new base area in the Northwest which until then had been a minor center of rural revolution.[5] During the course of this forcible relocation, Mao Tse-tung rose once more to the force of the movement. The magnitude of the setback is indicated by the estimates that after the consolidation of all forces and the expansion of base-area territory during 1935-36, the newly formed Northwest Soviet had a population of 1.4 million persons[6] and a Red Army of perhaps less than 50,000 fighters.[7]

The situation of the Chinese communist movement thus looked bleak indeed, even to so sympathetic an observer as Edgar Snow. But the Japanese aggression changed all that soon thereafter—drastically and fast. The agreement on a united front to resist Japan, reached after the kidnapping of Chiang Kai-shek in Sian in December 1936 and never fully spelled out, terminated all civil strife for the time being. It obligated the Chinese communists to stop their agrarian revolutionary practices. In return, it secured their headquarters area in the Northwest, now renamed the Shensi-Kansu-Ninghsia Border Region and subordinated *pro forma* to the national government as a special administrative unit. In addition, it provided logistic support for the three divisions (45,000 troops) of the Red Army, now re-named the Eighth Route Army and placed *pro forma* under the national military command.

Most importantly, however, the united front agreement gave the Chinese communist movement the seemingly legitimate op-portunity to infiltrate the Japanese occupied territory and to organize "anti-Japanese base areas" which resembled in many respects the soviets of before. The Chinese communists tried hard to make the most of this opportunity, and once more they apparently experienced spectacular initial successes. The base areas behind Japanese lines proliferated and expanded so that by 1940 they contained 100,000,000 people and supported 500,000 troops according to Mao Tse-tung.[8]

Such advances irritated not only the Japanese but also the Kuomintang-dominated national government. The Japanese, who found their rear operations interfered with by expanding and intensifying guerrilla warfare, waged an extermination campaign which produced a substantial contraction of com-munist-held territory during the following two years. The popu-lation of the various base areas shrank to less than 50,000,000 people, and the number of troops declined to 300,000 men, again according to Mao Tse-tung.[9]

The national government and the Kuomintang worried not only about the war against Japan but also about postwar rela-tions with the communists. They therefore treated the growth of communist-dominated base areas and communist-commanded armies as a violation of the *status quo* provisions of the united front agreement. Unable to keep the communists by any other means from building their strength for the future as well as for the present conflict, the national government reverted to limited hostilities against them, at the same time that the Japanese mounted their campaign. The deterioration of relations result-ed not only in the famous New Fourth Army incident, but also in the termination of all support for the Eighth Route Army, in the reimposition of a partial blockade on the Shensi-Kansu-Ningshia Border Region, and even in the occupation of some of its territory (to which the communists responded in kind).

Neither the retaliation of the Japanese military nor the re-newed hostility of the Kuomintang government seems to have come as a surprise to the communist leadership. Nevertheless, both events found the communist movement at large less than fully prepared. To cope with the consequent setbacks in a hurry and to guard as much as possible against their recurrence, Mao Tse-tung and his followers initiated a "rectification" campaign which drew in many respects on the lessons learned in Kiangsi and on the Long March.[10] Its principal intent was to modify the behavior not only of the communist movement but also of the people in the base areas, so that both would be mobilized for the cause of national liberation under "new democratic" auspices, and to such degrees that they would become highly invulnerable to the combined onslaught.

Mao Tse-tung and his followers were evidently successful in this undertaking.[11] Moreover, their efforts were facilitated by Japan's growing preoccupation with the Pacific theater of war as well as by the Kuomintang's continuing inability to adapt to similar circumstances on a larger scale. It was thus for external as well as internal causes that the base areas expanded again. In spring 1945, when the end of the Pacific War appeared in sight, they were said to contain once more a population of 94,000,000 persons.[12] At the same time, they were reported to field an even larger army than ever before, viz. 900,000 regular troops plus 2,200,000 militia.[13] On the eve of the resumption of civil war, the Chinese communist movement thus possessed unprecedented strength.

The Economic Problem

To build and maintain this strength with the resources of their base areas proved to be a continuous headache for the Chinese communists. The complexity of the task becomes apparent in the following generalization of base-area existence:

After an inaccessible area on the periphery of two or more provincial centers of power has been prepared for such an event, a communist military unit occupies this "border region" territory and establishes a state within the state. During the soviet period (1927-1936), the unit redistributes land and other assets from the landlords and from other "exploiters" to their tenants and to other "toilers," thereby liquidating the power of the rich and, so they hoped, incurring the allegiance of the poor. Moreover, to assure the domination of the latter over the former and thus safeguard the new relationships within the region, the unit creates new political institutions: soviets of peasants and workers plus Red Army men. During the anti-Japanese period (1937-1945), the unit moderates these changes and thereby broadens its potential base of support. It redistributes to a more limited degree income rather than assets, and it reforms the political institutions so that they represent all patriotic elements of the population, whether they are rich or poor.

In response to this challenge of their authority and their interests, the threatened "host" governmental institutions attempt to suppress the insurrection in their territory by all available means. In particular, they try to deprive the communist movement of popular support. To this end they invade the region and ravage it, thereby making it difficult for the communists and the indigenous population to sustain themselves with internal means. In addition, they blockade the region in order to isolate both segments from essential external resources. In such campaigns, the "host" governmental institutions find collaborators among those who have suffered from revolutionary change or who have reason to expect disadvantages from it.

In reaction, the base-area government must devise ways and means of coping with the problems of invasion and blockade in order to retain popular support. Ravaged territory must be rehabilitated, and efforts must be made to prevent invasions by defensive actions. The additional resources for this purpose can also be obtained by offensive actions outside the base area. Yet temporary occupation, confiscation, and recruitment there are likely to further antagonize the merchants and officials whose collaboration is required for endeavors to break the blockade. On the other hand, a greater reliance on internal contributions of men and materials for this reason necessitates a degree of allegiance on the part of the indigenous population which the redistribution of land or of income alone may fail to generate. Rather, such support may depend on more comprehensive improvements in the people's living as the result of the good government which the revolutionary actions are meant to bring about.

The strategic solution to this tactical dilemma is the achievement of territorial autarky by the base area. Such a state of self-sufficiency can be approached in two ways. On the one hand, it is possible to develop production in order to increase the variety, quantity, and quality of goods of internal origin. Particularly important for the base-area government is the growth of import-substituting production for public purposes. Because of the region's backwardness and isolation, production must be developed by technically primitive methods with internally produced means of production, which are relatively ineffective, even though they are efficient in the circumstances. Their use in turn sets narrow limits to increases in the amount and variety of intraterritorial supplies. Most severe appear to be the constraints on the production of weapons.

Severe supply constraints require on the other hand the imposition of corresponding restrictions on the intraterritorial demand for goods and services. In other words, the base-area government must adapt its expenditure to the productive potential of the region and to its ability to generate surplus. If it cannot gain the full support of the people without improving their living, the government must not reduce their personal consumption below previous levels. On the contrary, it may have to increase such consumption as well as the collective consumption of health, education, and welfare services. Of course, at least the latter improvements require investments. As a consequence, the residual surplus, which remains available for the administration and defense of the base area in soviet times cannot exceed the sum of the former incomes of the enemies: landlords, rich merchants, and public officials. Moreover, it must be even less during anti-Japanese times, when many landlords, merchants, and officials retain their positions as well as large parts of their incomes.

In both instances, the base-area government adapts to this limitation by instituting methods of administration and forms of warfare which match the techniques of production and the ways of living in the territory. Most importantly, the government induces its administrative and military personnel to share the life of the people in as many respects as is possible in their circumstances. Rations of food, clothing, and housing which are comparable to those of the people not only serve to support surprisingly large numbers of them but also tend to associate them with the people. Numerous productive activities which contribute notably to the region have the same effects. In the extreme, i.e., in the unusual situation of armed truce, most members of the public sector are encouraged to engage in production to the extent of becoming self-supporting. Even though the goal of public autarky may rarely be reached, various public services nevertheless appear more and more as net benefits to the people.

Public service of this extraordinary magnitude requires extremely high commitment among the members of the public sector. As a rule, this commitment does not emerge spontaneously but must be inculcated by continuing indoctrination. In addition, substantial efforts on the above pattern necessitate returns to specialization in any activity which are small in comparison with the returns to activism in all activities, so that the combination rather than the division of labor becomes the socially efficient solution. Returns in such proportions, which reflect the technical backwardness of the region, are related to seasonality in production, especially in farming, which employs most of the people part of the time and affords opportunities for additional supplementary work outside the public sector, too. In contrast with the public-sector members, however, the people at large are less responsive to ideological incentives. As a consequence, their activism must be stimulated to a greater degree with material rewards.

The attainment of the ideal state of territorial autarky, which is a most difficult task in the best of circumstances, involves in all cases a good deal of time. In the interim, the government has to cope with its problems less definitively. So long as the region continues to depend on external supplies, blockade running has to be organized. The smuggling, moreover, must be promoted in both directions, for imports as a rule must be paid for with exports. Increases in the cost of trade and other changes even tend to cause the development of production for this purpose. In spite of these efforts, however, imports may exceed exports to such an extent that an external payments problem arises. The latter tends to be associated with an internal payments problem due to a budget deficit. Both may be solved temporarily by a simultaneous depreciation and inflation of the base-area's currency.

Such financial solutions to payments problems reflect the government's real inability to make ends meet. Because they concern primarily external relations, depreciation and inflation may not interfere much with the subsistence-oriented activities of most of the people. To the extent that they do affect their living negatively, however, they can be expected to jeopardize the people's support of the government. In order to avoid this disaffection, the government must try to restrict the undesirable effects of deficit financing. Moreover, it must strive to make do without this means as soon as possible. For the longer run, of course, the aim must be to create an exportable surplus which can be contributed to the revolution or liberation of other areas. In the circumstances, this contribution is likely to be spent on food, clothing, housing, and training for cadres who then may be sent to further the causes of the communist movement in other parts of the country.

The Course of Inquiry

In the following seven chapters, these problems of guerrilla economy and the Chinese communists' solutions to them will be studied at length with reference to one specific base area, the Shensi-Kansu-Ninghsia Border Region, which served as the headquarters base of the Chinese communist movement during the period of the war against Japan (1937-1945).

Chapter 2 depicts in detail and as unequivocally as possible the initial conditions in the Northwest, where the Chinese communists established themselves after their Long March. It ignores the brief time of rapid territorial expansion after the Long March and focusses on the longer period of greater territorial stability during the anti-Japanese war. For this reason, most of the benchmark estimates refer to the territory, population, assets, and income of the Shensi-Kansu-Ninghsia Border Region on the eve of its formation (1936) and after a major territorial change (1940). An inventory of its resources reveals the extraordinary backwardness of the region, but a review of their utilization indicates specific opportunities for agricultural as well as nonagricultural development which were by no means negligible.

Chapter 3 describes the state of mind which the Chinese communists brought to bear on this situation. It traces their growing familiarity with the problems of survival in the countryside and shows that they had devised a promising strategy well before they were forced to give up their bases in the Central South. The Chinese communists transferred this know-how to the Northwest, and they did not modify their approach greatly when they terminated their efforts at land reform in accordance with united-front agreements. In fact, comparing development programs of the late Kiangsi with the early Yenan period indicates continuity in most every respect. But it also reveals one important innovation: the proposed use of cadres, students, and troops in subsistence production. This policy arose originally out of the truce with the nationalist government, which kept the soldiers in the Shensi-Kansu-Ninghsia Border Region garrisoned, but it soon was extended to the base areas in Japanese-occupied territory, in the expectation that greater activism would manifest itself not only in more output but also in better soldiering.

Chapters 4 to 8 deal with the implementation of this development strategy and its effects. Chapter 4 studies the organizational instruments and the motivational stimuli which the Chinese communists used in pursuit of their varied objectives. It finds that they operated on a dualistic pattern which took into account the evident differences in interest, talent, and circumstance between the public and the private sector. Of course, cooperation was stressed as ideal everywhere. But whereas it was tied to ideological incentives in the public sector, it tended to be associated with material rewards in the private sector. Moreover, material incentives in the latter were not dependent on particular forms of behavior, and cooperation seems to have been relatively rare in most circumstances.

Chapter 5 looks at the principal means by which production could be increased under conditions of isolation: additional human effort. It first enumerates its sources and estimates the contributions made by immigration, internal migration, rationalization, the intensification of work efforts, the absorption of women, institutional participation in production, and the rehabilitation of vagrants. The consequent changes in employment cannot be identified completely, but those which are evident tend to match the changes in organization. The reported increases in import-substituting and export-supplementing activities were relatively small and account for less than the increases in labor-force availability. In particular, peasant women engaged increasingly often in home spinning and weaving, but the effects of such changes on their other activities remain uncertain. In contrast, cadres, soldiers, and students added unequivocally and substantially to total work efforts.

Chapter 6 identifies the effects of changes in work efforts insofar as possible. It traces increases in inputs other than labor, most of which were own produced, changes in input relations, which apparently could not be great in the circumstances, and the resulting increases in output, including those of producer goods for own use. The discussion covers most of the materially productive sectors: agriculture, salt extraction, manufacturing and mining, road construction, and transportation. The assembled data suggest substantial advances in all lines of production, especially in import substitution and in export supplementation. Unfortunately, these data are incomplete as well as of questionable quality. And they do not suffice to substantiate asserted achievements in relation to autarky, the level of living, etc. which may well be true. Once again, however, the extraordinary contribution of the members of the public sector appears to be least in doubt.

Chapter 7 examines the effects of increases in production on public revenues, in the context of changing external relations. Trade opportunities varied from an initial blockade during the soviet period to free trade during the united-front interlude to renewed economic warfare after 1940. Deterioration of the terms of trade during the last period contributed to the severe payments problems which accounted at least in part for the rapidly rising inflation. The diminution, then termination, of nationalist financial aid, which had been granted under the united-front agreement, had the same consequences. In addition, it produced a budget deficit which aggravated the inflation. The Chinese communists attempted to close the inflationary gap by reintroducing taxes which they had eliminated at first and by promoting the self-sufficiency of the public sector.

The available data indicate that they were remarkably successful in this undertaking.

Chapter 8 tries to determine the impact of changes in land-ownership, production, external relations, and public finance on the structures of incomes and expenditures. The information for the public sector points to the attainment of benchmark levels in 1938 as well as in 1943. But it also reveals a sharp decline during the years in between. In addition, the public sector experienced a narrowing of income differentials which was so extreme that common soldiers, for example, continued to live better in 1941 than in presoviet times. The changes in the private farm and nonfarm sectors may have paralleled this development, though probably in a less extreme form. However, the evidence to this effect is far from complete and satisfactory. What is clear is merely that soldiers' incomes improved relative to those of peasants and factory workers' incomes relative to those of craftsmen. It is also clear that the positions of many who had been privileged in the past, notably landlords and public officials, deteriorated.

Chapter 8 shows, in addition, that besides maintaining, re-gaining, or increasing consumption and consumption-related investment, the Chinese communists tried to accumulate exportable surplus for the liberation of additional territory. To this end, they promoted the saving of one annual crop within a few years. To this end, they also supported the training of substantial numbers of cadres and experts who could be sent behind enemy lines. The latter outlay may be viewed as the greatest contribution of the Shensi-Kansu-Ninghsia Border Region to the cause of the Chinese communist movement.

The study of Chinese communist economic strategy and of its effects on the Shensi-Kansu-Ninghsia Border Region ends essentially on this note. Chapter 9 adds to it merely a brief review of the related question whether these developments were representative of the changes which occurred in the much more extensive base areas in Japanese occupied territory, the true guerrilla economies. Reasons and some evidence are provided in support of the view that there was strategic unity as well as tactical diversity, both of which were necessary for the success.

Throughout this introduction, reference has been made to the scarcity, incompleteness, and unreliability of information on the Shensi-Kansu-Ninghsia Border Region. Such remarks should not be surprising. Indeed, it would be unreasonable to expect—and worrisome to find—much more from a nascent government which emphasizes self-help in backward surroundings. As a consequence, however, there is ample opportunity for the intrusion of bias in various forms. Its more explicit appearance may be limited by efforts to refrain as much as possible from personal estimation. Moreover, its implicit presence may be diminished by a self-critical approach to writing. May the reader beware of the remainder!

II

Initial Conditions
in the Northwest

Any appraisal of the Chinese communists' accomplishments in the Shensi-Kansu-Ninghsia (SKN) Border Region requires information on the situation which the movement encountered when it first occupied this territory. For an assessment of their impact on the region's economy in particular, it seems important to go beyond the general impressions that the entire area was poverty-stricken, even though it had once been quite prosperous, that it had experienced a severe drought recently, and that it suffered badly from banditry, high taxes, traditional government, landlordism, and so on.

Unfortunately, a more detailed description is a highly problematic task. The twenty-three hsien (administrative districts) in the provinces of Shensi, Kansu, and Ninghsia, which were incorporated into this successor to the Northwest Soviet in 1937,[1] qualified as backward in the sense of both remote and retarded. The national statistical authorities did not know much about that part of the country, and their limited information had been rendered more uncertain by recent disaster.[2] John Lossing Buck's investigators, who gathered detailed data on *Land Utilization in China* during 1929-33 in so many locations, bypassed most of the area. They conducted comprehensive surveys merely in Tingpien Hsien at the northern and in Hsunyi Hsien at the southern border of the territory which subsequently became the SKN border region.[3] The Rural Reconstruction Commission of the nationalist Executive Yuan investigated within these boundaries only four villages in Suite Hsien.[4] And the SKN border region government, which perhaps could have provided a great deal of information about the initial circumstances, published relatively little. The only com-

14

prehensive village study known is that of a complex of six hamlets in Michih Hsien.[5] The consequent lack of evidence makes it impossible to establish some of the fundamental attributes of SKN unequivocally.

Area and Population

Territory. Uncertainty arises already when one attempts to delineate the territory of the SKN border region on the loess plateau inside the big bend of the Yellow River to the south of the Great Wall (see maps). In comparison with other base areas of the Chinese communists, this region appeared highly stable. But its territory, which had expanded substantially during the influx of communist forces until 1936, did not remain entirely the same from 1937 to 1945. According to Chinese communist claims which were never confirmed by the Chinese nationalists, SKN rule was to extend over twenty-six hsien.[6] However, the actual SKN domain seems to have been smaller at all times. At least three of the twenty-six hsien did not come fully under SKN control prior to March 1940.[7] And part or all of the territory of six other hsien was lost to national government troops during winter 1939 and spring 1940.[8]

The net effect of these changes is hard to assess, as the data of table 2.1 show. The SKN border region government has not provided information on the size of its territory prior to the events of 1939/40. The gross area data of the national government suggest that the border region experienced a substantial net loss of territory. But in the opinion of the SKN government these data understate the size of SKN, possibly because they fail to account for the fact that the SKN boundaries did not coincide with those of its peripheral hsien. The discrepancy is rather large, however. And Yung Ying Hsü, who attempted to correct for the mistaken inclusion and exclusion of territory, concluded that much of it appears to be attributable to faulty mapping by the SKN border region government.[9]

Households and population. The estimates of households and of population are correspondingly precarious. The data of the national government suggest that the number of households increased notably due to the territorial changes of 1939/40. The SKN border region government has not made public estimates of the number of households in the pre-1939/40 area. Its 1941 and 1944 estimates exceed the 1932 estimate of the national government for the post-1939/40 area. But they also appear to be inconsistent with each other. The same may be said of the 1941 and 1944 population estimates of the SKN border region government. A 1941 reference to 600,000 persons prior to 1939 seems to refer to the year 1935, since it conflicts with the 1937 estimate of 1,400,000 persons for spring 1937 as well as with Edgar Snow's best guess of 1936 that the base area was ". . . thinly populated, with perhaps less than 2,000,000 inhabitants."[10]

Table 2.1

GROSS AREA, HOUSEHOLDS, AND POPULATION.*

Item	Designated Area	Area until 1939/40	Area after 1939/40
Gross area			
National gov't, 1932 data [a]	83,146 km²	77,965 km²	71,265 km²
SKN government, 1944 data [b]	129,000 km²	n.a.	99,000 km²
Yung Ying Hsü, 1945 estimate [c]			84,650 km²
Households			
National gov't, 1932 data [a]	268,500 units	221,700 units	234,300 units
SKN government, 1941 data [d]			254,100 units [f]
" " Dec. 1944 data [e]			312,987 units
Population			
SKN government, 1937 data [g]		1,400,000 persons	
" " 1941 data [d]			1,352,175 persons
" " 1944 data [b]	2,000,000 persons [d]		1,480,000 persons
" " Dec. 1944 data [e]			1,595,065 persons

* SKN estimates do not include persons in administrative organs, armed forces, factories, and schools. One km² equals 0.386 square miles.

a. Derived from Buck, *Land Utilization in China. Statistics,* pp. 21 ff., 416 ff. (Hereinafter cited as Buck, *Statistics*). Designated area: Twenty-seven hsien (cf. reference 6. Shenmu and Fuku are counted in full). Area until 1939/40: Designated area minus Suite, Chingchien, Wupao. Area after 1939/40: Designated area minus Yuwang minus one half of Chenyuan, Ninghsien, Chengning, Hsunyi, Chunhua.

b. *Brief Account,* p. 2.

c. Hsü, *A Survey,* pp. 15-16 (2.59 times 32,685 square miles).

d. *Shan Kan Ning 1939-1941,* pp. 11-15, 55.

e. Chung-kuo k'o-hsueh yuan, li-shih yen-chiu suo, ti-san suo. *Shan Kan Ning pien ch'ü ts'an-i hui wen-hsien hui-chi,* (Peking: K'o-hsueh Press, 1958), pp. 4, 379. (Hereinafter cited as *Shan Kan Ning (1958)*.

f. Households in Michih and Chia Hsien estimated on the premise that the average household size was the same as elsewhere in SKN.

g. Bisson, *Yenan in June 1937,* p. 30.

Population density. The 1932 data of the national government in table 2.1 imply densities of 3.23 households per km^2 in
the designated area, of 2.84 households per km^2 in the area
until 1939/40, and of 3.29 households per km^2 in the area after
1939/40. The last number is comparable to the average of 3.16
households per km^2 which the 1944 estimates of the SKN border region government yield. But it exceeds the average of
2.56 households per km^2 which follows from the 1941 estimates.
The average household size was 5.3 persons in 1941 and 5.1
persons in 1944 according to the SKN border region government. These magnitudes are comparable to the estimates made
for the early 1930s by Wang Shih-ta and by Liu and Yeh.[11]
Moreover, the December 1944 data also yield a sex ratio of
112.5 which is lower than Wang Shih-ta's 1932/33 estimate and
the same as Buck's finding for the Shensi-Kansu area in 1929/
31.[12]

Natural change. Information on the fertility and mortality of
the population in SKN is incomplete. But the indications are
that there was no natural growth. Buck, who did not attempt to
determine rates of birth and death by agricultural area, noted
this pattern of change for 1929/31: whereas 58 percent of the
sampled localities in China and 53 percent of those in the *wheat
region* of China reported increases in population, 54 percent of
the sampled localities in the *spring wheat area* and 61 percent
of those in the *winter wheat-millet area* listed decreases in population.[13] The SKN border region was located in these two
areas.[14] The population losses were related to observations of
abandoned buildings, banditry, death, famine, and sickness.[15]
The severe drought of the time, which is also mentioned, may
have been the primary cause of all of these phenomena. However, problems of survival appear to have been severe in the
area at most times. Chairman Lin Pai-ch'ü of the SKN border
region government stated as late as in 1944 that ". . . up to this
day there still exist dreadful mortality rates of three percent
(adults) and of sixty percent (infants) . . ."[16] According to Buck,
a crude death rate of 2.7 percent and an infant mortality rate of
16 percent were normal for China during 1929-1931.[17] Chairman Lin did not mention the rate of birth and the age structure
of the population in the SKN border region. If one assumes a

crude birth rate near 4 percent and a share of adults twenty
or more years old of about 55 percent,[18] one can infer that
the deaths of infants plus adults probably equalled the births
in the SKN border region. Since one has yet to account for
adolescent mortality, it seems reasonable to conclude that
the population in SKN at best experienced natural stagnation.[19]

Population estimates. In the absence of agreement on the
size of the border region, it is possible to form estimates as
follows. First, one may assume that the December 1944 data,
which were compiled after four or eight or more years of intensifying administration by the border region government, are
most likely to be correct. Second, one may accept as probable
that the SKN population did not grow naturally from 1936 to
1944. The migration data, which are also incomplete, permit
the estimate on this basis of a total population of about 1.5
million persons for the end of 1940 and one of 1.4 million
persons for the end of 1936.[20] The estimate for 1940 exceeds
the 1941 data in table 2.1 by about 10 percent. But the unusually low population-land ratio for the 1941 data suggests that
they may understate the actual population to such a degree.
The estimate for 1936 appears to be consistent with the change
which one can infer from the household data in table 2.1.

Urban-rural structure. The SKN border region government
has not published information on the distribution of population
by size of residential community.[21] The hsien surveys which
Buck conducted yielded data on the distribution of all *families*
among cities, market towns, and farm villages or hamlets.
These data do not pertain to the SKN border region directly,
with the exception of Tingpien in the Northwest. However,
information for the *spring wheat area* and the *winter wheat-
millet area* indicate the state of affairs in SKN which formed
part of both agricultural areas. In the *spring wheat area* the
share of urban residents and especially that of city residents
was comparatively large. In the *winter wheat-millet area* the
opposite was true. These deviations from the national and the
wheat-region averages tended to offset each other. The SKN
border region averages, which can be estimated on the basis of
Buck's area data and the national government's household
data, do not differ greatly from the aggregate averages:

Relative share of all families residing in	Area until 1939/1940[22]	Area after 1939/1940[23]
Cities	10.6	10.1
Market towns	9.4	9.4
Villages and hamlets	80.0	80.5

Due to the low population density, these cities and towns were of course comparatively small. The average hsien in the SKN border region incorporated about 10,000 households,[24] close to 20 percent of which were distributed among at least one city, i.e., the seat of hsien administration, and one or more market towns. The possibility of a disproportionate loss of cities and towns during winter 1939 and spring 1940 implies in addition that the preceding estimates may well overstate the degree of urbanization of the SKN border region during 1940-1945.

Occupational structure. Systematic accounts of the occupational structure of the SKN population are lacking. In their absence, one may form an estimate by combining Buck's data on the occupational distribution of persons of seven or more years of age in North China with a personal estimate of the share of those in the category zero to six years of age. The estimate of table 2.2 modifies Buck's presentation further in regard to the classification of domestic service. Because women working in *domestic service* did so "principally in their own homes,"[25] it is best to treat them as dependents and consequently reduce the share of all employed persons from 77.0 percent to 54.1 percent of the total population. 68.3 percent of those employed engaged in agriculture only or in agriculture plus domestic service, apparently also primarily in their own homes. Both the share of all employed persons and the share of those in agriculture may be exaggerated for the reason that many persons in agriculture plus domestic service worked mainly in the latter area and therefore could be classified as dependents.[26] Correspondingly, the relative importance of all other occupations may be understated for this reason as well as due to the omission of various subsidiary activities of farm households.[27] As a consequence, persons engaged in agriculture plus nonagricultural occupations may have exceeded the 12.1 percent of

Table 2.2

**ESTIMATED DISTRIBUTION OF
POPULATION ACCORDING TO OCCUPATION**

Population	Per cent of total [a]	Thousand persons 1936	1940
Total	100.0	1,400.0[b]	1,500.0[b]
Employed	54.1	757.4	811.5
Agriculture only	23.0	322.0	345.0
plus domestic service	14.0	196.0	210.0
subtotal	37.0	518.0	555.0
Agriculture plus trade	3.2	44.8	48.0
plus manufacturing	1.0	14.0	15.0
plus transportation	0.8	11.2	12.0
plus home industry	0.7	9.8	10.5
plus professions	0.6	8.4	9.0
plus public service	0.2	2.8	3.0
subtotal	6.5	91.0	97.5
Nonagricultural professions	4.4	61.6	66.0
domestic service, male	2.6	36.4	39.0
trade	1.7	23.8	25.5
home industry	0.8	11.2	12.0
manufacturing	0.6	8.4	9.0
public service	0.4	5.6	6.0
transportation	0.1	1.4	1.5
subtotal	10.6	148.4	159.0
Dependent	45.9	642.6	688.5
Domestic service only, female	22.9	320.6	343.5
Idle plus unknown	8.0	112.0	120.0
Ages 0-6	15.0[c]	210.0	225.0

a. Derived from Buck, *Land Utilization in China,* p. 372 (North China, 1929-1933), and reference c.

b. Personal estimates. Cf. text.

c. Personal estimate. See Buck, *Land Utilization in China,* p. 377 (share of persons under ten in total population of North China in 1929-1931: 24.1 percent). Note that due to the extraordinarily high rate of infant mortality, the share of ages 0-6 may have been larger than estimated.

all employed persons which table 2.2 implies, and persons engaged in nonagricultural occupations only may have accounted for more than 19.9 percent of this total. However, such qualifications do not change Buck's principal conclusions which apply to all of China:

> The occupational composition of the surveyed communities is extremely simple. Virtually every able-bodied person seven or more years of age worked; and agriculture, domestic service, trade, and professional service were the only important occupations.[28]

By relating to the percentage distribution in table 2.2 the estimates of total population in 1936 and in 1940, one arrives at estimates of the absolute numbers of persons engaged in agriculture only, in agriculture plus nonagricultural occupations, and in nonagricultural occupations only for those bench-mark dates. These estimates are necessarily rough approximations which share the shortcomings of the percentage distribution.

Education. The SKN border region government noted in 1944 that "before the revolution, most places, with the exception of the Suite sub-region, were extremely backward in culture. . . ."[29] And it asserted that the illiteracy rate in the area had been 99 percent originally.[30] Such a high rate was evident for women in North China according to Buck, but the rate for men was much lower. On the average, 85.2 percent of the population of North China were illiterate, and 76.5 percent of them had not had any schooling.[31] It is possible that the border region government's reference to 99 percent was polemical. However, even a rate of 90 percent, which has been mentioned for the SKN border region troops,[32] depicts the degree of retardation clearly.

Farm Sector

Population. Buck determined the relative share of farm *families* in all *families* during 1929-1933 for a sample of hsien which included from the SKN territory merely Tingpien. The national government reported in 1932 for every hsien the number of all *households* and the number of farm *households*. In those hsien of the *spring wheat area* and the *winter wheat-millet area* for which both Buck and the national government provided estimates, the percentage of farm households differed as a rule not only greatly but also irregularly from the percentage of farm families. The shares of both units were comparatively small in the *spring wheat area* and comparatively large in the *winter wheat-millet area*. When one weights these area averages as previously,[33] one arrives at the following estimates for the SKN border region:

Buck's sample of hsien	Area until 1939/1940 %	Area after 1939/1940 %
Share of farm families[34]	83.6	84.0
Share of farm households[35]	76.9	77.1

A counting of the households and farm households in the hsien which approximated the SKN border region yields somewhat lower shares: 74.6 percent for the area until 1939/1940 and 76.8 percent for the area after 1939/1940.[36] The corresponding farm family shares may be estimated as 81.1 percent and 83.7 percent, respectively.[37] The share of the farm population in the total population of the SKN border region appears to have been somewhat larger for the reason that the average size of farm families seems to have exceeded that of nonfarm (landlord plus other) families. Buck's population data for North China permit the inference of a share of farm population in total population of 82.8 percent in the area until 1939/1940 and one of 85.5 percent in the area after 1939/1940.[38] Because of the need to rely primarily on Buck's data in a discussion of the farm sector, it is best to choose to operate with these population shares rather than with the household shares of the national government.

Urban-rural structure. Information on the urban-rural distribution of the farm population is hard to come by. The Rural

Reconstruction Commission determined that of all the house-holds in the four villages in Suite, nonfarm households (i.e., landlord households plus "other" households) accounted for 6.8 percent in 1928 and for 5.5 percent in 1933.[39] These shares were large in comparison with those found in two locations in Central Shensi.[40] But they fell far short of the share discovered in Yang Chia K'ou of Michih Hsien.[41] One may guess that about 5 percent of the rural households were nonfarm house-holds. Such a guess implies that at least 25 percent of the urban households were farm households according to primary oc-cupation.

Labor utilization. In the farm sector as elsewhere, the share of employable and employed persons was much smaller ac-cording to the Rural Reconstruction Commission than accord-ing to Buck. Of the members of rich, middle, and poor peasant households in four villages in Suite, the Rural Reconstruction Commission classified as *employable* 51 percent in 1928 and 42.5 percent in 1933.[42] Buck's data on man-work and man-equivalents make it possible to derive that employed persons accounted for 46.3 percent of the population of all farm house-holds in Hsunyi and for 42.6 percent of this total in Tingpien.[43] The estimated SKN border region averages of about 45 percent in table 2.3 do not differ greatly from the aggregate averages which are implicit in Buck's data. Close to 60 percent of all employed persons were men who did more than three-quarters of the total work. Children accounted for more than one-quarter of the employed and made about one-seventh of the total effort. Women contributed the rest, and their contribu-tions were so limited for the reason that their domestic work, which most of them carried on as an exclusive occupation, was not counted.[44] Domestic service as a subsidiary occupation seems to have been omitted, too. Such an omission could ac-count for the difference between the shares of employed per-sons in table 2.2 and in table 2.3.[45]

Farm work absorbed the majority of the employed as well as the greater portion of their efforts. But the importance of this activity varied within the region.[46] The estimated SKN border region averages of farm employment are small by the standard of table 2.2, apparently for the reason that many of those occupied in agriculture plus domestic service according to Buck's population survey were not counted as farm workers by his farm survey.[47] The share of farm workers in table 2.3 is also large in comparison with other data,[48] probably because the latter excluded children. The estimate of 360,000 adult persons in farm work, which can be derived for a farm population of 1,282,500 persons from the sources of table 2.3, is somewhat larger than the estimate of 338,760 *full agricultural labor powers* which the SKN border region government made public in January 1944.[49]

Subsidiary work involved a minority of the employed and the smaller portion of total efforts. Its importance, too, varied within the region,[50] as did its structure.[51] The estimated SKN border region averages appear to be large by the standard of table 2.2, principally for the following reasons. The number of farm population employed in home industry is substantially larger than the number of total population so occupied. And the number of farm population employed as merchants is slightly larger than the number of total population engaged in trade.[52] These discrepancies may reflect local peculiarities. But they also point to differences in classificatory practice. Many home industry workers in table 2.3 may have engaged in subsistence production. Many merchants may have been persons who merely attended periodic markets regularly.[53] Others perhaps were counted in table 2.2 as being engaged in transportation.

Finally, there is evidence that many of those who were employed were not fully utilized by urban industrial standards. In his earlier study, *Chinese Farm Economy,* Buck determined for North China that the equivalent of an able-bodied man on the average spent 95 (median) to 120 (mean) ten-hour days per annum in farm work.[54] If farm work accounted for about 75 percent of the total work effort,[55] the man-equivalent spent in addition 30 to 40 days in subsidiary work. In terms of ten-hour days, he therefore worked one-third to one-half the days in a year—much less than the possible total. However, men worked larger numbers of days, and the fewer days and shorter hours that women and children worked account for much of the average underutilization of the farm labor force.[56]

Table 2.3

ESTIMATED DISTRIBUTION OF
FARM POPULATION ACCORDING TO EMPLOYMENT

Farm Population	1936		1940	
	Percent of total [a]	1,000 persons	Percent of total [b]	1,000 persons
Total	100.0	1,159.2 [c]	100.0	1,282.5 [d]
Employed				
Men	25.8	299.1	26.0	333.5
Women	6.8	78.8	6.6	84.6
Children	12.4	143.7	12.5	160.3
Total	45.0	521.6	45.1	578.4
Farm work only	29.2	338.4	29.6	379.6
Farm + subsidiary work	8.4	97.4	8.1	103.9
Subsidiary work only	7.4	85.6	7.4	94.9
Subtotal: subsidiary work	15.8	183.2	15.5	198.8
of which [e]				
Merchant	6.1	70.7	5.8	74.4
Home industry worker	4.6	53.3	4.9	62.8
Farm laborer	2.8	32.5	2.6	33.3
Skilled laborer	0.9	10.4	0.9	11.5
Unskilled laborer	0.7	8.1	0.6	7.7
Professional	0.3	3.5	0.3	3.8
Scholar	0.2	2.3	0.2	2.6
Official	0.1	1.2	0.1	1.3
Soldier	0.1	1.2	0.1	1.3

a. Derived from Buck, *Statistics*, pp. 303-305, 309, Buck, *Land Utilization in China*, p. 475, and reference 14. Estimate: .354 times Tingpien data plus .646 times Hsunyi data.

b. Derived from *ibid.* Estimate: .315 times Tingpien data plus .685 times Hsunyi data.

c. Estimate: .828 times 1.4 million persons. See references 20 and 38.

d. Estimate: .855 times 1.5 million persons. See references 20 and 38.

e. Derived from reference a. Additional assumption: The share of all persons employed in subsidiary work on a full-time or part-time basis equals the share of all farm families listing subsidiary occupations.

Arable and cultivated land. The SKN border region government has stated that its territory contained about 40 million *mou* (according to present-day standards, 2.67 million hectares or 6.6 million acres) of arable land, more than 20 percent of which were being cultivated in the beginning.[57] Buck's investigators also found extensive areas of uncultivated land which were arable, notably in Tingpien.[58] Much of this unused land appears to have been upland which was comparatively fertile due to its loess composition but also relatively arid because of the limited rainfall in the area. In the absence of artificial irrigation its expected yield was therefore low. The reclamation

Table 2.4

ESTIMATES OF CULTIVATED LAND AND ITS USES.

Unit: million *mou**

Estimate	Area until 1939/1940	Area after 1939/1940
Cultivated land		
SKN border region gov't, 1936 [a]	8.431	
National government, 1932 data [b]	6.652	5.579
Buck's investigators, 1929-1933 [c]	15.293	15.621
Buck's Farm Survey data times our		
farm population estimates d		
Farm area	8.845	9.426
Crop area	8.091	8.657
Cropped area	7.419	8.067
Grains area	6.654	7.259

* One *mou* equals 0.0614 hectare according to Buck who applied this standard to the data of the national government. See Buck, *Statistics,* p. 29. But the size of the *mou* varied considerably within China. In particular, it measured 0.06067 hectare in Tingpien and 0.06574 hectare in Hsunyi. See *ibid.,* p. 473. The standard used by the SKN border region government is not known. The standard used in China today is 0.0667 hectare.

a. *Shan Kan Ning (1958),* p. 283.

b. Derived from Buck, *Statistics,* pp. 21-22.

c. Derived from *ibid.*

d. Derived from *ibid.,* pp. 172, 286, 300, reference 14, and table 2.3. Estimates: Area until 1939/1940: 1,159,200 times (.354 times average area per farm household member in Tingpien plus .646 times average area per farm household member in Hsunyi). Area after 1939/1940: 1,282,500 times (.315 times average area per farm household member in Tingpien plus .685 times average area per farm household member in Hsunyi).

of land *per se,* although simple enough to do, was consequently not very promising. The construction and operation of irrigation works, on the other hand, was complicated by the highly erosive properties of the loess, which accounted for the unusually high embankments of rivers (as well as for problems of silting and flooding with respect to the lowlands).[59]

There is less agreement on the extent to which land was being tilled. The differences between Buck's investigators, the SKN border region government, and the statistical authorities of the national government, which are made evident in table 2.4, are fairly extreme. In contrast, the estimates of cultivated land per household or per member of the farm population do not conflict nearly as much. The 1932 data of the national government yield averages of cultivated land per farm household of 40.2 *mou* (about 2.68 hectares or 6.62 acres) for the area until 1939/40 and of 31.0 *mou* (about 2.07 hectares or 5.11 acres) for the area after 1939/40. The probable averages per capita of the farm population are 7.7 *mou* (about 0.5 hectare or 1.25 acres) and 6.0 *mou* (about 0.4 hectare or 1.0 acre) respectively.[60]

Buck's farm survey results are of similar magnitude. A weighting of his findings for Tingpien and Hsunyi with the farm household shares of the *spring wheat area* and the *winter wheat-millet area* within the SKN border region yields the following SKN averages per capita of the farm population: 7.0 *mou* of crop area and 6.4 *mou* of cropped area in the territory until 1939/40; 6.8 *mou* of crop area and 6.3 *mou* of cropped area in the territory after 1939/40.[61] In comparison, the SKN border region government estimate of cultivated land and the personal estimate of farm population imply an average of 7.3 *mou* of cultivated land per capita of the farm population in 1936.[62] It thus appears that the total of 8.431 million *mou* of cultivated land is plausible. In addition, one may guess that the initial total in the area after 1939/40 may have reached nine million *mou* of cultivated land. (The approximate hectare and acre equivalents are fifteenths and sixths of these numbers).

Distribution of land. The SKN border region government has provided surprisingly little information on land tenure, farm size classes, and related indicators of rural social structure. In 1936, Edgar Snow was given the following information on the structure of the rural population in North Shensi, without corresponding data on the distribution of land holdings:[63]

Landlords	1 percent
Rich peasants	3-4 percent
Middle peasants	20-30 percent
Poor peasants	40-50 percent
Farm workers	7-8 percent
Others	5-10 percent

The findings of Buck differ from these data as well as from those of the Rural Reconstruction Commission in categorical and substantial terms. However, since Buck's farm-size classes appear to correspond reasonably well with the peasant household classes of others,[64] these two variables are correlated in table 2.5. Although the standards of classification are necessarily arbitrary, the data of table 2.5 suggest that the share of the poor was larger in Suite and that it had increased there drastically due to the drought. Correspondingly, the share of rental land was larger in Suite and had grown similarly for the same reason. Moreover, tenancy, which had been much more frequent in Suite, became increasingly so. In addition, rental land was concentrated much more heavily on poor peasants there than it was on smaller farms in Tingpien or in Hsunyi.[65] Accordingly, part-ownership of farms was apparently not as important in Suite as in the other two locations.[66] The shares of landlord households cannot be derived from Buck's information. But the following general contrast is indicated: whereas landlordism did not prevail in Tingpien and in Hsunyi according to circumstantial evidence, it was highly important in Suite according to the Rural Reconstruction Commission of the Executive Yuan, and clearly dominant in Yang Chia K'ou according to the Yenan Rural Survey Group.[67] Hired labor contributed relatively little in all four locations.

All of the conflicting observations are of course marginal to the SKN border region in terms of time as well as of place. Moreover, whereas the Rural Reconstruction Commission

Table 2.5

INDICATORS OF THE SOCIAL STRUCTURE OF THE FARM SECTOR IN TINGPIEN, HSUNYI, AND SUITE DURING THE LATE 1920s AND EARLY 1930s.

Unit: percent

John Lossing Buck's data [a]				*Data of the Rural Reconstruction Commission* [b]	
Relative share of . . .	Tingpien 1930	Hsunyi 1931	Suite 1928	Suite 1933	Relative share of . . .
farms					peasant households
very large and larger	—	10	4-5	4	rich
medium-large and large	35	31	20-22	14-15	middle
medium and smaller	65	59	76-73	82-81	poor
rental land in total					rental land in total
farm area	11.4	19.1	39.8	53.4	cultivated land
tenant farmers in					peasant-tenants in
all farmers	8.0	9.0	48-43	58-55	all peasants
farm work done by					land cultivated by
hired labor	12.5	4.5	11.2	13.5	hired labor

a. Derived from Buck, *Statistics,* pp. 55, 57, 289.
b. Derived from tables A.1, A.2. The share of *poor peasant-tenants* includes a minority of part-owners. The shares for Suite vary with the inclusion or exclusion of *poor peasant laborers* who are part-owners.

found much less tenancy and inequality in Central Shensi, Buck's investigators discovered conditions similar to those in Suite in several hsien of the *spring wheat area* and the *winter wheat-millet area.* In addition to such local variations, Buck's data indicate that the distribution of farm sizes in Hsunyi—rather than in Tingpien—conformed closely to the national, regional, and relevant area patterns. The shares of rental land in Tingpien and Hsunyi exceeded their respective area averages somewhat. Yet both fell short of the national average and of almost all other area averages.[68] Because it can be seen also that the average share of rental land varied from area to area with the average farm product and thus with the potential surplus over subsistence which could be collected as rent,[69] it is reasonable to consider Buck's finding of relatively small shares of rental land in the low-yielding Northwest plausible. Such a conclusion does not preclude that the findings for Suite and Michih indicate greater absentee ownership of the more fertile lowlands within the SKN border region.

Land use. Buck's data indicate that in Hsunyi as well as in Tingpien close to 96 percent of the total farm area was productive land. But whereas all of this land was crop area in the former location, 7.5 percent was pasture land in the latter.[70] Much of the crop area in Tingpien remained unharvested or idle, and little of the crop area in Hsunyi was cultivated more than once during the year. The estimated ratio of cropped area to crop area therefore was less than one for the SKN territory, viz., 0.91 in the area until 1939/40 and 0.93 in the area after 1939/40.[71] Correspondingly, very little land was irrigated, according to Buck[72] as well as according to the SKN border region government,[73] apparently because it might alkalize the land, at least in part of the region.[74] Close to 90 percent of the total sown land was given over to various grains, with the share of grain land larger in Hsunyi and smaller in Tingpien. Most important among the grain crops were wheat in the former, millet in the latter, and buckwheat in both locations. All other crops accounted for about 10 percent of the land, among them oil seeds for close to four percent, legumes for close to two percent, and vegetables for about one percent. According to Buck, fibers were not among the remaining crops.[75] The SKN border region government also observed that there was no cotton-growing in the region at the time of its formation, even though cotton-growing had been common once in the Eastern region (i.e., Yenchang, Yenchuan, and Kuling).[76]

Crop product. Buck determined four measures of yield per unit of land for crops found on 20 percent or more of all farms: the most frequent yield, the average yield during the year of investigation (1930 in the case of Tingpien and 1931 for Hsunyi), the normal yield, and the best yield. His findings imply that the most frequent yield of grain crops in Hsunyi was twice as high as that in Tingpien.[77] They also show that the yield varied much more drastically in Tingpien than in Hsunyi.[78] In particular, the average yield in Tingpien in 1930 was merely 30.3 percent of the most frequent yield. By weighting data for these two hsien as previously, it is possible to derive yield estimates for the SKN border region. The estimates in regard to the structure of land uses permit the conversion of yields per *mou* of land sown to all grains into output per *mou* of total crop land.[79]

Measure of grain yield	Area until 1939/40		Area after 1939/40	
	Kg* of grain per *mou* of . . .			
	grain area	crop area	grain area	crop area
Most frequent	39.5	32.4	40.5	33.9
Average, 1930/31	32.6	26.8	34.5	28.9
Normal	53.1	43.2	54.4	45.6
Best	59.2	48.6	59.9	50.2

*One kilogram (kg) equals 2,2046 pounds (lbs.).

In comparison, the SKN border region government's estimates of total grain output and total cultivated land in 1937 imply averages of 25.9 kg or 21.9 kg per *mou* (i.e., about 856 lbs. or 724 lbs. per hectare and 343 lbs. or 290 lbs. per acre), depending on whether one uses the original or the revised production data.[80] In the absence of information on environmental conditions in 1937, these averages could be considered compatible with the findings of Buck, even though they would point to a very poor year.[81] Yet the downward revision of the official estimates *ex post facto* also poses the problem that this manipulation of Buck's survey data may not have produced representative yields. Table 2.7 shows that the corresponding estimates of total grain output differ similarly from each other. And it indicates in addition that the total crop product of the SKN border region seems to have been hardly any larger than its total grain product, always according to Buck.

Animal stock. The SKN border region government has stated that prior to the anti-Japanese war, there were more than 100,000 oxen plus donkeys and 400,000 to 500,000 sheep within its territory.[82] Both the vagueness of this statement and the claims of much larger totals for subsequent years, which are evident in table 2.6, intimate that the initial stock of farm animals may have been larger than estimated. However, variations in the incidence of disease and other consequences of the civil war may have caused an abnormal decline in the stock.[83] Buck's farm survey results imply much larger totals, as table 2.6 shows. And the plans of the SKN border region government to increase the number of cattle by 400,000 and the number of sheep to ten million suggest that these implied totals were feasible.[84] Yet there are also indications that they overstate the actual stock of some animals considerably.[85]

Table 2.6

LIVESTOCK ESTIMATES

Kind of animal	SKN data 1938 [a]	SKN data 1940 [a]	Buck's data, Area until 1939/1940 [c]	1930/1931 [b] Area after 1939/1940 [d]
Oxen	102,676	148,408	160,200	174,200
Horses	n.a.	n.a.	4,800	4,800
Mules	1,468	1,817	10,400	11,300
Donkeys	70,810	94,334	202,800	218,000
Camels	1,254	2,458	3,000	3,000
Hogs	n.a.	n.a.	68,200	72,800
Sheep	751,464	1,625,170	4,194,600 [e]	4,242,300 [e]
Chickens	n.a.	n.a.	362,200	406,200

a. *Shan Kan Ning 1939-1941,* p. 43.

b. Derived from Buck, *Statistics,* pp. 122, 300, reference 14, and table 2.3.

c. 1,159,200 times (.354 times animals per farm household member in Tingpien plus .646 times animals per farm household member in Hsunyi).

d. 1,282,500 times (.315 times animals per farm household member in Tingpien plus .685 times animals per farm household member in Hsunyi).

e. Note that Buck considered the average number of sheep per farm in Tingpien as unusually large.

Table 2.7
FARM PRODUCT ESTIMATES

Kind of farm product	Unit of measure- ment	SKN data 1937 or 1938	1940	Buck's data Area until 1939/40 most frequent	Area until 1939/40 average 1930/31	Area after 1939/40 most frequent	Area after 1939/40 average 1930/31
All grains	million piculs	1.49 or 1.26 [a]	1.43	1.75 [b]	1.44 [b]	1.96 [b]	1.67 [b]
All crops	million piculs				1.48 [c]		1.72 [c]
Animals [d]							
Oxen	thousand head	11.7	17.4		18.2		20.4
Horses	thousand head				0.6		0.6
Mules	thousand head	0.5	0.6		3.3		3.9
Donkeys	thousand head	14.0	18.6		40.2		43.0
Hogs	thousand head				42.4		44.4
Sheep	thousand head	181.7	393.5		1,014.1		1,027.3
Chickens	thousand head				114.1		128.0
By-products							
Wool	million catties		2.0 [e]		7.3 [f]		7.4 [f]
Eggs	million eggs				15.3 [g]		18.3 [g]

a. *See Ching-chi yen-chiu,* No. 2 (1956), p. 108 and *Shan Kan Ning 1939-1941,* p. 42. The original estimate of 1.12 million piculs @ 400 catties has been converted into 1.49 million piculs @ 300 catties
@ 500 grams.
b. Derived from table 2.4 and reference 79. One picul equals 150 kg or 300 catties.
c. Grain equivalent. Derived from table 2.8.
d. Derived from table 2.6 and reference 86. Note the omission of camels due to the absence of young
animals.
e. See *Shan Kan Ning 1939-1941,* p. 50.
f. Estimate: 2.5 catties times 0.7 times number of sheep. See Liu and Yeh, *Economy of the Chinese
Mainland,* p. 314.
g. Estimate: 90 eggs times 0.5 times number of chickens. See Liu and Yeh, *Economy of the Chinese
Mainland,* p. 313, and table 2.6.

Animal product. In his count of farm animals, Buck distinguished between adult and nonadult animals. His data permit the inference of the following percentage shares of nonadult farm animals in all farm animals by previously used
methods:[86]

Kind of animal	Tingpien 1930	Hsunyi 1931	Area until 1939/1940	Area after 1939/1940
Oxen	6.6	15.4	11.4	11.7
Horses	12.5	0.0	12.5	12.5
Mules	0.0	60.0	32.0	34.6
Donkeys	21.1	18.4	19.8	19.7
Camels	0.0	0.0	0.0	0.0
Hogs	73.0	48.1	62.1	61.0
Sheep	23.9	25.6	24.2	24.2
Chickens	31.5	0.0	8.8	7.7

The SKN averages for oxen and horses conform to the national averages[87] as well as to common estimates of animal utilization rates.[88] The area averages for mules and donkeys exceed both of these measures, probably for the reason that the SKN region specialized in their breeding. The area averages for hogs and sheep plus the Tingpien share for chickens are comparable to the national averages but fall short of the common estimates of animal utilization rates. Possible explanations for such discrepancies are extraordinarily high death rates among young animals as well as maturation periods of less than one year.[89] Although Buck's data may therefore understate the rates of reproduction of some kinds of animals, one may use his findings in estimating the annual animal product. Because the stock estimates of Buck and of the SKN border region government are multiplied by the above shares, it follows that the totals of table 2.7 conflict as much with each other as those of table 2.6. The same is true of by-products of animal husbandry such as wool. Unfortunately, it appears to be impossible to resolve this discrepancy.[90]

Subsidiary income. According to Buck, subsidiary work absorbed 36 percent of the man-equivalents per farm in Tingpien and 18 percent of those in Hsunyi.[91] The SKN shares which can be derived from this information by previous methods come close to 24 percent.[92] Subsidiary income accounted for 42 percent of the net income per farm in Tingpien, but its share in Hsunyi is not known. However, there appears to have been a close correlation between the share of subsidiary work effort and the share of subsidiary income in the sampled locations.[93] One therefore may guess that subsidiary work provided about 20 percent of the net income of farms in Hsunyi and about 25 percent in the whole SKN border region. All of these percentages exceed the relevant area, regional, and national averages.

Buck did not publish estimates of the absolute value of net income or of subsidiary income. But he determined the value of farm wages in Tingpien as well as in Hsunyi. Farm wages were relatively high in the former and relatively low in the latter location.[94] Because the difference relates in large measure to the estimated value of board, one may guess that it reflects primarily a difference in the price of food between a grain-deficit area and a grain-surplus area. In both locations, however, the earnings of day laborers and even their money wages were higher than those which the SKN border region government reported. It stated for the prerevolutionary period working men's wages of 0.15 to 0.20 *yuan* per day without specifying the value of board, other fringe benefits, and the date of inquiry.[95]

Information on the prices of grains and on the grain-equivalent of earnings in Tingpien and in Hsunyi is lacking. In lieu of the local data, it is possible to use the agricultural area averages of the wheat-equivalent of annual farm labor earnings. If one weights the 562 kg per man in the *spring wheat area* and the 666 kg per man in the *winter wheat-millet area* as previously,[96] one arrives at SKN averages of 629 kg for the area until 1939/40 and of 633 kg for the area after 1939/40.[97] An underestimate is risked by assuming that these rates represent the average subsidiary earnings per man-equivalent in the respective areas. On such a premise, one finds subsidiary incomes per farm household of 506 kg in Tingpien, of 333 kg in Hsunyi, of 394 kg in the area until 1939/40, and of 387 kg in the area after 1939/40.[98] The coarse-grain equivalent of money earnings may have been higher.[99]

Total income. By dividing subsidiary incomes by their relative shares in net incomes, one derives estimates of the grain equivalent of the net incomes in 1930/1931 of farm households in Tingpien, in Hsunyi, and in the SKN territory before and after 1939/40.[100] By subtracting subsidiary income from total income, one arrives at net income from farming. And by deducting from the crop product estimates the estimates of production costs,[101] hsien taxes, and land rent, one determines the net income from crop-growing. The difference between farm income and crop income may be attributed to animal husbandry. The results, which appear in table 2.8 in per capita terms, are at least as problematic as the subsidiary income estimates. But they are plausible in two important respects. The residuals seem to reflect correctly the importance of animal husbandry in Tingpien, and the estimates of total net income appear consistent with Buck's data on food consumption which are presented in table 2.9.[102]

Table 2.8

ESTIMATES OF PER CAPITA INCOMES
OF FARM HOUSEHOLDS

Unit: Kg of grain*

Item	Tingpien	Hsunyi	SKN territory [a] until 1939/40	after 1939/40
Grain product [b]				
most frequent	184.6	250.2	226.1	228.8
1930/1931	55.8	260.5	187.1	195.1
All crops, 1930/1931				
product [c]	55.8	267.6	192.6	200.9
cost [d]	18.5	25.0	22.6	22.9
hsien taxes [e]	5.1	26.5	18.9	19.8
land rent [f]	2.6	20.7	14.3	15.0
Net income, 1930/31				
crops	29.6	195.4	136.8	143.2
other (animals)	73.1	23.3	40.9	38.9
farm	102.7	218.7	177.7	182.1
subsidiary [g]	74.4	49.7	58.4	57.5
total	177.1 [h]	268.4 [i]	236.1	239.6

* One kg equals 2.2046 lbs.
a. Derived from data for Tingpien and Hsunyi plus reference 14.
b. Yield per unit of land times land per person. See references 77 to 79 and Buck, *Statistics,* pp. 286, 300.
c. Product per man-equivalent times man-equivalents per farm divided by persons per farm household. Derived from Buck, *Statistics,* pp. 297, 300-302.
d. Estimate: 10 percent of most frequent grain product. See Liu and Yeh, *Economy of the Chinese Mainland,* p. 414, for similar magnitudes.
e. Kg of wheat per yuan times yuan of hsien tax per unit of land times area of land per person. Derived from Buck,

Statistics, pp. 157, 165, 291, 300 (Hsunyi: medium grade of land; Tingpien: most usual land), and Buck, *Land Utilization in China,* pp. 305-306 (one silver dollar equals 7.52 kg of wheat in the spring wheat area and equals 8.68 kg of wheat in the winter wheat-millet area).

f. Estimate: Per capita crop product times 50 percent of share of rental land in farm area minus per capita hsien taxes times share of rental land. See Buck, *Statistics,* p. 55.

g. Income per farm divided by persons per farm household. See *ibid.,* p. 300, and reference 98.

h. Estimate: 506 kg divided by 42 percent times 6.8 persons. See reference 98 and Buck, *Statistics,* p. 309.

i. Estimate: 333 kg times 2.7 man-equivalents divided by 0.5 man-equivalents times 6.7 persons. See *ibid.*

Income distribution. Buck's data do not permit a performance of the same operations for each of the five farm-size classes which he distinguishes. However, his information on average farm sizes for these classes in combination with his estimates of most frequent yields suggests that as a rule, more than 10 percent of the farm population in Hsunyi, about 50 percent of the farm population in Tingpien, and by implication at least 20 percent of the farm population in the entire SKN area were unable to feed themselves merely by crop-growing.[103] This implication is consistent with the practice of the SKN border region government to exempt 21 percent of all farm households, regarded as *poor,* from agricultural taxation.[104] Moreover, about 30 percent of the farm population in Tingpien must have experienced extreme difficulties staying alive by any means.[105] The degree of income differentiation seems to have been comparatively small in both locations,[106] probably because agriculture yielded little surplus. The data for Suite and Michih support conflicting interpretations.

Hsien tax. At the average price for the respective agricultural area, the wheat equivalent of hsien tax accounted for 9 percent of the crop product in Tingpien in 1930 and for 10 percent of the crop product in Hsunyi in 1931. Such burdens, which were surprisingly high by national standards, were not unique. The information for Suite Hsien implies comparable levies for 1933.[107] And Buck as well as the Rural Reconstruction Commission observed that the fiscal imposition in this part of the country was severe.[108] Weighting the estimates of per capita tax payments in Tingpien and Hsunyi as previously and multiplying the SKN averages by the farm population estimates results in farm sector contributions of hsien tax revenues at 1930/1931 rates of about 146,00 piculs (or 21,900 metric tons) in the territory until 1939/40 and of 169,000 piculs (or 25,350 metric tons) in the territory after 1939/40.[109] The data for Suite yield estimates of 17,400 tons and 19,200 tons, respectively.[110]

Land rent. Net of hsien tax, the payment of land rent probably required less than 5 percent of the crop product in Tingpien in 1930 and close to 8 percent of that in Hsunyi in 1931. These shares were small in comparison with the national average and with the share of land rent in Suite.[111] The data for Tingpien and Hsunyi suggest total payments of land rent net of hsien tax of about 111,000 piculs (or 16,650 tons) of grain in the territory until 1939/40 and of 128,000 piculs (or 19,200 tons) of grain in the territory after 1939/40.[112] By the standard of Suite, which one should not accept, the total payment would have been twice as large.

Interest. Interest payments by the farm sector cannot be determined with confidence. There is evidence that the interest rate was near 3 percent per month. However, information on the length of the period of borrowing is lacking, and the available information on the share of borrowers and the extent of their borrowing is inconsistent with that on the share of lenders and the extend of their lending, even though most of the borrowing and lending apparently occurred among friends, relatives, and neighbors within the farm sector.[113] Because this borrowing and lending was intrasectoral, however, one's inability to estimate the interest payments is not so consequential.

Food consumption. Buck's data indicate that food consumption on the farms varied strongly with farm production—in quantity as well as in quality. In both Tingpien and Hsunyi, members of the farm population derived close to 95 percent of their total caloric intake from grains. Legumes and animal products supplied most of the very small residual in Tingpien. Vegetable oil accounted for most of the similarly small remainder in Hsunyi. Most of the grain and much of the legumes and meat were produced on the farm whereas most of the oil was purchased.[114] The average caloric intake per person was much higher in Hsunyi than in Tingpien, but it was quite low in both locations. Even in Hsunyi it merely approximated Buck's minimum standard of 2,800 calories per diem per adult male.[115] His data yield the rations of table 2.9. The corresponding total

Table 2.9

ESTIMATES OF PER CAPITA FOOD CONSUMPTION IN FARM HOUSEHOLDS

| Item | Tingpien [a] | Hsunyi [b] | SKN territory [c] | |
	1930	1931	until 1939/40	after 1939/40
Grams per diem				
Grains	366	559	491	498
Legumes	14	6	9	9
Oil	0	13	8	9
Vegetables	35	82	65	67
Animal products	7	5	6	6
Fruits	0	9	6	6
*Kg per annum**				
Grains	133.6	204.0	179.1	181.8
Legumes	5.1	2.2	3.2	3.1
Oil	0.0	4.7	3.0	3.2
Vegetables	12.8	29.9	23.8	24.5
Animal products	2.6	1.8	2.1	2.1
Fruits	0.0	3.3	2.1	2.3

* One kg equals 2.2046 lbs.
a. Buck, *Statistics,* p. 87.
b. *Ibid.,* p. 93.
c. Derived from references a, b, and 14.

consumption of grain by the farm population may be estimated as 1.38 million piculs (or 207,000 tons) for the area until 1939/40 and as 1.55 million piculs (or 232,500 tons) for the area after 1939/40. On the assumption that the nonfarm population consumed grain at the same rate, total grain consumption in the territory may be placed at 1.67 million piculs (or 250,500 tons) and 1.82 million piculs (or 273,000 tons), respectively.[116] These totals exceed the grain production estimates for 1930/31, and they approximate the estimates of most frequent production according to Buck. They also exceed the estimates of the SKN border region government for 1937/38 and 1940, as table 2.7 shows. The consumption of grain in Tingpien in 1930 was probably unusually low. Moreover, seed and feed have yet to be accounted for.[117] It thus appears that the SKN territory at best was barely self-sufficient in grains originally.

Level of living. Information on other expenditures is lacking or at least difficult to compare. But the data of tables 2.8 and 2.9 provide some insight, especially when they are compared with estimates for all of China:

Average per capita of the farm population	Kg of grain equivalent	
	China 1929-1933[118]	SKN 1930-1931[119]
Crop product	446	197
Subsidiary income (farm wages)	68.6	58
Total net income	490	238
Grain consumption	220	180
Residual	270	58

The data show that the crop product and the net income per capita of the farm population were more than twice as high in China on the average. The consumption of grain was somewhat lower in the SKN area than in all of China. But grains contributed more than 93 percent of the total caloric intake in the SKN area, in comparison with 83 percent in all of China.[120] Moreover, farmers in China on the average retained a much more substantial income share for other expenditures. The per capita residual in all of China was more than four times as large as that in the SKN area. It thus is evident that the SKN territory was an extraordinarily poor area within China.

Nonfarm Sector

Population. The estimates of total population and of farm population imply that the nonfarm population accounted for 17.2 percent of the total population in the area until 1939/40 and for 14.5 percent of the total population in the area after 1939/40.[121] The initial absolute numbers may be placed at 240,800 persons for 1936 and at 217,500 persons for 1940.[122] A decline in the size of the initial nonfarm population is also plausible since the SKN border region lost a disproportionate share of its urban sector during 1939/40.

Employment. In the absence of direct information, it is possible to derive employment estimates by subtracting the full-time plus part-time subsidiary employment of the farm population according to table 2.3 from the full-time plus part-time nonagricultural occupations of the total population according to table 2.2. Categoric and territorial differences render the results questionable,[123] but not all of the residuals in table 2.10 are implausible. The implication that most members of the professions did not reside in farm households appears to be consistent with the findings of the Rural Reconstruction Commission.[124] The implication that relatively large shares of all persons occupied in trade, transport, and manufacturing resided in farm households seems to conform with these results as well.[125] The numbers of nonfarm population occupied in trade and in home industry are obviously understated, for reasons mentioned previously.[126] Appropriate adjustments of their numbers do not change the principal conclusion which is inherent in the data of table 2.10. The nonfarm population, which must have been primarily urban population,[127] was engaged mostly in various professions, secondarily in domestic service, and only to a minor degree in materially productive activities. In particular, the surprisingly small number of persons employed in manufacturing appears consistent with estimates of the SKN border region government.[128] Almost all of them worked in small handicraft workshops, and very few were employed in large enterprises prior to the formation of SKN.[129]

Table 2.10

ESTIMATED DISTRIBUTION OF NONFARM
POPULATION ACCORDING TO EMPLOYMENT

Unit: 1,000 persons

Occupation of total population (Table 2.2)		Residual: Nonfarm		Employment of farm population (Table 2.3)
		1936		
Professions	70.0	64.2	5.8	Professions + scholars
Domestic service	36.4	36.4	— — — — —	Domestic service
Public service	8.4	6.0	2.4	Officials + soldiers
Trade	68.6	-2.1	70.7	Merchants
Transportation	12.6	12.6	— — — — —	Transportation
Manufacturing	22.4	3.9	18.5	Skilled + unskilled
Subtotal	103.6	14.4	89.2	Subtotal
Home industry	21.0	-32.3	53.3	Home industry
		1940		
Professions	75.0	68.6	6.4	Professions + scholars
Domestic service	39.0	39.0	— — — — —	Domestic service
Public service	9.0	6.4	2.6	Officials + soldiers
Trade	73.5	-0.9	74.4	Merchants
Transportation	13.5	13.5	— — — —	Transportation
Manufacturing	24.0	4.8	19.2	Skilled + unskilled
Subtotal	111.0	17.4	93.6	Subtotal
Home industry	22.5	-40.3	62.8	Home industry

Natural resources. The SKN border region contained fields of coal, iron, oil, and salt in several locations.[130] Most of these resources were being exploited prior to the establishment of the soviet, but apparently to minor degrees. In the case of salt, which was the most important resource, the SKN border region government reported that

> Before 1938, there were 461 salt fields in Kaochih, not even one in Laochih (people used to produce salt in the old lake), and only a few salt fields in Nannichih, Lienhuachih, Oupachih, Wawachih, Hant'anchih, etc. At that time, output of salt was very little, only amounting to several ten thousand loads (muleloads) a year.[131]

This output accounted for a few percent of the estimated production capacity of more than one million loads per annum.[132] In the case of oil, the production claims of the SKN border region government suggest that its total output could be increased drastically, too.[133] Evidence on the extent of iron and coal mining is lacking.

Income. The information on the structure of earnings of the nonfarm population is extraordinarily sketchy. The data of table 2.11 indicate that unskilled workers earned about as much and skilled workers (craftsmen) close to twice as much as the farm laborers did. The same earnings relations are inherent in the nationwide estimates which Liu and Yeh compiled. It is possible to determine the wheat equivalents of these earnings.[134] By multiplying them with the ratio of earnings of farm laborers in the SKN area and in China according to Buck,[135] one may derive earnings estimates for the SKN area in the early 1930s. These data appear in table 2.12. In the absence of an overall average for the professions, one may operate with the average of earnings in education and in medicine. In combination with the data of tables 2.10 and 2.12, this estimate yields average earnings of 1,124 kg of wheat per employed person[136] and of 575 kg of wheat per capita[137] of the nonfarm population. The latter amount is equal to 2.4 times the quantity of wheat earned per capita by the farm population.[138] A relation of this magnitude is indicated for China during the early 1950s,[139] so the conjectures are not implausible.

Expenditure. For lack of information, it is impossible to describe the impact of taxation and the structure of consumption. But one may note that the level of income of nonfarm households in the SKN area apparently did not exceed the level of income of farm households in all of China greatly.[140] Such an observation suggests an unusually low level of living for the nonfarm sector, too.

Table 2.11

DAILY AND ANNUAL WAGES OF VARIOUS OCCUPATIONS

Occupation location period	Cash payments		Total wages		Price of kg of wheat
	Money value Yuan	Wheat equiv. Kg*	Money value Yuan	Wheat equiv. Kg*	Yuan
Daily wages					
Yang Chia K'ou, 1931-36 [a]					
Carpenter	0.223	3.0			0.074
Mason	0.235	3.2			0.074
Bricklayer (1930)	0.250	2.5			0.100
Blacksmith	1.000	13.5			0.074
Laborer, male	0.133	1.8			0.074
Laborer, female (1936)	0.034	0.4			0.115
Farm Laborers, 1929-33 [b]					
Tingpien (1930)	0.26		0.46		
Hsunyi (1931)	0.20		0.38		
Spring wheat area	0.21	1.6	0.41	3.1	0.133
Winter wheat-millet area	0.25	2.2	0.41	3.6	0.115
China	0.24	2.4	0.46	4.6	0.099
Annual wages					
Yang Chia K'ou, 1931-36 [a]					
Laborer, male	32.7	44.2			0.074
Laborer, female (1936)	11.0	9.6			0.115
Farm laborers, 1929-33 [b]					
Tingpien (1930)	36.00		98.00		
Hsunyi (1931)	19.00		40.50		
Spring wheat area	32.32	243	74.77	562	0.133
Winter wheat-millet area	36.93	321	76.71	666	0.115
China	39.02	394	85.58	850	0.099

* One kg equals 2.2046 lbs.

a. Derived from Yen-an nung-ts'un tiao-ch'a t'uan, *Mi-chih hsien*, pp. 128-129 (wages) and p. 149 (price of wheat).

b. Derived from Buck, *Statistics*, p. 328 (wages) and Buck, *Land Utilization in China*, pp. 305-306 (prices of wheat).

Table 2.12

ESTIMATES OF NET VALUE ADDED PER PERSON
IN VARIOUS OCCUPATIONS [a]

Net value added per person employed in	Wheat-equivalent
Professions	
Old-style tutoring	577 kg*
Private school teaching	1,977 kg
Education, average	1,025 kg
Medicine	1,977 kg
Law, accounting	8,235 kg
Domestic service	535 kg
Public service	
Soldier	494 kg
Official	2,470 kg
Average	1,153 kg
Trade	
Stores	1,918 kg
Peddlers	1,070 kg
Average	1,499 kg
Transportation, old-style	906 kg
Handicraft production	1,070 kg

* One kg equals 2.2046 lbs.

a. Derived from Liu and Yeh, *Economy of the Chinese Main-land,* pp. 154, 161, 164-166, 600, 608 (wages, net value added) and 332 (price of wheat) as well as reference 96 and table 2.11. Assumption: wheat-equivalent of net value added in SKN equals wheat-equivalent of net value added in China times 630/850.

Summary

The available evidence on the initial state of the SKN border region is incomplete as well as imperfect. The bench-mark estimates which could be formed on its basis are therefore not necessarily firm. However, the sources which could be used in this undertaking appear to agree on the following principal facts:

(1) The area was characterized by a low density of population, a low fertility of land, and a backward state of the arts, all of which reflected themselves in low levels of productivity and income and thus in low rates of surplus over subsistence.

(2) Partly due to preceding declines, in response to drought, disorder, and deteriorating communications, the area contained unutilized natural resources in substantial quantities. In particular, there were large areas of uncultivated arable land and salt, iron, coal, and oil deposits which could be developed.

(3) Many technical production possibilities were not exploited anymore. Crops could be irrigated and cotton could be grown in selected parts of the area, as they once had been. Moreover, spinning and weaving could then be reactivated.

(4) Due to extraordinarily high infant mortality rates, the area's population stagnated. The realization of the area's larger productive potential therefore required the better utilization of a constant labor force and/or immigration.

(5) Prior to the arrival of the Chinese communists, the area had experienced heavy taxes and poor public service. This unfavorable balance of governmental costs and benefits could be changed, and both could also be redistributed.

(6) The extent of landlordism in the area is at issue. The low income level, the high tax rates, and the existence of uncultivated arable land all suggest that land tenure problems were not so pressing. Nevertheless, they could be solved by land reform.

The preceding points identify the major strategic limitations and opportunities which the Chinese communists faced in the Northwest, but they do not reveal the sentiments of the area's population directly. Buck's survey of the "special conditions" in various localities provides this evidence to some extent, but for broader areas. In comparison with respondents elsewhere, those in the *spring wheat area* and *winter wheat-millet area* were concerned to extraordinary degrees about problems of backwardness such as the lack of good schools, bad sanitation, prevalence of superstition, and inconvenient communications. Complaints about disasters (droughts, wind, insects, floods) and disorder (trouble with bandits or soldiers) were not voiced unusually often. Heavy taxes were objected to relatively frequently.[141] Opinions on land-tenure problems have not been made public.[142]

In general, Buck's findings are not as dismal as the impressions which other Western observers formed.[143] It is impossible to explain the discrepanices between these two views fully,[144] but it may be noted that both suggest the existence of opportunities as well as support for policies aiming at economic development and political stability. Moreover, disagreement on the seriousness of the land problem in SKN is compatible with the recognition of interest in land reform among the poor peasants who stood to benefit from it.

III

Evolution of
Economic Policy

The Chinese communists were quick to recognize these opportunities for economic development in their new base area in
the Northwest, and they attempted at once to realize them. By
the time they had consolidated their forces, expanded their
territory, and secured a state of truce with the Kuomintang-
dominated national government, they were also ready to institute a comprehensive development program in the newly constituted SKN border region. They were able to act so con-
structively so soon because the situation in the Northwest was
not altogether unfamiliar to them. They had encountered similar circumstances in their previous base areas in the Central
South, and they had devised their policies to suit those conditions. Measures which had proved successful or promising
could be reenacted at once, with few modifications. Needless
to say, such solutions took time to formulate, during the years
1927-1934, but after the Long March to the Northwest, it was
easy to reformulate them and later modify them to conform
with united-front agreements.

Uncertain Beginnings

From the very beginning the Chinese communist movement
had to solve two basic economic problems in order to survive in
the countryside. It had ". . . to feed and equip the Red Army,
and to bring immediate relief to the poor peasantry. Failing in
either, the Soviet base would soon collapse. To guarantee success at these tasks it was necessary for the Reds, even from
earliest days, to begin some kind of economic construction."[1]
Yet a good deal of time elapsed before this recognized need

was followed by action. Relief for the poor peasantry was to come first, but for quite a while this was to result primarily from the principal event of the agrarian revolution, the redistribution of land. And problems of base-area supply remained baffling to Mao Tse-tung as late as one year after the permanent shift to the countryside:

> The shortage of necessities and cash has become a very big problem for the army and the people inside the White encirclement. Because of the tight enemy blockade, necessities such as salt, cloth and medicines have been very scarce and dear all through the past year in the independent border area, which has upset, sometimes to an acute degree, the lives of the masses of the workers, peasants and petty bourgeoisie, as well as of the soldiers of the Red Army. The Red Army has to fight the enemy and to provision itself at one and the same time. It even lacks funds to pay the daily food allowance of five cents per person, which is provided in addition to grain; the soldiers are undernourished, many are ill, and the wounded in the hospitals are worse off. Such difficulties are of course unavoidable before the nation-wide seizure of political power; yet there is a pressing need to overcome them to some extent, to make life somewhat easier and especially to secure more adequate supplies for the Red Army. Unless the Party in the border area can find proper ways to deal with economic problems, the independent regime will have great difficulties during the comparatively long period in which the enemy's rule will remain stable. An adequate solution of these economic problems undoubtedly merits the attention of every Party member.[2]

By the time Mao felt compelled to make these statements in fall 1928, some advice was beginning to flow in. The Sixth Congress of the Chinese Communist Party, which was held in Moscow from 18 June to 11 July 1928, passed a resolution on the agrarian question which, like other policy initiatives of the congress, seems to have been prepared by the COMINTERN.[3]

The resolution demanded not only the redistribution of land and related assets plus the cancellation of usurious debts and exploitative contracts, all of which were to benefit the poor peasants the most, but also the earmarking of land and working capital for allotments to the soldiers of the Red Army. In addition, all previous taxes and levies were to be abolished, while a unified progressive (income) tax was to be instituted in its place. And there was a call for state assistance to agriculture, specifically for ". . . (a) organization of agriculture, (b) improvement and expansion of the irrigation system, (c) assistance in the struggle with natural calamities, (d) governmental organization of migration, (e) organization of cheap credit through agricultural banks and credit cooperatives, (f) organization of market and supply cooperatives, and (g) establishment of a unified monetary system and a unified system of weights and measures."[4]

The proposed measures added up to a simple rural development program which could serve to improve the living conditions of both the people and the communist units in the base areas. But they apparently were not meant to cope with the effects of the Kuomintang government's counterinsurgency strategy. How to respond to the blockade remained one of the principal issues in the base areas throughout their existence, and it soon involved much more than merely questions of supply.

Goods could be obtained from the outside either by launching forays into enemy territory or by blockade-running. Confiscating the wealth of the rich and requisitioning on the outside were as such much less costly than trading with the enemy on adverse terms. Yet they also offered strictly momentary gains, since foraging tended to exhaust at once not only the stocks of needed items but also the goodwill of those who could make them available again. For the longer run, therefore, smuggling had the advantage if enough surplus could be raised within the base areas for this purpose. Of course the cultivation of such business relations necessitated the acceptance of the business partners, and this more lenient approach to the petty bourgeoisie inside as well as outside the encirclement posed fundamental ideological issues.

To complicate matters, rapprochement with these "intermediate classes" was scarcely promising in view of the expropriation that had already taken place and was continuing with respect to "local tyrants" and other remaining enemies. The circumstances made it most difficult to distinguish clearly between potential friends and foes among the propertied classes.

The need for a more positive policy toward the petty bourgeoisie as well as the problems of appealing to them effectively became apparent fairly soon, at least to Mao Tse-tung.[5] In late 1928 and early 1929 directives were issued against the "reckless burning and killing" by the Red Army, for the "protection of the interests of the middle and small merchants," and the like. The impact of these evident changes in orientation is hard to determine, however. Recent Chinese sources assert that trade redeveloped and that expropriation became less important as a source of revenue.[6] But statements at the time suggest that confiscated wealth continued to fund a major portion of public expenditure throughout the soviet period,[7] even in the Northwest.[8] Moreover, *serious doubts have been voiced about the extent to which any policy was implemented prior to the establishment of an adequate administrative structure late in 1931.*[9]

Institutionalization of the Revolution

Such improvements in organization followed the convocation of the First Congress of Soviets of Workers', Peasants', and Red Army Representatives of China. It convened in Juichin, Kiangsi Province, in December 1931, established the Chinese Soviet Republic, and elected Mao Tse-tung its chairman. The principal norms which the congress enacted, mainly in the form advocated by the COMINTERN,[10] did not differ much from those adopted on previous occasions, e.g., by the sixth party congress. This was true in particular of the principles of economic policy as they were stated most generally in articles 5 to 7 of the Constitution of the Chinese Soviet Republic:[11]

> 5. It shall be the purpose of the Soviet Government radically to improve the standard of living of the working class, to pass labour legislation, to introduce the eight-hour working day, to fix a minimum wage and to institute social insurance and state

assistance to the unemployed as well as to grant the workers the right to control industry.

6. In setting itself the task of abolishing feudalism and radically improving the standard of living of the peasants the Soviet Government in China shall pass a land law, shall order the confiscation of the land of the landlords and its distribution among the poor and middle peasants, with a view towards the ultimate nationalization of the land.

7. It shall be the purpose of the Soviet Government in China to defend the interests of the workers and peasants and restrict the development of capitalism, with a view to liberating the toiling masses from capitalist exploitation and leading them to the socialist order for society. The Soviet Government in China shall free the toiling masses from all burdensome taxation and contributions introduced by previous counter-revolutionary governments and shall put into effect a single progressive tax. It shall adopt every conceivable measure to suppress all attempts at wrecking and sabotage on the part of either native or foreign capitalists; it shall pursue an economic policy which shall be directed towards defending the interests of the worker and peasant masses, which shall be understood by these masses and which shall lead to socialism.

In accordance with these norms, the first congress passed a labor law which was progressive by any standard and thus contrasted sharply with the backward conditions in the base areas that limited its applicability even in the public sector.[12] The first congress also enacted a land law which apparently reversed previous changes toward a more lenient treatment of the rich peasants without modifying other regulations substantially.[13] In addition, the congress adopted various resolutions in regard to the Red Army. The "Regulations Concerning the Privileges Extended to the Chinese Workers' and Peasants' Red Army" provided in detail for the support of Red Army men and their dependents through land grants, free cultivation of land, freedom from taxation, various free services, price reductions, medical care, pensions, burial, aid to dependents, etc.[14]

The first congress also passed a fairly comprehensive resolution on economic policy which apparently went well beyond previous development proposals.[15] With respect to industry, it secured at least temporarily the position not only of Chinese but also foreign capitalists in industrial, handicraft, and home-industry production on the condition that they would remain loyal to the Soviet and submit to worker control. Moreover, it urged the "utmost" development of industry in general and of enterprises serving the Red Army in particular. The latter point was reinforced by a separate instruction on the importance of developing an armaments industry:

> In order to guarantee the Red Army's supply of all requisite weapons and munitions, the necessary enterprises for the manufacture of munitions as well as arsenals and centralized supply departments shall be created.[16]

In addition, the resolution on economic policy promised internal freedom of trade, subject to the same general conditions and so long as speculation and price inflation could be kept within proper bounds. It placed trade with the non-Soviet area under governmental control and required the licensing of silver exports. Furthermore, it abolished chambers of commerce, prohibited private monopolistic practices, encouraged the formation of cooperatives, and called for the development of some state trade.

In the fiscal and monetary sphere, the resolution called on the Soviets to abolish all existing taxes and to "introduce a single progressive tax which shall mainly be levied upon the bourgeoisie." Army men, workers, and poor people were to be exempted. A Workers' and Peasants' Bank with the right of note issue was to be created as the financial instrument of the Soviet government. Private banks could continue to issue banknotes. Usury was forbidden, pawned articles were to be returned to their owners unconditionally without payment, and all pawnshops became Soviet property. Finally, the resolution provided for rent reductions for the urban poor as well as for the confiscation and redistribution of enemy houses in the cities.

Additional ordinances by the government affirmed and specified the right to invest and to engage in business subject to licensing. They also regulated the organization of cooperatives which were described as "one of the chief forms of development of Soviet economy,. . ." The regulation distinguished between consumers' cooperatives, industrial cooperatives, and credit cooperatives. It viewed all of them as weapons in the struggle against capitalists (traders, industrialists, usurers). A third ordinance regulated lending and in particular the rate of interest on loans. It limited the monthly maxima to 1.2 percent on short-term loans and to 1 percent on long-term loans, at a time when in "normal" circumstances elsewhere the prevailing rates appear to have been twice as high.[17]

In summary, the actions taken by the first congress and its organs show that by the time the Chinese communists were in a position to constitute their Chinese Soviet Republic, they also were familiar with most of the measures which could serve to solve their economic problems. However, *they still had to implement most of these solutions effectively.* And they had yet to agree with Mao that their revolutionary extremism—in subsequent party history referred to as the "third left line" and attributed to the "Russian returned students"—limited the effectiveness of such efforts in several respects.[18]

The Emerging Mass Line

Statements which point to a growing awareness that revolutionary extremism limited effectiveness appeared close to two years later, after determined steps had been taken to improve the administrative organs in the economic sphere, notably the finance department.[19] The seemingly greater "realism" of those in charge of economic policy then may have been enhanced by their struggle against bureaucratism, corruption, and dogmatism (as well as incompetence). But it appears to have been strengthened even more by the experience of a rapidly tightening blockade, which made it unavoidable to rely more and more on internal resources. To mobilize them, the soviet government first organized in spring 1933 the People's Commission for National Economy with a hierarchy of administrative departments down to the hsien level.[20] It then promoted in summer 1933 an economic construction campaign.

The change in orientation which accompanied these events was spelled out most clearly by Mao Tse-tung at the Second National Congress of Workers' and Peasants' Representatives in January 1934:

> Our central task at present is to mobilize the broad masses to take part in the revolutionary war, overthrow imperialism and the Kuomintang by means of such war, spread the revolution throughout the country, and drive imperialism out of China. Anyone who does not attach enough importance to this central task is not a good revolutionary cadre. If our comrades really comprehend this task and understand that the revolution must at all costs be spread throughout the country, then they should in no way neglect or underestimate the question of the immediate interests, the well-being, of the broad masses. For the revolutionary war is a war of the masses; it can be waged only by mobilizing the masses and relying on them.
>
> If we can only mobilize the people to carry on the war and do nothing else, can we succeed in defeating the enemy? Of course not. If we want to win, we must do a great deal more. We must lead the peasants' struggle for land and distribute land to them, heighten their labor enthusiasm and increase agricultural production, safeguard the interests of the workers, establish co-operatives, develop trade with outside areas, and solve the problems facing the masses —food, shelter and clothing, fuel, rice, cooking oil and salt, sickness and hygiene, and marriage. In short, all the practical problems in the masses' everyday life should claim our attention. If we attend to these problems, solve them and satisfy the needs of the masses, we shall really become organizers of the well-being of the masses, and they will truly rally round us and give us their warm support. Comrades, will we then be able to arouse them to take part in the revolutionary war? Yes, indeed we will."[21]

The specific means to this end, which had been set out already during the economic construction campaign,[22] were restated by the second congress in its "Resolution on Soviet Economic Construction" of January 1934.[23] Its introductory survey over achievements in economic work during the preceding year served to make the point that the substance of the resolution had already proved its worth. The remainder dealt not only with economic construction but reiterated in eleven points most of the policies which had been advocated on previous occasions. It thus became the most concise and systematic statement on economic strategy yet and is paraphrased below for this reason.

Point One concerned methods of increasing agricultural production. It advocated the year-round cropping movement, demanded solutions to the peasants' difficulties caused by the shortage of draft animals, seeds, fertilizer, water, tools, capital, labor power, etc., and urged to this end the widespread formation of mutual aid groups and cooperatives (e.g. labor-aid groups, animal and fertilizer cooperatives). It called on the government to operate agricultural experiment stations and animal stations. It also demanded the beginning of instruction in insect and flood control, the cultivation of necessities such as cotton, and forest preservation.

Point Two emphasized the simultaneous need for developing the small handicraft industry. It focussed on the production of armaments, exportable goods, and necessities. It listed specifically tungsten, coal, iron, lime, paper, soda, cloth, camphor, drugs, tobacco, oil, sugar, wood, and agricultural implements. It called on the government to assist every potential or actual producer, to form cooperatives, and to direct the flow of the masses' capital into these pursuits. It also advised the government to encourage private capitalists to invest and enlarge production in most of these branches of industry, and it even permitted the rental or sale of confiscated enterprises to them. It advocated state management for special cases (e.g., the tungsten mines, weaving mills, paper manufacturing plants, and various armaments industries). In general, however, it endorsed cooperatives as the appropriate form of organization in the current backward circumstances.

Point Three demanded raising and spreading the labor spirit of the worker and peasant masses. Under this heading, it called on activists to scatter in order to raise production, on the government to distinguish model units and encourage emulation, on the female masses to increase their participation in agriculture and industry, and on workers in private capitalist enterprises to increase their labor productivity. Moreover, it called on all the worker and peasant masses to understand that under the soviet system improvements in living cannot be separated from the development of production. In addition, this point of the resolution dealt with the formation of communist attitudes toward labor through education and related questions.

Point Four stressed the need to break the economic blockade and develop the external trade of the soviet region. Tungsten, paper, lumber, and rice were to be exported, while daily necessities such as oil, salt, and cloth were to be imported. For this purpose, the resolution required the establishment of an external trade bureau, of various trade corporations, and of purchasing stations. Their leadership and their organizational work were to be strengthened. Point Four advocated the utilization of private and cooperative capital in external trade and the maintenance of appropriate relations with these agents. It promised them freedom of trade within the limits set by tariff policy, and it encouraged everybody's initiative in external trade.

Point Five attributed special significance for the development of commerce within the soviet to the formation of consumer cooperatives. Through them, the worker and peasant masses would be able to buy more cheaply and sell more dearly (than through the conventional middlemen), and they thus could improve their living. Cooperative organizations were to be established at the hsien, provincial, and central levels, and they were to receive as much manpower and financial aid as possible. In conclusion, the call went out for improvements in cooperative work, in the interest of improving the living of the masses.

Point Six stressed in this connection that the primary task of soviet economic construction was solving the grains problem. To improve the situation, the grains department was to engage in price regulation as well as in investigation, collection and storage, transportation, and other activities relating to grains. Moreover, the existing organization of the grain trade was called inadequate, and the formation of grains cooperatives as the mass basis for the grains department was considered desirable for the solution of the problem.

Point Seven dealt with the shortage of capital as one of the great difficulties in the development of soviet economy. But it also noted the inadequate utilization of mass capital and private capital by the soviet government. The government's performance in the financial sphere was criticized and the formation of credit cooperatives was advocated both as a method of overcoming the capital shortage and as a powerful weapon in the struggle against usury. In addition, Chairman Mao's call for the issuance of three million yuan of bonds was endorsed.

Point Eight advised extreme caution in the issuing of bank notes. It acknowledged that during prolonged periods of war, deficit financing was one way of making ends meet. But it emphasized that the soviet government had to choose a method which placed the burden of the revolutionary struggle on the exploiting classes and increased various kinds of tax revenues during the course of the development of soviet economy. Increases in the money supply were to be determined by the requirements of external and internal trade, subject always to maintaining the value of the currency.

Point Nine warned that the imperialists, landlords, and capitalists not only imposed war and an economic blockade from the outside but also engaged in obstruction on the inside. It called for resolute struggle against such reactionary practices as shop closings, work stoppages, discrediting the currency, disturbing finances, speculating, and raising prices. It also demanded proletarian vigilance against the subversive activities of reactionary elements in the state organs as well as in the cooperatives, the prosecution of such actions, and so forth.

Point Ten directed that the leadership of the department of national economy, the department of finance, the department of grains, and the state bank be strengthened in order to speed and improve the fulfilment of certain concrete tasks. With respect to economic construction, it opposed the "left right opportunistic" and bureaucratistic leadership in these departments, urged training and placement of many new cadres, advocated strengthening the leadership of the proletariat, recommended greater use of women on the economic front, and called for work conducive to the transition to socialism.

Point Eleven stressed finally that economic construction could not be separated from the revolutionary struggle. It had to meet its needs and leave many economic problems unsolved until the day of victory. Only then would it be possible to follow the road of soviet socialist construction, to the final liberation of China's toiling masses.

In summary, the first eight points outlined a comprehensive development program which could serve to meet the "immediate interests of the masses." Of course, the last three points added to this program once again considerations which were more characteristic of the "third left line." Similar manifestations of strategic incongruity had appeared earlier, during the land investigation drive of summer 1933, which had been undertaken to facilitate the economic construction campaign.[24] Both phenomena indicate that the Chinese communist movement had yet to complete its reorientation from the COMINTERN's "class line" to Mao's "mass line" approach when it was about to lose its base areas in the Central South. Moreover, *the repetitousness of the pronouncements suggests that many proposals had yet to be implemented shortly before this territory had to be abandoned.*

From Kiangsi to Yenan

When the Chinese communists ventured on their famous Long March to the Northwest, they took along with them the lessons which they had learned during seven years of struggle in the Central South. Included among these intangible possessions was a comprehensive development program for rural base areas plus valuable experiences with its implementation which could readily be used in the new territory. However, the extreme setbacks of 1934, the experience of the Long March, and the unsettled state in the Northwest added to this know-how a sense of caution which was most clearly expressed by Mao Tse-tung in his lectures on "Problems of Strategy in China's

Revolutionary War" of December 1936[25] Mao called attention
to a principal consequence of mobile warfare which may not
have been so apparent to him and others previously:

> Fluidity in the war and in our territory produces
> fluidity in all fields of construction in our base areas.
> Construction plans covering several years are out of
> the question. Frequent changes of plan are all in the
> day's work.

> It is to our advantage to recognize this charac-
> teristic. We must base our planning on it and must
> not have illusions about a war of advance without
> any retreats, take alarm at any temporary fluidity of
> our territory or of the rear areas of our army, or
> endeavour to draw up detailed long-term plans. We
> must adapt our thinking and our work to the cir-
> cumstances, be ready to sit down as well as to march
> on, and always have our marching rations handy. It is
> only by exerting ourselves in today's fluid way of life
> that tomorrow we can secure relative stability, and
> eventually full stability.[26]

The choice of mobile warfare thus limited the ways in which
the Chinese communist movement could expect to realize the
"immediate interests of the masses" as well as its own interest in
the masses' support. And it made not only for short-term policies in general but for redistributive acts in particular as the
most appropriate solutions to economic problems. Shifts to
new territory made it possible to confiscate the wealth of even
more members of the enemy classes for the benefit of both the
masses and the movement. The loss of territory of course
meant that most if not all of the achievements of the agrarian
revolution would be undone under renewed counterrevolution-
ary rule. But this consequence did not have to diminish the
revolutionary orientation of the masses, and it could not be
prevented in any case. So far as the communist movement itself
was concerned, the more it could live off the enemy, the less it
would be damaged by the need to move on. It was, therefore,
unwise to come to depend on the resources of any base area for
long, even if they sufficed to meet all requirements.[27]

The Long March represented this situation of terrial fluidity in the extreme.[28] But the initial period in the Northwest also lacked stability. Pockets of revolutionary activity became contiguous, and the total territory of the soviet grew as the various units of the Red Army arrived in succession at the new location. The principal revolutionary changes had yet to be made systematically in this expanding area. Wealth, especially land, had to be redistributed, and new political institutions had to be formed for this and other purposes. Moreover, since the territory lacked many essential resources, such supplies had to be obtained from external enemies, notably through raids into the neighboring territory of the warlord Yen Hsi-shan.[29] For all of these reasons and because the new base area, too, remained threatened at least until the united front against Japan began to take shape, economic construction was stressed less than it had been in the Central South, although it was not ignored[30] Moreover, since the interval between the end of the Long March and the establishment of the united front was extraordinarily short, *the actual accomplishments in economic policy had to be quite limited.* The same may be said of the results of efforts to institutionalize the revolution.[31]

Strategic Continuity and Strategic Innovation

The formation of the united front against Japan changed the options of the Chinese communist movement drastically. As their contribution to the settlement of all internal strife for the duration of the war, the communists, according to Mao, made the following four pledges:

(1) the Communist-led government in the Shensi-Kansu-Ningsia revolutionary base area will be renamed the Government of the Special Region of the Republic of China and the Red Army will be redesignated as part of the National Revolutionary Army, and they will come under the direction of the Central Government in Nanking and its Military Council respectively;

(2) a thorough democratic system will be applied in the areas under the Government of the Special Region;

(3) the policy of overthrowing the Kuomintang by armed force will be discontinued; and

(4) the confiscation of the land of the landlords
will be discontinued.[32]

In exchange, the communists were assured their base area,
most parts of which had been exposed to land reform already,[33]
and they secured financial and logistic support for their army.[34]
For some time to come, they thus experienced unusually favorable conditions in which to demonstrate the lessons they had
learned along their way. With much less internal strife, they
could build a model base for mobilizing resistance against
Japan as well as for improving the people's material and cultural lives. With the agrarian revolution delayed for the duration of the war, they could even call on "patriotic gentry,"
landlords, and capitalists to join in this endeavor.[35]

Of course, such unprecedented external security and outside
support might tempt the movement to become overly dependent on both and to lose its self-reliant orientation. Tendencies to react in this manner were displayed by some of the
"Russian returned students"[36] and shared by many bureaucrats,
including intellectuals who had come to Yenan in search of
national salvation.[37] But they evidently ran counter to official
policy. In his report on the work of the government to the first
representative assembly of the SKN border region, which met
belatedly due to the war in January 1939, Chairman Lin Pai-
ch'ü enumerated the methods that had been used during 1937
and 1938 to build a defense economy and to improve the living
of the people under conditions of backwardness:[38]

1. With respect to agriculture: activate the people
to form labor-aid groups in order to regulate labor
power. Activate women and children to participate
in production in order to increase labor power. Encourage labor emulation in order to raise the masses'
labor spirit. Support the peasants in solving difficulties concerning draft animals, farm tools, and seeds,
and extend rural credit in order to circulate rural
capital.

2. With respect to handicrafts: eliminate oppressive taxes. Encourage handicraft production. Strictly
prohibit speculation, monopoly, and cornering of the

market. Protect regular commercial profit. Lower
taxes and interest rates. Develop the cooperative
movement. Repair and extend public roads in the
interest of transport and communications.

3. With respect to public enterprises: strengthen
the development of petroleum and coal mining. Enlarge the scale of the paper factory. Establish a refugee factory. Improve the equipment and technique of
the printing plant so that it becomes a modern factory.

Moreover, the implementation of these measures constituted
only the beginning of an increasingly active policy of import
substitution. In his specification of the tasks of the SKN border
region government during the new stage of the war of resistance, Chairman Lin formulated the following seven targets for
the campaign to enlarge production:[39]

1. Increase cultivated land, in 1939 by 600,000
mou, and double cotton and hemp production. To
reach these goals, it is necessary to broadly rise the
labor spirit, to mobilize women to study production,
and to encourage labor emulation.

2. Mobilize the administrative organs, schools, and
rear units of the army to produce for themselves, so
that they reach self-sufficiency in grains and vegetables.

3. Develop animal husbandry so that the stock of
animals doubles. Peasants are to be called upon to
gather capital to buy ewes, cows, and jenny asses. The
export or slaughter of ewes is to be forbidden.

4. Develop handicrafts and modern industries,
promulgate laws that encourage handicraft production, invite businessmen from the outside to come to
the border region to invest, and promulgate laws
which protect capital.

5. Develop public enterprises. The textile factory
in *Ch'uan-k'ou* is to be added to and enlarged so as
to enable it to meet the clothing needs of the administrative organs, schools, and army units. Improve and enlarge the production of paper. Develop

farm tool-making, oil-pressing, leather-making, and other handicrafts so that they meet the needs of the people and organs.

6. In the case of petroleum and coal mining, strengthen management, increase production, and raise quality.

7. Develop cooperation in production and consumption.

The first border region assembly, in its resolution on the work of the government, endorsed these points and broadened them. It in fact adopted a comprehensive development program for the purposes of defense and material wellbeing. In the context of specifying the tasks of defense mobilization, which also involved military manpower mobilization and spiritual mobilization, the assembly recognized six tasks of resource mobilization:[40]

1. Enlarge the cultivated area, develop irrigation schemes, improve methods of cultivation, increase agricultural production.

2. Develop animal husbandry, increase the quantity of animals.

3. Develop handicrafts and military industries, improve and enlarge the production of handicrafts, raise the quality of military industries.

4. Develop transportation and communications, improve public and side roads, develop cooperative activities, let the markets abound and flourish.

5. Encourage commercial investment, protect commercial enterprises, in the interest of commercial development.

6. Enforce vigorously in public finance increases in income and decreases in expenditure, initiate in all organs, schools, and rear army units a production movement and an economizing movement, help solve difficulties with wartime expenses.

In addition to the above six tasks of resource mobilization for the conduct of the war, the assembly propagated seven measures to improve the people's living:[41]

1. Effectively preserve the benefits which the people obtained from the land reform, as well as cause them to solidify and develop.

2. Develop production, raise production technique, increase the people's real income.

3. Raise the labor spirit, induce women to study production.

4. Ration foods and important daily necessities.

5. Develop cooperation in production and consumption.

6. Strengthen the work of aiding refugees and relieving invalids, do not turn them into homeless vagrants, develop sanitation and health-protection services so as to increase the health and strength of the people.

7. Strengthen child-care work, pay attention to children's health, cause them to grow up in good health.

The preceding excerpts appear in such repetitive detail because they serve to demonstrate the strategic continuity from Kiangsi to Yenan. A comparison of these 1939 statements with those of January 1934 attests to this fact. But it also reveals one important innovation. In order to reduce their imposition on the border region, all units of the border region government (organs, schools, rear army) were called upon not only to make do with as little as possible but also to produce as much as possible for their own sustenance. This policy, which subsequently became the core of the campaign for "better troops and simpler administration,"[42] was feasible because the garrison in the SKN border region did not engage in warfare so long as the truce with the national government lasted. The Chinese communists thus initiated the production movement in the army apparently for tactical reasons. However, at least Mao Tse-tung soon came to believe that production did not serve merely as an alternative to confiscation during the war of resistance.[43] In opposition to those who thought that the policy jeopardized the quality of the army Mao argued that it actually made them "better troops." By 1945, he put his position in the following form:

Some people say that if the army units go in for production, they will be unable to train or fight and that if the government and other organizations do so, they will be unable to do their own work. This is a false argument. . . .

Thus it can be seen that in the context of guerrilla warfare in the rural areas, those army units and government and other organizations which undertake production for self-support show greater energy and activity in their fighting, training and work, and improve their discipline and their unity both internally and with the civilians. Production for self-support is the outcome of our country's protracted guerilla war and this is our glory. Once we master it, no material difficulty can daunt us. We shall grow in vigour and energy year by year and become stronger with every battle; we shall overwhelm the enemy and have no fear of his overwhelming us."[44]

The Chinese communists reiterated the above policies in varying form on several occasions during the course of the war of resistance against Japan, with minor modifications and shifts in emphasis to match the changing circumstances inside as well as outside the SKN border region. Because their implementation of this economic development program lagged well behind its initial adoption, however, the impression arose that fundamental changes in orientation occurred later in the war, in response to growing necessity.[45]

Summary

The indications are that the Chinese communists had no ready solution to their economic problems when they first took to the hills of South Central China. But by trial and error they rapidly learned to survive there, with and at times against the advice of the COMINTERN. By the end of the Kiangsi era at least Mao Tse-tung and his followers within the movement had reached a rather profound understanding of their situation.

Mao's doctrine of the immediate interests of the masses attributed critical importance not only to the agrarian revolution but to the direct improvement of all aspects of life. In this connection, it viewed economic development as a means of achieving logistic as well as popular political support. The resolution on economic construction plus numerous detailed instructions outlined the methods by which such development was to be brought about. The program of rehabilitation, import substitution, trade promotion, and financial regularization could be termed "neo-mercantilistic." The methods of labor mobilization and income redistribution were of course of the soviet type. The constitution, various laws and regulations, and again the resolution on economic construction designated the organizational instruments which were to implement the development program. It is noteworthy that they limited the extent of state management to a few strategic activities, promoted cooperation in most other activities, and tolerated or even encouraged private enterprise almost everywhere.

The Chinese communists had to abandon their base areas in the Central South before they could derive substantial benefits from this strategy. But they took their knowledge with them to the Northwest, and when the united-front era afforded them the opportunity to try again, they wasted little time in attempting to implement the lessons which they had learned during the soviet period. Their economic development program for the SKN border region resembled previous plans in most respects, with one modification: all members of the movement—functionaries, soldiers, students, and teachers—were called upon to participate in production to support themselves, in addition to continuing in their primary occupations.

Of course, the propagation of all of these measures soon after the formation of the SKN border region by itself did not assure their implementation. Realizing the program required the formation of appropriate organizations and the provision of suitable incentives.

IV

Organization of Development

To implement their development program, the Chinese communists likewise drew on their experiences in the Central South. They not only instituted representative government, first in the form of soviets and then along lines more consistent with the united-front agreement,[1] but they also promoted purposive organization and conscious cooperation on a dualistic pattern which reflected the diversity of interests in the region. In the case of activities which were believed to be in the immediate interest of the people, which were familiar to them, and which could be improved considerably by minor changes in tools and techniques, mass organization and voluntary cooperation were prescribed. In the case of activities which served the communist movement directly, which were new to the people, and which required more modern means and methods of production, state organization and directed cooperation were chosen. The Chinese communists quite clearly favored these more socialistic approaches, but did not rely on them exclusively. They also tolerated and even encouraged private initiative in many spheres, by providing psychic as well as material incentives for the improvement of individual performances.

Mass Organization and State Administration

The organizational success of the Chinese communists seems to be indicated by their claim that as of June 1939 more than 90 percent of the entire population of the SKN border region belonged to the *Anti-Enemy Rear Support Association.* This united-front organization was said to coordinate at least twenty-five mass organizations with overlapping functions and memberships. Numerically most important were the General Union with 48,000 members, the Patriotic Youth Association with 168,023 members, the Women's Federation with 173,878 members, the Peasants' Association with 421,000 members, and the *K'ang Ta* (Anti-Japanese Military Academy) Alumni Association with 20,000 members.[2]

Most of the larger organizations and the united-front association as well were said to maintain elaborate structures of territorial and functional subdivisions.[3] Moreover, practically all of them performed overlapping "patriotic" or war-related duties in addition to their primary tasks and in various ways served more than one principal policy objective.[4] They may thereby have extended the influence of the state administrative apparatus (and of the communist movement) well beyond formal limits, thus allowing both of the latter to remain relatively small in size. However, the scarcity of subsequent mentions of their work and the later propagation of mass campaigns without reference to them suggest that most mass organizations were probably relatively ineffective instruments.[5]

Whatever the division of labor between state administration and mass organizations may have been, the bureaucracy of both was relatively small, reaching only 7,900 in 1942, 8,200 in 1943, and 15,000 in 1945, exclusive of teachers.[6] The state administrative apparatus alone apparently employed close to 4,500 persons in 1944.[7] Although these numbers accounted for very small fractions of the total population, they were considered to be excessively large and subject to decrease.

Defense Organization

To defend the SKN border region, the Chinese communists not only maintained a garrison of the Eighth Route Army in its territory but also formed a militia-like *self-defense corps* with various supporting units. According to official claims, this corps had 224,325 members in 1939 and 145,000 members in 1943.[8] Its decline from about 15 percent to about 10 percent of the border region population cannot be explained. It apparently is not attributable to the inclusion in 1939 of auxiliary units. The women's self-defense corps, youth self-defense corps, and young vanguards added at least 50,000 and perhaps even 80,000 members to the defense forces in that year.[9] The self-defense corps was divided into regular and elite units. The regular units performed a variety of duties (guarding, settling veterans, supporting dependents of soldiers, mobilizing supplies for the army, etc.) in their localities. The elite units, estimated at 42,000 in 1939 and at 22,000 in 1943,[10] tended to be located near the front. At times, they were activated into the army.[11]

The size of the Eighth Route Army contingent was doubtlessly much smaller than that of the self-defense corps, but the approximate number of troops is somewhat in question. Snow estimated that the border region in 1936 held a total of 40,000 men which soon swelled to 90,000 men.[12] A large number of troops moved out to the front in fall 1937, but some units returned after 1938 to reinforce the garrison. Forman and Stein in 1944 were told of 40,000 to 50,000 troops.[13] Estimates of 33,000 men in 1938, 40,000 to 41,500 men in 1940, and 45,000 men in 1941 are related to these numbers.[14] The 1945 total of 20,000 troops,[15] which is matched by a 1939 reference to the fact that 20,000 households were affected by separation from production for military reasons,[16] indicates that about half of the garrison had been locally recruited.[17] It thus appears that regular military service, which remained voluntary during the period, diverted not more than 2 percent of the region's original population or not more than 4 percent of its indigenous labor force from civilian pursuits. But defense could impose more heavily on the product of the SKN border region—in the absence of outside aid and of self-sufficiency of the Eighth Route Army units. The effects of militia service on productive efforts and the allocation of products cannot be estimated with sufficient confidence.

Economic Organization

To develop the SKN border region economically, the Chinese communists not only created state-operated enterprises but also advocated the formation of various types of cooperatives on the largest possible scale. If the employment data of table 4.1 are chosen as indicators, it appears that cooperatives were the prevalent new form of economic organization. In 1937 there were only 270 employees in state-operated enterprises (exclusive of about 1,300 persons in army shops?),[18] while the number of cooperators approached 80,000 persons (inclusive of 20,000 persons who participated in labor-aid groups). By 1943 these proportions had changed notably. Whereas state-operated enterprises now employed 6,300 persons, all forms of cooperation accounted for more than 280,000 members. The cooperators thus continued to predominate. Of course, total numbers of participants constitute merely one measure of relative importance for these alternative forms of organization. For a more comprehensive view, these numbers need to be supplemented with information on the structure of state and cooperative activities.

Table 4.1

GROWTH OF NEW FORMS OF ENTERPRISE, 1937-1944

Year	Members of consumer cooperatives	Members of producer cooperatives	Members of all regular cooperatives	Members of CIC societies	Members of labor-aid groups	Employees of state enterprises
1937	57,847 [a]	70 [b]			20,000 [c]	270 [d]
1938	66,707 [a]	3,620 [b]				
1939	82,885 [a]	28,531 [b]	> 80,000 [b]	298 [b]		700 [d]
1940	123,279 [a]					1,000 [d]
1941	140,218 [a]					7,000 [d]
1942	143,721 [a]	73,000 [e] (?)		602 [f]		3,991 [g]
1943	150,000 [a]		200,000 [h]	1,591 [b]	81,128 [i]	6,300 [j]
1944	+ 182,878 [a]		250,000 [e]		*160,000 [i]	

+ February
* Planned.
a. Mao Tse-tung, "Ching-chi wen-t'i yü ts'ai-cheng wen-t'i," *Mao Tse-tung hsüan-chi,* 1947 ed., Vol. 5, p. 49, and Hsü, *A Survey,* Part 2, p. 121.
b. Nym Wales, *Notes on the Beginnings of the Industrial Cooperatives in China,* pp. 59-63 (Hereinafter cited as Nym Wales, *Notes*).
c. Edgar Snow, *Random Notes,* p. 38 (1936 data).
d. *Wei kung-yeh p'in ti ch'üan-mien tzu-chi erh fen-tou.* Shan Kan Ning pien ch'ü cheng-fu pan kung t'ing pien, October 1944, pp. 42-44 (Hereinafter cited as *Wei kung-yeh p'in*).
e. *Chieh-fang jih pao,* No. 1132 (28 June 1944), p. 1.
f. Mao Tse-tung, "Ching-chi wen-t'i," pp. 50-51.
g. *Shan Kan Ning (1958),* p. 283.
h. *Brief Account,* p. 12, and Forman, *Report,* p. 62.
i. *Brief Account,* p. 10.
j. *Wei kung-yeh p'in,* p. 48.

Table 4.2

COOPERATIVE SOCIETIES, 1937-1944

Cooperative activities	Number of cooperative societies							
	1937	1938	1939	1940	1941	1942	1943	1944 [a]
Consumption [b]	142	107	115	132	155	207?	260?	255
Production	1 [c]	4 [c]	146 [d]					212
Transport			1 [d]		17 [c]		119 [a]	302
Hostels								92
Credit								32
Medical								23
Farming								7
Total						190 [a]	260 [e]	923

a. *Chieh-fang jih pao,* No. 1132 (28 June 1944), p. 1.
b. Lyman P. Van Slyke, ed. *The Chinese Communist Movement,* p. 162.
c. Nym Wales, *Notes,* pp. 59-63.
d. *Ibid.* Not including public cooperative organizations, CIC, and workers' cooperative union.
e. *Shan Kan Ning pien ch'ü cheng-ts'e t'iao-li hui-pien,* pp. 26-27.

Forms of cooperation. The cooperative sector in the narrow sense originally consisted almost entirely of consumer (better, marketing) cooperatives, which tried to displace the traditional middlemen, especially in rural trade. The only other important form of cooperation in a broader sense was the rendering of mutual labor aid by individual peasant proprietors. Mutual-aid teams were built on previous forms of neighborhood aid which organized the exchange of labor by small groups of peasants for the duration of the agricultural season or a part thereof (e.g., spring plowing). Both forms of cooperation grew in importance over time, as the data of tables 4.1 and 4.2 show. Partial reports for subsequent years, which may be distorted by a good deal of double counting, suggest that the share of peasants involved in all kinds of mutual aid rose much more than planned in 1944 and fell in an equally drastic fashion thereafter.[19] The specific estimates are listed in Table 4.5.

Consumer cooperatives and mutual-aid teams were soon supplemented by producer cooperatives proper. From their beginnings, the latter consisted mainly of groups of peasant women who engaged in spinning and weaving as subsidiary occupations in their own households, thus forming putting-out systems under cooperative rather than capitalist auspices.[20] Cooperatives in all other branches of production accounted for a minor share of all the cooperators at all times.[21] In addition cooperatives were formed in several other sectors of the economy during the later years of the war. Transport cooperatives undertook primarily the transportation of salt by pack animal, hostel cooperatives catered in particular to the men and animals of the transport brigades, credit cooperatives attempted to control rural finance, and medical cooperatives aimed at organizing medical care in the countryside. Cooperative farms (agricultural production cooperatives proper) were extraordinarily rare.

Cooperative integration. The appearance of such a variety of cooperative ventures had organizational consequences which were drawn first by the *South Ch'ü* cooperative of *Yenan Hsien.* This organization developed from a simple consumer cooperative in 1936 into a complex cooperative during later years. By 1939, it incorporated nine economic units (consumer cooperatives, animal store, salt transport brigade, oil press, flour mill, sheep-shearing station, credit cooperative) in four localities. In 1941 it also undertook the production of cotton cloth, and during the years 1939-1942 it implemented a variety of financial and administrative reforms which transformed it into a territorial holding organization. By fall 1943 it had become a hsien-wide organization with eight component cooperatives and eighteen economic units in addition to its salt transport and marketing units. This form of organizational integration of various cooperative activities on a territorial basis, which Mao Tse-tung himself endorsed, became the model for cooperative reorganization in the SKN border region in 1942.[22] By 1943 about 15 percent of the cooperatives in the region had adopted the *South Ch'ü* form.[23] The structure which emerged toward the end of the period is evident in table 4.3. By 1944 territorial cooperatives had been formed in all the hsien and in 75 percent of the ch'ü but only in 17 percent of the hsiang in the region.[24] This meant that cooperative integration and perhaps even cooperation generally had yet to be extended to most of the localities.

Chinese Industrial Cooperatives. The labor-aid, spinning, weaving, and other groups did not exhaust the forms of producer cooperation. There was also the Yenan workers' cooperative union,[25] and there were cooperative organizations for the productive activities of the rear army and of other basically nonproductive units.[26] Most importantly, however, there was a branch of the Chinese Industrial Cooperatives (CIC or Indusco) which began to operate in the SKN border region in the spring of 1939.[27] CIC provided technical assistance in the form of a few experts and teaching materials. In the beginning, it also supplied most of the funds for local operations through gifts from abroad. Both contributions were welcomed by the Chinese communists. Mao Tse-tung endorsed the idea of CIC unequivocally in the fall of 1939,[28] and the Chinese communists in December 1939 are said to have subordinated all of their cooperatives to the CIC headquarters.[29] However, assistance from the outside decreased sharply in 1941,[30] and the subordination of all cooperatives under CIC did not imply that a standardized form of cooperative organization developed. The CIC units, which in contrast with most cooperatives in the SKN border region were owned collectively by their members, were treated as industrial enterprises comparable to those operated by the state. Table 4.1 shows that although CIC membership grew substantially, it did not assume large proportions. CIC activities were more diversified than those of the other producer cooperatives,[31] but they, too, remained strongly focussed on textile production.[32]

Table 4.3

COOPERATIVE ORGANIZATION, 1944 [a]

Hsien cooperatives	32 units
Ch'ü cooperatives	158 units
Hsiang cooperatives	213 units
Branch cooperatives	17 units
Total	420 units

a. *Chieh-fang jih pao,* No. 1132 (23 June 1944), p. 1.

State-operated enterprises. Unlike the common cooperatives but like the CIC units, state-operated enterprises in the narrow sense appeared principally in the industrial sector.[33] In the broader sense, of course, the institutional households of the army, organs, and schools were also forms of state enterprise. Moreover, as in the case of the South Ch'ü cooperative of Yenan Hsien, many or even most of the state-operated productive units were formed or at least sponsored by these state-operated consumption units. In many cases, especially in those concerning army units, such activities served to meet logistics requirements.[34] During the course of the autarky campaign, however, self-sufficiency acquired a much broader meaning. Institutional households now also engaged in production (as well as in commerce) for the purpose of making profit, and this profit rather than the product itself supported the institutional households.[35] As a result, the enterprises of most units became similar to those "regular" ones that had been formed to supply a wider market and—it was hoped—contribute to the general fund of public revenue.

Table 4.4 indicates that most of the state-operated enterprises were formed during 1940-1941, in response to the renewed blockade. After an initial phase of "blind expansion," the enterprises were consolidated in 1942, so that they might grow again "consciously" thereafter. Like the other new forms of organization, state-operated enterprises most often engaged in textile production. But they also pioneered in many other branches of industry, and they evidently dominated in industrial production from the beginning. By 1943-1944 they were said to account for 78 percent of the employment in the industrial sector, in comparison with 20 percent for the CIC units and with 2 percent for capitalist enterprises.[36] Of course, attribution of the term "industrial" to this sector is not entirely accurate because industrial as a rule signifies technical modernity and the use of mechanical power. Such a source of energy usually was lacking in the SKN border region, and most enterprises were therefore technically manufactories. The distinction between industry and handicrafts was consequently made in terms of ownership and/or size of establishment, apparently not always in an unequivocal fashion.[37]

Table 4.4

STATE-OPERATED ENTERPRISES, 1937-1943

Branch of industry	1937 [a]	1938 [a]	1939 [b]	1941 [c]	1942 [d]	1943 [e]
Textile		1	1	22 [f]	7 [g]	21
Garment	1	1	1	14	8 [g]	14
Paper		1	1	12	12	12
Printing	1	1	1	3	3	4
Machines + tools		1	1 }	6 }	9?	4
Machine repair	1	1	1			3
Wood				10	n.a.	7
Pottery		1		4		4
Leather	1	1		5		3
Drugs		1		2	12 [h]	2
Soap		1		2		2
Oil refining	(1)	1	1	1		1
Alcohol refining				2		n.a.
Matches				n.a.		1
Coal mining			3		12	6
Iron refining					1 [i]	3
Other		1 [j]	1 [k]	14 [l]	n.a.	9 [m]

a. *Wei kung-yeh p'in,* p. 42. Note that Snow lists a much larger number of enterprises for 1936: "Soviet industries, when I visited Red China, included clothing, uniform, shoe, and paper factories at Pao An and Holienwan (Kansu), rug factories at Ting-pien (on the Great Wall), mines at Yung P'ing which produce the cheapest coal in China, and woollen and cotton spinning factories in several hsien . . ." plus the oil wells at Yung P'ing and Yen Ch'ang. See Snow, *Red Star,* p. 268.
b. *Shan Kan Ning (1958),* p. 32.
c. *Wei kung-yeh p'in,* p. 44.
d. Mao Tse-tung, "Ching-chi wen-t'i," pp. 92, 142.
e. *Wei kung-yeh p'in,* p. 48.
f. *Chieh-fang jih pao,* (12 November 1941), p. 3.
g. *Wei kung-yeh p'in.* p. 45, refers to a total of sixteen textile and garment plants.
h. Plus one glass plant.
i. *Wei kung-yeh p'in,* p. 45.
j. Technical training plant.
k. Flour-milling plant.
l. Flour-milling, rug-making, and rope-making plants.
m. Oil presses.

In summary, the formation of various types of cooperatives and of state-operated enterprises changed the pattern of economic organization in the SKN border region substantially. But the magnitude of this change cannot be ascertained as precisely as is desirable, because of problems of measurement. Such problems come to the fore when one attempts to relate data on the number of cooperators to estimates of the size of the relevant population segment. The data on total cooperative membership tend to exaggerate the extent of cooperation because it was possible to hold membership in more than one functional organization. The available data on relative sectoral shares, which are listed in table 4.5, do not suffer from this shortcoming. But their interpretation, too, is complicated by problems of delineation. In the case of the consumer cooperatives, for instance, it would be helpful to know whether membership normally was held by household heads for all household members or whether other members also joined individually. Moreover, in the case of manufacturing and mining, it seems to make a great deal of difference whether or not one distinguishes between industry and handicraft as the Chinese communists did.

Table 4.5

SOCIAL ORGANIZATION OF ECONOMIC ACTIVITIES

Unit: Percent of reference group

Activity or sector	Year	State-operated	CIC-operated	Cooperative	Private-operated	Reference group (100%)
Consumption [a]	1941			9.3 (55)		Total population
	1944	5.9		10.8 (58)		(total households)
Production [b]	1939	0.09	0.04	3.5		Civilian employed
	1942	0.49	0.07	9.0		population in 1940
	1943	0.78	0.20			
Agricultural labor [c]	1943			#23.9		Agricultural labor
	1944			#50-70		force
	1945			#28-45		
Salt transport [d]	1942			2		Total number of
	1943			15		pack animals
Industrial	1943	78	20		2	Industrial employees [e]
employment	1943	18	4.5		0.6	Industrial plus handi-craft employees [f]
Weaving [g]	1938	1.9	—	*97.4	0.7	All persons employed
	1939	2.7	0.3	*95.4	1.8	and self-employed in
	1940	7.6	0.7	*90.0	1.7	weaving
	1941	12.0	2.3	*84.4	1.3	
	1942	7.1	2.5	*88.4	2.0	
	1943	3.1	1.6	*94.4	1.6	

\# Mutual-aid team members.
* All persons engaging in home industry, mostly through cooperative putting-out systems.
a. Derived from chapter 2, note 20, and tables 2.1, 4.1.
b. Derived from tables 2.2, 4.1.
c. Derived from tables 4.1, 5.2, and Selden, *The Yenan Way*, p. 248.
d. Derived from Mao Tse-tung and others, *New Life in New China* (Calcutta: Purabi Publishers, no date), pp. 128-129.
e. Stein, *The Challenge*, p. 180.
f. Derived from *ibid.* and table 5.2.
g. Derived from table 6.6.

However, irrespective of such problems and of constraints resulting from incomplete coverage, the data of table 4.5 quite clearly support the following point: not only state-operated enterprises but also producers' cooperatives assumed importance mostly in the case of import-substituting activities, notably in textile production. Practically all other activities continued to be carried out mainly in their traditional forms. It thus appears that the campaigns to organize and to cooperate as a matter of principle were less than fully successful. The lack of claims for 1944 and 1945 suggests that this state of affairs did not change substantially during the final phase of the war.

Educational Organization

To advance the SKN border region educationally, the Chinese communists at once instituted a school system of their own. Because education was to serve their objectives of political, military, and economic development by affecting youths as well as adults at various levels of educational attainment, the system had to be organized in a fairly complex fashion. Most important were the following two dimensions.

Full-time versus part-time education. To accommodate both youths who could engage in learning as their primary occupation and adults who had to pursue education as a secondary activity, the government created full-time schools for the former and various part-time schools (literacy groups, night schools, half-time schools, winter schools) for the latter. Table 4.6, which depicts enrollments in both systems, is incomplete in that it omits soldiers participating in elementary educational programs of the army. Since most soldiers were illiterate initially and became involved in learning efforts,[38] it seems reasonable to infer that the part-time schools as a whole enrolled about twice as many persons as listed in table 4.6. In addition, various government organs instituted extension programs to improve techniques.[39]

Mass versus expert education. To conform with the policies of political, military, and economic development, the school system had to provide elementary education in a practical form for the masses as well as advanced training, also in a practical form, for a few experts. The data of table 4.6 reveal the numerical preponderance of elementary education. They further imply that most of the primary school students were beginners,[40] that a substantial share of the middle school students were immigrants,[41] and that a majority of the other students were in a sense beginners, too. Table 4.7 indicates that almost all of the students of higher educational institutions participated in military and political training programs of relatively short duration. Most of these cadres had had very little schooling, and many of them were barely literate.[42] In comparison, the numbers of prospective specialists, who were enrolled in the other institutions of higher education, were extremely small.[43]

The formation of the system (as well as its reformation in 1942)[44] doubtlessly increased the population's exposure to formal education considerably, but it is once again difficult to determine the magnitude of the change more precisely, partly because the initial state of educational attainment is so uncertain.[45] The data of table 4.6 point to a very rapid growth of enrollment in full-time schools until 1941 when enrollment fell, apparently for reasons related to the 1942 reform.[46] Primary school attendance did not regain the 1940-1941 level during subsequent years, but middle school enrollment increased strongly, especially in 1945. In spite of this growth of the full-time system, enrollment remained far from all-inclusive. By 1944-1945 children who attended the first three grades of primary school probably accounted for about one-third of the normal age group.[47] However, they were drawn from a much wider range of ages.[48] Senior primary schools and middle schools absorbed extremely small shares of the teenage population. Enrollment in higher educational institutions, which apparently did not vary greatly after a period of initial growth,[49] involved about 2 percent of the entire labor force. The program in part-time education, finally, which experienced a change from efforts to achieve literacy to broader forms of elementary education, reached from 5 to 10 percent of the border region population. By necessity, the impact of educational organizations thus remained rather limited, even though it went far beyond any previous experience in the area.

Table 4.6

SCHOOL ENROLLMENT, 1936-1945

Unit: Students

Year	Full-time school system [a]			Part-time school system [b]			
	Primary Schools	Middle schools	Higher schools	Literacy groups	Night schools	Half-time schools	Winter schools
1936	500 [c]						
1937	10,396			39,983 [d]	1,917 [d]	919 [d]	10,337
1938	16,725	400 [e]	13,700 [f]		8,245	3,994	12,824
1939	22,089			24,107	8,086	3,323	17,750
1940	43,625	1,000		23,725	8,706	5,833	33,689?
1941	40,366 [g]	1,436 [g]		12,259	7,905	5,990	20,919
1942							
1943							
1944	31,790 [g]	1,772 [g]	16,300 [f]	34,000 [h]			
1945	32,500	2,800					

a. Unless otherwise indicated, *Shan Kan Ning (1958)*, pp. 26-27, 89-90, 222, 286.
b. Unless otherwise indicated, *General Survey of National Education in the Shensi-Kansu-Ninghsia Border Region* (translated manuscript, no date), p. 15.
c. *K'ang Jih chan-cheng shih-ch'i chieh-fang ch'ü kai-k'uang* (Peking: Jen-min Press, 1953), pp. 18-19.
d. Ch'i Li, *Shan Kan Ning pien ch'ü shih-lu*, p. 33.
e. Estimate: 200 middle school students plus 200 normal school graduates. See *Shan Kan Ning 1939-1941*, p. 67, and Snow, *Random Notes*, p. 24.
f. See table 4.7.
g. *General Survey of National Education*, pp. 1, 2.
h. *Shan Kan Ning (1958)*, p. 223.

Problems of Organizational Effectiveness

The formation of elaborate organizational structures in the administrative, defense, economic, and educational spheres as such did not assure the realization of the development program. The accomplishment of this task depended in addition on the appropriate functioning of the newly formed organizations which in turn required adequate performances by their functionaries. Questions of personnel policy therefore were of great concern—as they had been at least since the formation of the Kiangsi Soviet. Such problems were especially important when they affected the communist party itself, and they were discussed most often in this context. However, the remedies which were specified for them tended to be characteristic of general solutions.[50]

Cadre policy. Mao Tse-tung himself dealt with the problem of organizational effectiveness on numerous occasions, and also primarily with respect to the communist party.[51] He form-

Table 4.7

INSTITUTIONS OF HIGHER EDUCATION, 1938 and 1944

Institution	July 1938 [a]		1943-44	
	Course	Students	Course	Students
Anti-Japanese Military Academy	7 months	5,000-6,000	2 years	10,000 [b]
North Shensi Public School	4 months	5,000	6 months	
Women's Academy			to	1,300 [b]
Che-tung Youth Cadre School	4 months	1,000-2,000	2 years	
Lu Hsün Arts Academy		200	2 years [d]	300 [b]
Military Research College				
Science Research College			3 years [d]	50 [e]
Administrative College			3 years [d]	
Medical College				210 [b]
Nationalities College				
Japanese Workers' and Peasants' School				
Mobile Training School		1,000		
Communist Party School		500	1-2 years [d]	5,000 [d]
Total (incomplete)		12,700-14,700		16,300

a. Snow, *Random Notes*, p. 24.
b. Forman, *Report*, pp. 51, 86, 195.
c. *Shan Kan Ning (1958)*, p. 91. The three institutions were merged to form Yenan University.
d. Stein, *The Challenge*, pp. 151, 264.
e. Claire and William Band, *Two Years with the Chinese Communists* (New Haven: Yale University Press, 1948), p. 253 (Hereinafter cited as Band, *Two Years*).

ulated his norm of cadre conduct concisely in his concluding speech at the National Conference of the CCP on 7 May 1937. An excerpt from his comments on "The Question of Cadres" reads as follows:

They must be cadres and leaders versed in Marxism-Leninism, politically far-sighted, competent in work, full of the spirit of self-sacrifice, capable of tackling problems of their own, steadfast in the midst of difficulties and loyal and devoted in serving the nation, the class and the Party. It is on these cadres and leaders that the Party relies for its links with the membership and the masses, and it is by relying on their firm leadership of the masses that the Party can succeed in defeating the enemy. Such cadres and leaders must be free from selfishness, from individualistic heroism, ostentation, sloth, passivity,and sectarian arrogance, and they must be selfless national and class heroes; such are the qualities and the style of work demanded of the members, cadres and leaders of our Party.[52]

Mao stressed the importance of his point by quoting Stalin's statement that "cadres decide everything." Of course, such a legitimation of his concern did not change the fact that the standard was hard to live up to, especially in circumstances which had long favored different norms of behavior. So long as the responses of the functionaries remained less than fully satisfactory, the issue of their conduct had to be raised time and again. Mao's report on "The Role of the Chinese Communist Party in the National War," which was made to the CCP central committee in October 1938,[53] not only reiterated the merits of activism, frugality, and integrity, but also emphasized strongly the importance of the *mass line* in sentences such as these:

> Every Communist working among the masses should be their friend and not a boss over them, an indefatigable teacher and not a bureaucratic politician. . . .It must be realized that Communists form only a small section of the nation, and that there are large numbers of progressives and activists outside the Party with whom we must work. It is entirely wrong to think that we alone are good and no one else is any good. . . .Communists should set an example in being practical as well as far-sighted. For only by being practical can they fulfil the appointed tasks, and only far-sightedness can prevent them from losing their bearings in the march forward. Communists should therefore set an example in study; at all times they should learn from the masses as well as teach them. Only by learning from the people, from actual circumstances and from the friendly parties and armies, and by knowing them well, can we be practical in our work and far-sighted as to the future.[54]

Besides exhorting cadres to act in accordance with these rules, the report pointed to methods which would enable them to do so. The list of ways which it enumerated[55]—guidance, upgrading, supervision, persuasion rather than struggle, and assistance—in fact constituted a comprehensive process of learning by doing which could become a profoundly formative experience—with the cadres' cooperation. Inadequate involvement in this process justified the call for the *rectification movement* of 1941-1942, which brought the underlying theory of knowledge to the fore. Previously enunciated rules of conduct were shown to follow from the proper understanding of Marxism-Leninism. Upon attaining such an understanding, the cadres could be expected to draw the necessary inferences by themselves and act accordingly. A reform of the cadres' "style of study" (as well as of their styles of writing and of social relations) was therefore essential to the improvement of their "style of work."[56]

The impact of the campaign cannot be measured directly. The editors of Mao's *Selected Works* assert that it was an unqualified success which ". . . consolidated the position of proletarian ideology inside and outside the Party, enabled the broad ranks of cadres to take a great step forward ideologically and the Party to achieve unprecedented unity. . . ."[57] Mao's own assessment of 1943 on the other hand suggests also that rectification itself was in need of rectification.[58] In the end, of course, its success or failure had to manifest itself in more tangible results which may constitute indirect measures of its effects.

Education. Although problems of cadre conduct were viewed with extraordinary concern when they affected the party, they were not taken lightly when they appeared in other organizations. Moreover, because they were attributed to the same causes, they also were to be solved by the same methods. For this reason, rectification was not limited to the party but was extended to the entire educational system of the SKN border region. The attack on the form of education and especially on the orientation in higher education followed the line of Mao's "Talks at the Yenan Forum on Literature and Art" of May 1942.[59] The traditional elite orientation in education was held to reflect itself in the tendencies of elementary school curricula to be preparatory for middle school studies, of middle school curricula to be preparatory for more advanced studies, and of

more advanced curricula to be largely self-serving. Against
these tendencies the *mass line* stressed that for the vast majority of students at any level the curriculum was terminal. The
appropriate objective in education at each level was therefore
to prepare students for their work rather than for further
studies. This objective was to be achieved for the masses by
making elementary education more practical and more related
to production;[60] the revisions affected both full-time and part-
time curricula.[61] Moreover, the goal was to be reached for the
prospective teachers of the masses[62] by transforming all normal
schools, middle schools, and higher educational institutions
into cadre schools on the pattern which the Anti-Japanese Military Academy had developed successfully.[63] The reports of
Stein and Forman indicate that most of these changes had been
made by the time of their visit in 1944, apparently with positive
results.[64]

Production. Rectification and the reformation of the educational system were meant in particular to mobilize additional
labor efforts and thereby increase production, which was
viewed as the most pressing problem at that time. In his endorsement of the policy of "better troops and simpler administration" of 7 September 1942,[65] Mao Tse-tung called for this
kind of activism among the soldiers and functionaries in the
border region. He repeated his call in his summary comments
on "Economic and Financial Problems in the Anti-Japanese
War" of December 1942[66] as well as on subsequent occasions,
apparently for the reason that the reorientation toward production encountered some resistance. Participation in production
added substantially to the burdens of soldiers, functionaries,
teachers, and students. It imposed to an ever greater degree on
the cadres who not only had to understand and accept the need
for the change in order to make it understandable and acceptable to others, but who also had to learn how to produce in
order to teach others, and who had to be models in all their
activities. For them in particular, adaptability and flexibility
were therefore essential qualities, as Mao did not fail to stress:
". . . men's minds are liable to be fettered by circumstance and
habit from which even revolutionaries cannot always escape. . .
. .When the weather changes, it becomes necessary to change

one's clothing. . . . ."[67] Yet men do not shed their habits as easily as their garments, and Mao had to call again for such adjustments. In his directive to "Spread the Campaigns to Reduce Rent, Increase Production and 'Support the Government and Cherish the People' in the Base Areas" of 1 October 1943, he insisted:

> At all levels, the leading personnel in the Party, government and army organizations and in the schools should master all the skills involved in leading the masses in production. No one who fails to study production carefully can be considered a good leader. Any soldier or civilian who is not serious about production and who likes to eat but does not like to work cannot be considered a good soldier or a good citizen. Village Party members who are not diverted from production should realize that one of the qualifications for becoming a model among the masses is to work well in increasing production. . . .[68]

Mao made his point even more strongly in his enumeration of "nine wrongs" which followed this statement and which reiterated the model of cadre conduct in "thou shalt not" style.[69] At almost the same time, however, he also noted that ". . . great achievements and advances have been scored in every field of production this year [1943] . . ."[70] as a result of the campaign. And he expressed confidence that the campaign was taking hold so that even more progress would be made in 1944. The impressions of Stein and Forman suggest that this anticipation was justified,[71] and the reported data on increases in production, for instance by the army, confirm it as well.[72] It thus seems that the cadres conducted themselves rather appropriately in this respect toward the end of the period. Nevertheless, efforts to rouse them continued, and Mao felt the need for tempering his commendation of labor heroes with the admonition not to become conceited.[73]

Administration. The promotion of a production mass movement appears to have been the most important part of the policy of "better troops and simpler administration." However, rectification also affected the implementation of the administrative simplification program, which had made little headway previously in official opinion.[74] Various laws and regulations were intended to bring about five changes.[75] First, the state administrative apparatus was to be *rationalized* by conventional methods, such as the simplification of procedures, the merging of offices, the reassignment of officials, the reduction of personnel, and the transfer of those in excess to production or schooling. Second, the *leadership* in administration was to be *unified* in accordance with the principles of democratic centralism. The realization of this objective necessitated changes in the lines of authority as well as in the form in which authority was exercised. Third, it was considered necessary to *oppose bureaucratism* and in so doing *improve the leadership work style.* Such an improvement required activism, initiative, integrity, mass orientation, and other new personal attributes. Fourth, the *efficiency* of administrative work was to be *raised* by improving the morale of the less committed functionaries as well as by eliminating subversive elements. And fifth, there was to be more *economizing* in the state sector so that the impositions on private households in the SKN border region could be reduced.[76]

By promoting all of these changes, the government in fact applied the principles of party cadre policy to the entire state sector, apparently with positive results. By 1944 it claimed that ". . . the work of last year enables us to say definitely that the five objectives mentioned above have been realized to a great extent."[77] The observations of visitors such as Stein and Forman tend to support this claim.[78] But there also is evidence which raises doubts about the profundity of some changes. In particular, it should be noted that employment in state administration and in mass organizations apparently could not be reduced lastingly.[79] At the very least, it thus appears that in matters of simplification, it was continuously necessary to reinvigorate the cadres.

State enterprises. The simplification program referred primarily to the state organs and mass organizations. But the efforts to rationalize the administration and make it dynamic extended to the state-operated enterprises. Cadre policy again constituted the principal instrument in pursuit of this objective.

State enterprises were called upon simultaneously to increase the quantity, improve the quality, and reduce the cost of production.[80] To this end, they were asked in particular to diminish their administrative personnel, to induce administrators to participate in production, and to transform administration into a (subsidiary) part-time activity of productive personnel.[81] Such an integration of administrative and productive work was considered most conducive to the study of techniques of production by all employees, and improvements in technology were viewed as the key to the attainment of all three goals.[82] The mass line thus appeared as an especially important part of the solution to the problem of organizational efficiency in state enterprise.

The campaign to adopt the mass line in the management of state enterprises appears to have met with resistance, allegedly for two reasons. On the one hand the technical elite (scientists, engineers, technicians) took an elitist position. They did not believe in the creativity of the masses and did not develop an adequate interest in their training. At the same time many workers accepted this position and were quite satisfied with the existing state of affairs.[83] Although it was claimed that attitudes had improved so that progress had been made in technical learning and in economizing which resulted in increases in productivity and decreases in production costs,[84] it seems much remained to be accomplished. At least, there was again cause for vigilance—by continuing the campaign against bureaucratism and by promoting more business-like behavior (ch'i-yeh-hua) in the state-operated enterprises.[85]

Incentive Problems

Cadres could be activated and induced to function appropriately by rectification, the preferred means. But there were other methods which could be used, notably the granting of social distinction and the provision of material rewards for suitable performance. Moreover, the choice among these incentives was important in the case of the masses as well. They, too, presumably could be exposed to rectification, so that they would act properly in the interest of the social cause. Or they could be rewarded with status or income so that they would act correctly in pursuit of their personal interests. In either case, the problem of which incentives to choose was a familiar issue since the days of the Kiangsi Soviet. And in both cases, the principal solutions to the problem date also from that period.

Cadres. In the very beginning, officers and men of the Red Army appear to have been kept on extremely small rations by physical necessity. Other functionaries may have fared similarly then for the same reason. And the equal treatment of officers and men seems to have had positive incentive effects in the circumstances.[86] But the decision to restrict the living of cadres to low levels also followed from ideological necessity. It was hard to come close to the masses if one did not live as they did. The income levels of workers and peasants therefore were standards which could not be exceeded by much. And rectification consequently appeared preferable not so much because it was the cheaper method immediately but because it was more consistent with the mass line and therefore potentially more effective in the end. In October 1938 Mao stressed the importance of frugality in combination with activism as follows:

> Every Communist engaged in government work should set an example of absolute integrity, of freedom from favoritism in making appointments and of hard work for little remuneration.[87]

Of course, the preference for the ideological incentive did not imply that material and other incentives were rejected entirely in favor of work for the sake of liberation and revolution. Mao had already in 1929 condemned absolute equalitarianism as uncalled for by the circumstances.[88] He also emphasized the importance of providing adequately for cadres in cases of need.[89] And he stressed as one of the "wrongs" in 1943:

> It is wrong to consider it dishonorable and selfish either for Communists in the countryside to engage in household production in order to support their families or for Communists in government organizations and schools to engage in private spare-time production in order to improve their own living conditions, for all such activity is in the interests of the revolutionary cause. . . .[90]

At the same time, however, such activity was narrowly circumscribed. Members of the army were not to engage in *individual* production, probably because it would tend to destroy the social cohesion of the troops. Moreover, trade on an individual basis was objected to in principle, presumably for the reason that it threatened to undo the cadres' ideological progress.[91] The majority of them, who lived without dependents as members of institutional households, apparently experienced conditions similar to those in which the teaching staff of the Anti-Japanese Military Academy found itself. In addition to common rations of room, board, and clothing, which did not differ substantially from those of the soldier-students, the staff received allowances of from 2.5 to 7 yuan per month in 1938, in comparison with 1 yuan pocket money per soldier.[92] The minority of the staff, who lived elsewhere, received comparable incomes (in kind or cash equivalent) for themselves as well as for possible dependents.[93] At 1938 prices, the staff allowances bought from 30 to 80 catties (33 to 88 lbs.) of millet, 1 catty being about equal to 1.1 lbs.[94] And the highest allowance, which exceeded the standard maximum of 5 yuan,[95] tended to be equivalent to the supplies plus pocket money per soldier.[96] Since most cadres probably received substantially less than the maximum,[97] material incentives were doubtlessly rather insignificant in the beginning. This situation appparently did not change greatly.[98] Moreover, cadre status varied officially with behavior, and appropriate behavior could yield unusual material returns only in unusual circumstances.[99]

State employees. The supplies plus allowances system which was used to support cadres also served to compensate most other state employees in the SKN border region. As a consequence, the degree of income differentiation was similarly small and independent of performance not only in administration and education[100] but even in the state-operated enterprises, many of which, of course, were run by the army, organs, and schools. Rations of food and clothing varied in accordance with need, mostly with family size and structure. Wages apparently depended mainly on qualification. Forman reported ratios of 4:3:2 between the wages of foremen or department chiefs, skilled workers, and apprentices.[101] Stein discovered a wider range, ". . . from about 100 pounds of millet per month for highly skilled workers and heads of departments to 10 to 20 pounds of millet per month for apprentices."[102] However, 100 pounds of millet were hardly more than twice the monthly grain ration, and they probably did not exceed the value of all rations by much.[103] The ratio of highest to lowest incomes in state-operated enterprises was consequently near 2:1, just as in the Anti-Japanese Military Academy. Moreover, for the majority of workers, the degree of income differentiation was much smaller, since 75 percent or more of the total outlay on labor were paid in the form of rationed supplies.[104]

This "mixed" system of payment may have been appropriate for cadres. But its use in industry, apparently since 1942,[105] posed substantial incentive problems. Such difficulties were attributed for one to the fact that industry developed in part due to the immigration of workers from cities outside the border region. Immigrant workers brought badly needed skills but also the old labor attitudes. In contrast, workers from within the region, who normally came from the farms, often had sufficiently advanced attitudes but did not possess the requisite skills.[106] However, especially those new from the farms also were said frequently to lack a properly proletarian outlook.[107] More generally, then, ideological retardation for various reasons tended to account for an attitude of "kan pu kan, i chin pan!"—i.e., whether or not one does something, one gets a pound and a half!

To be sure, such backwardness was to be overcome by ideological work. But it also was to be taken into consideration in a revision of the system of payment. As the system least conducive to loafing and to other forms of waste,[108] the government promoted an all-wages system on the soviet pattern. In particular, this system was meant to cope with the following three important problems which the "mixed" system had failed to solve, apparently because the (standardized) supplies portion dominated.

Wage differentials between various branches of industry had not been large initially. Moreover, subsequent wage drift had reversed some relations. As a result, there appeared wage differentials, for instance between defense plants and textile plants in favor of the latter. This development was to be corrected so that heavy industry would be favored appropriately over light industry.[109]

Wage differentials between skill, seniority, and status groups had been very small from the beginning; in at least one instance they had even been reduced so that the wages of regular workers exceeded those of service workers and apprentices by at most 15 percent.[110] Such a manifestation of equalitarianism was to be eliminated by a system of wage grades which would class employees according to the three criteria of skill, seniority, and status.[111]

Since the payment of wages or supplies had not been tied to performance, the form of payment did not provide incentive. This shortcoming was to be remedied by relating wage grades to standards of quantitative and qualitative achievement.[112] Mao Tse-tung especially advocated the adoption of a progressive piece-wages system, apparently of the soviet type.[113]

In summary, the government evidently recognized the need for resorting to material incentives in stimulating industrial production. But it also was conscious of technological and ideological constraints to their use. Managers must have found it difficult to administer suitable wage-grade and piece-wages systems,[114] and they also may have considered it objectionable to rely on the "old-style" stimulants.[115] The "mixed" system appears to have been resilient for both reasons. Although Mao himself advocated progressive piece wages in December 1942, visitors such as Stein and Forman did not report on their use in 1944, and various organizations continued to promote their adoption. Nor did information on wage-grade systems appear. The one system that could be found did not concern state-operated enterprises. According to a regulation of 26 September 1943, communications workers in the SKN border region were to be paid as follows, usually in cash equivalent of millet:[116]

Wage Grade	Monthly Wages	Wage Ratio
4	195 catties	1.000
3	225 catties	1.154
2	255 catties	1.308
1	295 catties	1.513

The wage-grade differentials near 15 percent conformed with soviet practice. But the number of wage grades was comparatively small, perhaps on account of the size of the region. The system thus did not differentiate basic wages greatly, especially not since most of the workers probably appeared in the intermediate grades. Moreover, seniority pay did not enlarge these differentials substantially. The increment after one year of satisfactory service was 7.5 catties of millet per month, i.e., about 2.5 to 3.8 percent of the base pay. Various fringe benefits continued to be distributed according to need.[117]

Self-employed persons. The incentive problem which the government found difficult to solve in the case of its own employees did not arise for the vast majority of the people, who were and remained self-employed. In accordance with its anti-Japanese united-front policy, the government of course appealed to peasants, craftsmen, merchants, and housewives to cooperate for patriotic reasons. Yet it also did not fail to point out the material benefits which would accrue to them individually as a result of such cooperation. And it always tried to make certain that there were benefits to be reaped. A listing of the major inducements may serve to substantiate this point.

To further immigration, the border region government gave refugee farmers land, loans, three years of tax exemption, plus other forms of help in getting settled.[118] Correspondingly, it took steps to assure immigrant businessmen that their investments would be secure and provided nonagricultural workers with jobs in state-operated enterprises.[119] One of the first industrial enterprises formed was the refugee textile factory.[120]

To increase salt production, the government went even further. It not only granted land plus initial shelter, food, implements, and loans to immigrants as well as to migrants choosing to undertake salt farming on their own, but also provided interest-free loans to employers of additional salt workers. And it even rewarded recruiters of new salt farmers in proportion to the number of families recruited.[121]

In promoting textile production, the government resorted to similar methods. It stimulated cotton growing with loans and with the exemption of cotton land from taxation for three years.[122] In addition, it tried to encourage cotton spinning and cotton weaving by reducing the import duties on raw cotton and cotton yarn to 1 percent while raising the import duty on cotton cloth to 15 percent ad valorem.[123]

To advance industrialization more generally, the government went so far as to strongly support private initiatives. In particular, private industrialists were guaranteed profit at the rate of 20 percent.[124]

To develop agricultural production more generally, the government also promoted a rent-reduction campaign in those areas of the border region which had not yet been exposed to land redistribution.[125]

Even in regard to taxation, the government advocated the use of material incentives in a general way. Mao Tse-tung himself made the following statement: ". . . In the financial and economic field, the Party and government personnel at the county and district levels should devote nine-tenths of their energy to helping the peasants increase production, and only one-tenth to collecting taxes from them. If pains are taken with the first task, the second will be easy. . . ."[126]

The preceding measures, most of which were instituted by 1942, indicate that the border region government relied heavily on conventional incentive policy in its efforts to manipulate a multitude of small private ventures. Of course, the tariff revisions also benefitted the state-operated enterprises in textile manufacturing, thus accounting possibly for much of the wage drift in that branch.[127] At issue is the degree to which some of the provisions were implemented. In particular, local cadres called on eligible peasants to forsake tax exemption sufficiently often to arouse central concern.[128] Such resistance to the use of material incentives may have limited the efforts of many self-employed persons as well. For lack of more comprehensive information, however, this possibility cannot be explored satisfactorily.

Finally, even in instances where they were implemented properly, the government's incentive provisions tended to be dwarfed by market forces. As a result of the war and the renewal of economic warfare with the national government, the SKN border region experienced extreme changes in its terms of external trade and consequently in its internal price structure.

Table 4.8

PRICE INDEX RATIOS FOR SELECTED COMMODITIES AND MILLET, YENAN, 1937-44. [a]

June 1937 equal to 100

Date (year and month)	Millet/ millet	Salt/ millet	Pork/ millet	Cotton fiber/ millet	Home spun/ millet	Fine cloth/ millet	All commodities/ millet
1937 June	100	100	100	100	100	100	100
Dec.	100	100	156	111	115	98	—
1938 June	—	—	—	—	—	—	—
Dec.	100	128	181	86	156	184	126
1939 June	100	115	208	101	140	254	136
Dec.	100	179	192	146	174	364	224
1940 June	100	169	148	177	192	598	202
Dec.	100	395	202	262	256	621	236
1941 June	100	202	161	165	164	457	171
Dec.	100	127	293	220	202	683	194
1942 June	100	252	288	294	287	881	260
Dec.	100	218	276	291	235	783	237
1943 June	100	223	328	426	320	1072	360
Dec.	100	213	306	526	308	1061	380
1944 June	100	230	318	617	422	1883	591
Aug.	100	149	241	457	323	1274	399

a. Hsü, *A Survey.* Part 2, p. 11.

Table 4.8 makes these changes apparent. The extraordinary increases in the prices of most commodities relative to the price of millet reflected of course *ceteris paribus* the extremely limited production possibilities within the region. But they also provided powerful stimuli for individual efforts to overcome such obstacles, notably in cotton-growing, spinning, and weaving, especially since 1942. Interestingly, the price incentive to salt-farming did not develop similarly, and this difference may help explain the unusual recruitment rewards in the latter branch.

Summary

The Chinese communists apparently were quite successful in organizing the population of the SKN border region for purposes of administration, defense, economic development, and education on a dualistic pattern which made allowance for differences in interests, talents, and circumstances. They supplemented a small state administrative apparatus with mass organizations that involved most people. They added to a small garrison of regular troops a much more numerous militia-like self-defense corps. They complemented a small number of state-operated industrial enterprises with much larger numbers of cooperative ventures in import-substituting and export-promoting activities (especially textile manufacturing, salt transportation, and marketing generally). And they promoted expert as well as mass education in a somewhat complicated form which often combined work with study—not only by necessity but also by choice.

Substantial progress in the formation of new organizations did not entail the appropriate functioning of these new units. That depended decisively on the performance of their functionaries. Formulating and implementing norms of functionary conduct were therefore most important tasks of organizational policy. Central to Mao Tse-tung's solution to the conduct problem was a "cadre ethic" which called for activism, frugality, and closeness to the masses. Cadres were to learn to live up to these norms. Yet perhaps because the requirements contrasted so sharply with the traditional standards of conduct, they were not met with ease, and cadres were constantly in need of rectification and reinvigoration. This was even more true of nonparty personnel in positions of leadership who might not have been so strongly committed to the cause yet who experienced the same remolding approach.

Besides relying on "ethical" (ideological) incentives to performance, it was possible to provide material ones as well. The Chinese communists, by all indications, limited material incentives for cadres severely, apparently so as not to jeopardize the mass line. But they recognized that the ideologically less advanced segments of the SKN population, whether state-employed or self-employed, needed material rewards. This was especially apparent during the period of the mass campaign in production. However, there remain questions about the extent to which cadre zeal may have prevented the implementation of specific incentive policies in industry as well as in agriculture. And all incentive measures appeared small in comparison with some of the rewards which the market offered, especially during the years 1943-1944, when the mass campaigns in production took place.

In general, the available data point to an interesting process of transition which also accounts for much of their inconclusiveness. The small number of activists in the institutional households of the army, organs, and schools continued to be stimulated by "Maoist" means, perhaps with difficulty, while increasing numbers of the population at large, who became organized for more limited purposes, had to be rewarded in more tangible ways. Because it involved more and more of the less and less committed people, the growth of organization thus was associated with a change in the pattern of incentives, especially in the economic sphere. For the same reason, progress in organization also necessitated changes in the form of cooperation—away from the more spontaneous pattern appropriate for the subsistence activities of institutional households and toward the more coordinated pattern suitable for autarky on a larger scale. There are indications that this transformation toward larger scale autarky was attempted, starting at the latest with the propagation of administrative simplication.[129] Unfortunately, there is no information on the success of various integrative efforts planned for 1944 and 1945.[130]

V

Mobilization of
Human Efforts

The SKN border region contained various underutilized resources in substantial qualities. But the backwardness of the
region and its isolation from the more developed parts of China
by acts of war precluded their exploitation by modern means
and methods of production. Instead, they had to be utilized
more fully by primitive techniques which mostly meant substantial increases in common work efforts. Such increases could be
brought about in several ways, most of which had been tried
previously in Kiangsi. Particularly important were the following changes.

Immigration

The border region could accommodate additions to its labor
force and population through migration not only because it
branched out into new economic activities but also because it
had experienced population losses during preceding periods of
disaster.[1] The border region government therefore encouraged
immigration with few exceptions. As mentioned previously, it
invited businessmen to come and invest in its territory. It also
announced that as the border region had extra land, it would
welcome refugee farmers, especially those willing to undertake
salt extraction in addition to the cultivation of land. Industrial
workers were encouraged to immigrate, too, and one of the
first industrial enterprises formed in the region was the refugee
factory.[2]

Refugee farmers, workers, and businessmen from the war
zones in Honan and Shansi constituted the great majority of
immigrants, notably during the later years, but they were not

the only source of population influx. The Chinese communist movement itself, i.e., many of the cadres who staffed the state organs and mass organizations, half of the soldiers in the garrison, and most of the students, had come from the outside. In addition, substantial numbers of veterans and disabled soldiers plus their dependents were being settled in the SKN territory. The latters' total during 1938-1943 amounted to more than 9,625 persons according to one source and to 11,500 persons according to another source.[3] Common to veterans, students, soldiers, and cadres was that even though most of them participated in material production eventually, their contributions in this sphere were probably more limited than those of most refugees.

The data of table 5.1, which exclude the members of state administrative organs, schools, and rear army units,[4] indicate that the effect of immigration on the size of the border region's population and labor force was by no means negligible. During the years 1937-1944, the estimated average annual inflow exceeded 23,000 persons and surpassed 1.5 percent of the estimated population at the end of 1940.[5] By the end of 1944, the eight-year total number of immigrants accounted for close to 12 percent of the border region population (exclusive of members of state administrative organs, schools, and rear army units). The share of immigrants in the labor force was probably at least as high.[6] Specific data on emigration during the years 1937-1944 are lacking. But there are indications that the number of emigrants was insignificant.[7] It is therefore reasonable to treat the numbers of table 5.1 as approximate net gains.

Internal Migration

Although the border region as a whole lacked manpower, members of the labor force were not utilized equally well in all of its parts.[8] Total efforts could therefore be increased by inducing people to move from labor-surplus areas to labor-deficit areas. The border region government encouraged such movements, which often involved rural-urban migration as well as occupational shifts. Peasants in particular, who constituted the majority of the migrants, could move into areas with reserves of

Table 5.1

IMMIGRATION INTO THE SKN BORDER REGION

Year	Families	Persons	Laborers
1937			
1938			
1939		> 30,000 [a]	
1940			
1937-1940		100,000 [b]	
1941	7,855 [c]	20,740 [c]	
1942	5,056 [c]	12,431 [c]	
1943	8,021 [c]	23,030 [c]	8,800 [d]
1944	7,368 [e]	29,599 [e]	
1941-1944	28,300 [f]	85,800 [f]	

a. *Shan Kan Ning (1958)*, p. 12 (refugees from Shansi, Hopei, Honan, Suiyuan).
b. *Shan Kan Ning 1939-1941*, p. 44.
c. Mao Tse-tung and others, *New Life*, p. 125.
d. *Shan Kan Ning pien ch'ü cheng-ts'e t'iao-li hui-pien*, May 1944, p. 28.
e. Residual.
f. *Shan Kan Ning (1958)*, pp. 284-285.

reclaimable land,[9] but they also could enter salt production[10] or they could become workers in the newly developing manufacturing establishments, especially in textile mills.[11] Frequently the latter type of movement was not permanent resettlement but a prolonged working away from home by members of rural farm households. It thus constituted subsidiary work in the extreme.

The magnitude of internal migration cannot be ascertained with confidence. Official sources registered the movement of

2,538 persons during 1937-1938 from Suite, Michih, and Ch'ing-chien to Yenan (300 persons), Yenchang (440 persons), Yen-chwan (1,082 persons), and Anting (716 persons).[12] By 1941 Yenan alone was said to have gained 3,000 to 4,000 residents from other parts of the region.[13] Gunther Stein was told of the resettlement of 5,000 inhabitants in 1943.[14] Such numbers suggest that internal migration was of secondary importance in increasing work efforts, yet the data are apparently incomplete. Qualitative information does not add much to them. There are indications that persons moved on their own in response to earnings incentives, but there also is evidence that the existing earnings structure was not always conducive to labor mobility in the desired directions.[15]

Rationalization of Activities

In the larger units of organization, surplus labor existed hidden in the form of excessive numbers of administrative employees. Rationalization campaigns were waged to move unneeded administrative personnel from the state organs and state enterprises into materially productive work. However, the success of these campaigns is in question. The personnel of state administrative and mass organizations was to be reduced in 1942 from 7,900 persons to 6,300 persons,[16] yet the number of those left after the second screening was to be decreased from 8,200 persons in 1943 to 7,500 persons in 1944.[17] And again, a total number of 15,000 persons in 1945 was to be diminished to 10,000 persons in 1946.[18] The apparent growth contrary to intentions cannot be explained.[19] Aggregate data on personnel changes in state industry are lacking.[20] In general, it appears that the numbers of those who were considered dispensible were large in proportion to those who should be retained, yet state organs plus state enterprises employed a mere fraction of the total labor force. The rationalization campaigns cannot, therefore, have had a great impact on the occupational distribution of the total labor force. On the other hand, going *hsia hsiang* (to the villages) probably had a profound influence on those administrators (and students) who went as well as on the native villagers who came into close contact with them, and such changes in outlook were considered important for the success of the mass production campaign and the practice of the mass line generally.[21]

Intensification of Efforts

Besides removing persons who were underutilized from their locations or occupations, it was possible to encourage them to do more on the spot in their current lines of production and in supplementary undertakings. Workers in state enterprises, which attempted to plan their production activities, as a rule were exhorted to overfulfill their production plans as early and by as much as possible.[22] But there are indications that the response was not uniformly positive.[23]

Peasants, who by tradition worked relatively few full days per man per annum, also could be induced to exert themselves more fully more often. Greater efforts could be made by them in agricultural production as well as in various subsidiary activities. Within definite limits set by climate and soil conditions as well as by the state of farm technology, it was feasible to implement a rudimentary version of the agricultural development program of 1956. Land reclamation, irrigation, crop shifts, double cropping, deep furrowing, fertilizing, afforestation, and other practices could be undertaken by labor-aid groups in emulation campaigns similar to those used in industry.[24] The border region government encouraged such ventures, and while the resulting increase in farm work cannot be estimated with confidence, it seems to have been substantial.[25]

In addition, it was possible to mobilize peasants for work on public projects in construction and transportation. The border region government accomplished this task in a thoroughly traditional manner, by imposing a labor tax on able-bodied males. Men of ages 15-44 had to render three days of corvée per month, and these days could be cumulated annually.[26] Since members of this segment of the population probably did not work more than 180 days per annum on their own, the corvée could increase their efforts by 20 percent. And since the entire segment must have accounted for 20 percent of the population,[27] the corvée could increase total work efforts at least by 4 percent. The actual imposition of labor tax appears to have declined toward the end of the period,[28] apparently because the road-building program was completed[29] and changes had come about in transportation.[30]

Work in construction and transportation could be undertaken privately, too, as could work in a large number of other subsidiary activities. Unfortunately, there is little direct information on changes in such efforts. Most of the available data relate to the absorption of women into materially productive activities.

Absorption of Women

By tradition, women were preoccupied with domestic service, principally in their own homes.[31] The development of the border region could be furthered by diverting them from such activities to materially productive work, notably in agriculture and handicrafts. Efforts to involve women to a greater extent in farm work as well as in subsidiary work were made from the beginning according to Nym Wales,[32] even though the wide-spread practice of footbinding made it difficult for many women to work in the fields.[33] In subsequent years, the government promoted home-spinning and home-weaving as critical import-substituting activities. Its success in reviving these crafts, which had been nearly extinct in the area, is evident in table 5.2 for the years 1942-1945. A comparison of these data with the estimates of table 2.3 suggests that the number of employed women increased substantially. Information for earlier years and other activities is incomplete.

Institutional Participation in Production

In addition to the dependents of private households, there were approximately 100,000 members of public institutional households who were not materially productive. By inducing these functionaries, students, and soldiers to participate in production on a part-time basis, it was possible to add noticeably to total production. The border region government promoted participation in production practically from the beginning,[34] but the initial responses seem to have been relatively weak.[35]

Efforts were made in two directions. On the one hand, troops were used as an extraordinary workforce on various occasions. During 1941 and 1942 a few thousand soldiers participated first in the construction and then in the operation of new salt fields.[36] In 1943-1944 about one thousand soldiers mined iron ore, and others mined coal,[37] but there is no adequate information to measure total efforts in this direction.

On the other hand, troops as well as functionaries and students were encouraged to provide much or all of their food and clothing by themselves. Such efforts also cannot be measured directly; nor are the data on the results of their work sufficiently complete to derive time-series estimates.[39] However, the data on land cultivated by the border region garrison imply that at the rate of 18 *mou* per soldier,[39] cultivation required 1,400 soldiers in 1939, 5,000 soldiers in 1942, 17,000 soldiers in 1943, and 46,000 soldiers, i.e., virtually the entire garrison, in 1944.[40] Functionaries and students apparently did not exert themselves any more drastically than the troops did, and the decisive increase in efforts seems to have occurred everywhere in 1943 and 1944, according to data on the degree of institutional self-sufficiency.[41]

Rehabilitation of Vagrants

In addition to all the persons who were not fully utilized in legitimate occupations, the border region initially contained a substantial number of vagrants or "loafers" (erh-liu-tze). These people according to Forman ". . . were not merely parasites. Their wayward habits, their laziness, gambling, cheating, lying and stealing are sources of demoralization for others, and they have no place in the vigorous society for which the Communists are striving."[42] For all of these reasons, the government made great efforts to absorb vagrants into legitimate occupations. As a result, their number declined according to Forman from an estimated 70,000 persons in 1935 (which would account for 5 percent of the 1936 population!) to 9,554 persons at the beginning of 1943 and to 3,967 persons one year thereafter.[43] Other sources refer to an initial number of 6,424 persons in 1943 and to the rehabilitation of 4,500 persons during that year.[44] By either measure, there remained few candidates for rehabilitation in 1944 and 1945. Information on the pattern of absorption of vagrants during the preceding years is lacking, as is information on the number of those who evaded integration by emigrating to other territories.[45]

Changes in Employment

Although many if not all of the attempts to mobilize additional productive efforts were evidently successful, it remains difficult to specify their effects on the level and structure of employment satisfactorily. The border region government apparently did not inquire into the employment and occupations of its citizens in the two population counts which it conducted, and it also does not seem to have carried out a special census for this purpose. The data which could be assembled in table 5.2 from a variety of sources are therefore problematic in many respects. The available entries do not exhaust the range of occupations and states of employment, the categories are not standarized, the estimates are of varying quality, appear with varying frequency, and so forth. Such shortcomings not only reflect on the government's control of the situation, they also limit the extent to which indications of change during the war period can be compared with evidence on the initial state as presented in tables 2.2, 2.3, and 2.10. Fortunately, however, they do not render all comparisons meaningless.

Agriculture. The first available estimate of employment in agriculture, a reference to 180,000 labor powers in 1941, appears to understate the actual number of persons engaging in farm work grossly because it falls far short even of the likely number of peasant households.[46] The 1943 estimate of 338,760 persons comes close to the estimated number of those occupied in agriculture only (table 2.2), but it remains more than 10 percent below the estimated number of those employed in farm work only (table 2.3). The improvement in estimation may be attributable to the 1941 population count as well as to the increasing formation of labor-aid groups and other cooperatives. The 1943 source does not specify whether farm laborers, on whom information is available merely for 1939, are included in the total. The reference to 26,000 unionized farm workers, which excludes a minority of nonunionized workers,[47] appears to be consistent with the number of those who were farm laborers according to table 2.3. Persons who engaged in farm work on a part-time basis seem to have remained unaccounted for in 1943. On this premise and with due allowance for the uncertainty of all the data, it may be said that private employment in agriculture probably did not increase significantly.[48] The one significant addition to the agricultural labor force which can be detected was made in the public sector, mainly in the form of part-time work by soldiers of the border region garrison.[49]

Salt production. In view of the importance which salt production acquired, it is surprising that hardly any information on employment in this line of business could be found. Unfortunately, tables 2.2 and 2.3 do not contain evidence on the likely initial state, either.[50] According to one report, the four major deposits in Yenchih Hsien were worked in 1943 by 521 households with 2,037 members and 1,121 workers who engaged in salt extraction more or less regularly.[51] The four minor deposits in Suite Hsien occupied at the same time an additional 837 workers.[52] The fact that many of the households in Yenchih held immigrant status may have been responsible for their small average household size as well as for their relatively large average labor force share. Their involvement in salt production cannot be specified precisely, however, because many of their members undertook part-time work in salt production jointly with part-time work in agriculture.[53] There are indications that many peasants had shifted to farming during a preceding decline of the salt trade and that employment in salt production increased due to their resumption of this subsidiary work. The available evidence on salt fields in operation and on migration also points to a substantial growth of the number of persons engaged in salt production. Yet the statement that salt production still lacked one thousand adult labor powers in 1943 reveals limits to success in recruiting.[54] And the fact that soldiers and members of other public institutions, who were mobilized for work in the salt fields at least on a temporary basis, apparently outnumbered the private workforce in the sector at times by far, once again indicates the importance of the institutional population as a source of additional development efforts.

Table 5.2

CHANGES IN EMPLOYMENT, 1937-1945

Branch of Economy	1937	1938	1939	1940	1941	1942	1943	1944	1945
Agriculture									
"labor powers" [a]			>26,000		180,000		338,760		
farm laborers [b]									
Salt production									
employed persons [c]							1,959		
Industry (incl. mining)									
total [d]	700		2,800			7,000	8,000	12,000	>10,000
state-operated [e]	270		700	1,000		3,989	6,300		
cooperative (CIC) [e]					7,000	602	1,591		
capitalist [f]			298				109		
Crafts and Trades									
employed persons [g]			>20,000				5,000		
wage workers [h]			>10,000						
Home Industry									
spinners [i]					74,000		137,600		>150,000
weavers [j]		5,000	8,000	10,000	13,000	13,500	41,500		45,000
Construction									
corvee laborers [k]				(44,750)	(44,750)	45,400			

	1937	1939	1941	1942	1943	1944	1945
Transport and Communications wage workers [l]			>1,200				
Other Workers [m]			12,100				
Medical Professions [n]			>800				
State and mass organizations [o]			7,900				
Schools [p]				3,650	8,200	3,300	
Army [q]	33,000	40,750	45,000	45,000	46,000	46,000	15,000
employed in agriculture [r]		1,400		5,000	17,000		20,000
employed in salt production [s]				3,500	3,500		
employed in iron mining [t]					3,500	1,000	
Students [u] (total)	30,825				43,500	49,862	1,000

a. 1941: Nym Wales, *Notes*, p. 62. See *ibid.* for a total labor-force estimate of 202,293 labor powers. 1943: *Shan Kan Ning pien ch'ü cheng-ts'e t'iao-li hui-pien*, pp. 27, 30.

b. Union members. See Ch'i Li, *Shan Kan Ning pien ch'ü shih-lu*, pp. 83, 84. A minority of the agricultural workers were not unionized and are not accounted for.

c. Hsü, *A Survey*, Part 2, p. 109.

d. 1937, 1942, 1944: *Mao III*, p. 172; 1939: Ch'i Li, *Shan Kan Ning*, pp. 83, 84. All industrial workers were unionized and accounted for; 1943: Sum of components; 1945: *Shan Kan Ning (1958)*, p. 283.

e. Table 4.1.

f. Derived from *ibid.* and table 4.5, note e. Note that *Wei kung-yeh p'in*, p. 52, refers to 10,000 persons in "private industry of a relatively large scale" but apparently means capitalistic putting-out systems.

g. 1939 estimate: More than 10,000 wage workers times two persons per shop (Peter Schran, "Handicrafts in Communist China," *The China Quarterly*, No. 17 (1964): 170); 1943 estimate: About

15,000 persons minus persons in salt production and industry. See Hsü, *A Survey*, Part 2, pp. 108-109.

h. 1939: Ch'i Li, *Shan Kan Ning*, pp. 83, 84. The great majority of the workers was unionized and accounted for.

i. 1941: Mao and others, *New Life*, p. 48; 1943: *Shan Kan Ning pien ch'ü cheng-ts'e t'iao-li hui-pien*, pp. 27, 30; 1945: *Shan Kan Ning (1958)*, p. 283.

j. See *ibid.* plus table 6.6; 1945: Average, 40,000-50,000 persons.

k. 1942: Mao and others, *New Life*, p. 53; 1940 and 1941: derived from *ibid.*, pp. 53-55 (one-half of difference between total laborers during 1940 to 1942 and laborers in 1942).

l. Ch'i Li, *Shan Kan Ning*, pp. 83, 84. Very few workers were not unionized and not accounted for.

m. *Ibid.* implies a total of 50,000-55,000 workers, 48,000 of whom had been organized. The residual includes 7,600 organized workers of unspecified occupations.

n. *Shan Kan Ning (1958)*, p. 315.

o. 1942: Selden, *The Yenan Way*, p. 215; 1943: *Shan Kan Ning pien ch'ü cheng-ts'e t'iao-li hui-pien*, p. 9; 1945: *Shan Kan Ning (1958)*, p. 315.

p. 1937: Snow, *Red Star*, p. 254 (grade school teachers); 1943: *Shan Kan Ning pien ch'ü cheng-ts'e t'iao-li hui-pien*, p. 9.

q. Chapter 4, notes 13-15.

r. Estimate. Notes 39 and 40.

s. 1941: Estimate, same as 1942 (the reference is to several thousand soldiers); 1942: Average, 3,000-4,000 persons, including members of other institutions. See *Salt Production*, pp. 1, 2.

t. Forman, *Report*, p. 78.

u. 1938 and 1944: See table 4.6; 1943: 100,000 persons in army, organs, and schools minus those accounted for in notes o, p, q. See Stein, *The Challenge*, p. 133, and *Brief Account*, p. 3.

Industry. Changes in the employment of enterprises operated by the state, the CIC, and a few capitalists have been reported to a greater extent though also not in the desirable detail. The data of table 5.2 depict a very rapid growth from extremely small beginnings to near 1.5 percent of all employed persons as estimated in table 2.2. However, the 1937 estimate conflicts with Nym Wales' report of 1,300 persons in "national" factories,[55] and the information on the structure of employment, which is incomplete, raises questions about the accuracy of the aggregate series during later years. The available data on employment by branch of industry which appear in table 5.3, account in 1941 for 75 percent of the enterprises with 52 percent of the employees in the state sector. A similar discrepancy exists according to table 5.2 in 1942 between the number of employees in state plus CIC enterprises and the total number of industrial employees. In 1943, on the other hand, the number of employees listed by branch of industry in table 5.3 add up to more than their total according to table 5.2.[56] The available information does not suffice to explain these differences.

Irrespective of such uncertainties, tables 5.2 and 5.3 point first of all to the extraordinary importance of employment in textile and garment manufacturing. This is true not only for the state sector but also for the CIC sector, where units engaging in textile production accounted for an ever larger share of total sectoral employment.[57] Second in importance appeared paper-manufacturing plus printing, third were traditional chemical industries such as soap-making. In contrast, branches of heavy industry and armaments enterprises absorbed a comparatively small share of total industrial employment until 1943, when iron-mining and smelting developed. For lack of information, it is impossible to describe the details of this last development beyond 1943.

Common to most of the state and CIC-sponsored ventures was that they engaged primarily in import-substituting production which required few of the skills of established local craftsmen. Furthermore, there is evidence that many industrial workers were refugees who had immigrated into the SKN border region from other parts of China and that others had come to the new industrial towns from rural areas within the region.[58]

Table 5.3

INDUSTRIAL EMPLOYMENT, 1941-1943

Branch of industry	1941 state sector [a]	1942 state sector [b]	1942 state + CIC [c]	1943 total [d]
Textile }	2,400	1,425	1,924	2,433
Garment }		405	405	785
Paper	400	437	437	484
Printing	300	379	379	185 [e]
Machines + tools	?	237	237	} 1,026
Machine repair	?	?	?	
Wood	200	?	?	236
Chemical*	344	674	694	644
Oil refining	84	?	?	203
Drugs	167 [f]	?	?	?
Coal mining	?	432	432	1,891
Iron refining	—	?	?	600
Other	?	?	85 [g]	?

* Including pottery, leather, drugs, soap, oil refining, alcohol refining.
a. *Wei kung-yeh p'in,* p. 44.
b. Mao, "Ching-chi wen-t'i," p. 92.
c. Derived from *ibid.,* pp. 50-51, 92.
d. Derived from Hsü, *A Survey,* Part 2, pp. 102, 108-109.
e. Excluding print shop of the Anti-Japanese University. See Band, *Two Years,* p. 255, for a reference to 300 employees at the Central Printing Press.
f. Hsü, *A Survey,* Part 2, p. 97.
g. Including rug-making, flour-milling, oil-pressing.

Unfortunately, these indications do not suffice to preclude the possibility that the new industries also diverted substantial numbers of local craftsmen from their traditional pursuits. Such a possibility adds significance to the employment of soldiers in mining. They accounted for at least 10 percent of all industrial employees in 1944 and thus for an important share of the entire import-substitution effort.[59]

Crafts and trades. The number of persons employed in the traditional crafts and trades, which differed from industry in their form of ownership and size of establishment rather than in their technology, has not been reported. The partial data of table 5.4 make it possible to estimate totals of 13,500 shops and 27,000 employed persons for 1939.[60] If one doubles the number of (unionized) wage workers in all crafts and trades according to table 5.2 in order to account for the self-employed proprietors, too, one arrives at a total of "more than 20,000" craftsmen and tradesmen for the same year. In comparison, table 2.2 places the number of persons originally employed in manufacturing at 22,400 for the area of 1936 and at 24,000 for the area of 1940.[51] All data point to the prevalence of very small shops which were operated largely by self-employed proprietors with the help of family members. A reference for 1943 to 10,000 persons in relatively large private undertakings appears to concern persons associated with capitalistic putting-out systems, in other words home industry.[62]

The available data do not provide sufficient information on changes in employment in the crafts and trades sector. The increase from 1942 to 1943 which table 5.4 depicts is so unusually large in so many branches that it may be suspected of reflecting improvements in statistical coverage as well as real changes. Moreover, to the extent that it was real, the increase in hsien city employment may have resulted at least in part from the migration of craftsmen. The same possibility must be considered probable in the case of the capital city Yenan where the number of shops is said to have increased from 123 in 1936 to 473 in 1943, doubtlessly in connection with changes in population.[63] Data for the years 1937-1938 suggest an increase in handicraft activity and employment prior to the formation of most industrial enterprises,[64] but the scarcity of data for subsequent years prevents similarly definite statements for the period of "industrialization." As a consequence, it is also impossible to ascertain the development of manufacturing generally in an appropriate form.

Table 5.4

HANDICRAFT ESTABLISHMENTS
AND EMPLOYMENT, 1939-1943

Handicraft activity	Border Region [a] Establishments 1939	Thirteen Hsien Cities [b] Establishments		Employed Persons	
		1942	1943	1942	1943
Oil-pressing	2,500	45	73	149	237
Felt-making	1,000	26	49	91	145
Leather-making	2,000	33	72	149	338
Blacksmithing [c]	800	63	101	169	336
Wood-working	1,000	40	69	131	216
Subtotal	7,300	207	364	689	1,272
Shoe-making		29	33	51	85
Garment-making		10	32	23	74
Bag-making		18	36	92	152
Dyeing		45	92	72	201
Horsehoing		12	14	37	42
Coppersmithing		7	9	10	19
Hemp-cording		3	14	9	63
Flour-milling		63	43	106	85
Other	500 [d]	5	19	18	54
Total	(13,500) [e]	399	656	1,107	2,047

a. Ch'i Li, *Shan Kan Ning pien ch'ü shih-lu,* pp. 1-2.
b. *Wei kung-yeh p'in,* pp. 53-54.
c. See Nym Wales, *Notes,* p. 62, for an estimate of 1,000 blacksmiths in 1941.
d. Sugar-making.
e. Estimate: 7,300 x (399 + 656)/(207 + 364).

Home industry. The number of persons engaging in home industry for own consumption or for the market has not been reported, either. But the estimates of participation in home spinning and home weaving, which have been made public, permit the demonstration of a significant change. Estimates of the total numbers of persons involved, most of whom were said to have been cooperators,[65] appear in table 5.2. In addition, there is evidence of 28,326 cooperators in textile production in 1939, most of whom were engaged in home industry.[66] The number of private producers at that time is not known. The number of cooperators in 1939 exceeds the estimated number of all persons in home industry according to table 2.2, but it falls short of the estimated number of farm household members in home industry according to table 2.3. Such a relationship supports the claim of an increase in the commercialization of home industry, but it does not suffice to demonstrate an increase in total employment in this branch.[67] In contrast, the number of home spinners and home weavers for the years 1942-1945 is substantially larger than the estimated number of all home industry workers in farm households according to table 2.3. Such a discrepancy points to a significant expansion of total employment in home industry during the early 1940s. Capitalistic organizations appear to have involved a small minority of all home industry workers.[68] The efforts of soldiers, functionaries, and students, all of whom were encouraged to engage in home spinning etc., cannot be accounted for adequately, even though they seem to have been significant.[69]

Construction. The number of persons employed in construction cannot be determined, due to problems of classification. Members of traditional construction trades, such as bricklayers, carpenters, and stone masons, are included in table 5.3 among the wage workers in crafts and trades.[70] Unskilled workers such as excavation workers appear to be part of the category "other workers." Their numbers cannot be ascertained. Because table 2.2 also does not identify construction workers as a category, however, it may be assumed that their number was comparatively small. Efforts at construction for own use, which seem to have been more important, are not included in the two items. Also omitted are persons affected by corvée. Table 5.2 specifies the number of those mobilized for road work under such auspices during the years 1940-1942. Their number implicitly exaggerates their contribution to construction due to the fact that the period of corvée was limited to thirty-six days per annum.[71] Moreover, the inclusion of corvée as a secondary occupation also tends to distort total employment. Nevertheless, the change from earlier times, when few roads were repaired and no new roads were built, is worth registering on the input side as well. The use of corvée labor apparently diminished after 1942, upon the completion of the regional road-building program.[72]

Transportation and communications. The identification of persons employed in transportation poses problems, too. Table 5.2 specifies more than 1,200 wage workers in this sector for

1939, a number which excludes self-employed persons, who could not become union members,[73] water carriers, who were part of the crafts and trades sector,[74] and peasants who combined work in agriculture with work in transportation. In view of the first two omissions, the reference to 1,200 wage workers may well be compatible with the estimate of 1,500 persons employed in transportation only which appears in table 2.2. The corresponding estimate of 12,000 part-time transportation workers cannot be contrasted with data for later years. Changes in employment during the 1940s cannot be described fully, either. But it may be estimated that employment in salt transportation, which constituted the most important activity in transportation, grew from 2,600 persons in 1942 to 4,200 persons in 1943.[75] The changes from 1941 to 1942 and from 1943 to 1944 were probably much smaller.[76] The use of corvée labor in transportation and the efforts at transportation by the army, which assumed importance in 1943,[77] cannot be measured. The number of persons occupied in communications was apparently quite small.

Other workers. This category appears as a residual in a 1939 report on the structure of the proletariat in the SKN border region.[78] It seems to cover various types of common labor (e.g., excavation workers) as well as commercial employees outside the crafts and trades sector plus household laborers.[79] Tables 2.2 and 2.3 therefore contain no counterpart to it, and the item is important primarily because it raises the number of workers to 50,000-55,000 persons. This total accounts for 6 to 7 percent of the estimated number of all employed persons and thus reveals the backwardness of the region in yet one more dimension.

Various professions. Estimates of the total number of persons in professional occupations have not been made public, but table 5.2 contains entries for the estimated numbers of members of legitimate as well as illegitimate medical professions[80] and for the personnel of public schools. The latter seems to have grown substantially while the former may have declined.[81] In 1943 the two categories absorbed about 7,000 persons, thus accounting for about twice the number of professionals who were members of farm households according to table 2.3 and who seem to have consisted primarily of doctors and tea-chers.[82] Yet they included less than 10 percent of the total number of persons estimated to perform professional services according to table 2.2. The sources to table 2.2 unfortunately do not provide information on the structure of professions, so that it is impossible to specify the omissions. Other sources suggest that old-style teaching, secretarial service, the equivalent of "gentry service," old-style "scholarship," and priesthood may have made up much of the difference.[83] The evident backwardness of the territory and its initial exposure to land reform point to the alternative explanation that table 2.2, which represents the state of affairs in all of North China in 1929-1931, overstates the size of the professional sector in the SKN border region considerably.[84]

Public service. Table 5.2 provides information on the numbers of civilian and military personnel, both of which are subsumed in table 2.2 under "public service." The number of persons employed in state administrative organs only, which apparently reached 4,500 persons in 1944,[85] accounted for half of the public servants according to table 2.2. The employees of mass organizations added substantially to this number and increased total civilian employment to a level comparable to previous total employment in public service. However, their functional counterparts in previous times, i.e., "latter-day gentry" who performed mediation, charitable, and other services, probably appeared among the scholars or the idle persons in table 2.2. The addition of military personnel, which was several times as numerous as the civilian personnel, raised total employment in public service to a multiple of the initial state according to table 2.2, yet in this instance, too, the North China averages may be misleading because they refer to a "normal" state of affairs which the SKN border region had not experienced in a long time.[86] Nevertheless, it appears that the share of public service in total employment grew substantially due to the immigration of a large military contingent.

Ommissions. According to Buck, ". . . agriculture, domestic service, trade, and professional service were the only important occupations . . ." in China during 1929-1931 and presumably in the Northwest on the eve of the formation of the SKN border region.[87] As mentioned previously, table 5.2 includes some of the domestic servants and lists the membership of a few professions, but it does not account adequately for either occupation, and it fails to deal explicitly with trade. There are less specific indications that urban trade grew notably with the development of new manufacturing centers.[88] However, like domestic service, trade appears to have been primarily a subsidiary activity of farm households and perhaps often a form of hidden unemployment. In the absence of adequate information on changes in marketing activities, it may be noted that while the volume of sales and purchases by farm households may well have increased, production and cooperation campaigns aimed at reducing the number of persons engaged in buying and selling (as well as in domestic service), with uncertain success.[89]

Summary

There is evidence that the government was able to add to the labor force as well as to the productive efforts of labor-force members in the SKN border region in various ways. But the data on changes in the level and the structure of employment are far from complete. As a consequence, it is impossible to identify the effects of the labor mobilization strategy in the desirable detail, and it becomes necessary to rely on inferences from indirect information in many instances. The following specific points may be made.

The data of table 5.2 indicate that the government was able to increase employment in sectors, branches, and occupations to which it attached priority. Noteworthy examples were import-substituting industry and home industry, export-supplementing salt production and transport, plus services in public health, education, and — to an unintended degree — civil administration.

The data of table 5.1 imply that immigration alone sufficed to offset most of these changes in employment. The presumable labor-force members among the immigrants were more numerous than the additions of employees to industry, salt production and transportation, plus various public services. However, they did not match the increases in home industry employment.

The extent of subsidiary production activities by peasants appear to have increased. The growth in the numbers of home spinners plus home weavers and the reintroduction of corvée are evidence to this effect. At issue is whether these changes reduced other economic activities (e.g., marketing) or leisure-time activities.

In the absence of adequate direct information on most traditional activities, it may be noted that residual immigration, the rehabilitation of vagrants, and other measures suggest increases in labor-force availability. But there also is the implication that employment in agriculture seems to have stagnated.

The subsidiary production activities of institutional households (army, government organs, schools) increased drastically and constituted a major source of identifiable additional efforts, especially in agriculture. Unfortunately, such activities cannot be measured in the cases of officials, students, and teachers.[90]

In conclusion, it must be emphasized that changes in employment are not necessarily indicative of changes in productive efforts. In agriculture and in other traditional sectors especially, small variations in the number of employed persons may have been associated with substantial increases in the magnitude of their exertions. Such developments have been measured directly in an incomplete form in the case of part-time enrollment in schools (table 4.6), but they also could reflect themselves in increases of production, which will be studied next.

VI

Development of Production

The need to develop production within the SKN border region mainly by indigenous means had important implications for the structure of productive activities. Autarky demanded not only the expansion of familiar activities such as food-crop growing and livestock raising, it also required the growing and processing of industrial crops. In addition, it necessitated the establishment of an armaments industry. Moreover, the development of all types of consumer goods production depended in large part on the development of producer goods production. Finally, advances in all lines of production could be affected by technological improvements which might involve little more than the spreading of the best practice within the region. The emergence of these changes, which is already apparent in the preceding data on employment and education, can be described further with data on the production of the most important sectors of the SKN border region economy.

Agriculture

The development of production by additional efforts especially in producer goods production and by limited technological improvements is clearly evident in the case of agriculture. Here various government organs proposed and supported a set of measures which as such were not new.[1] Comprehensive implementation of this program required the organization of existing skills and energies on an unprecedented scale, an organizational problem the Chinese communists chose to solve by instituting cooperation in various forms. These as such were not new, either.[2] Their efforts to develop agricultural production on this pattern met with varying success.

Changes in land use. Essential to the development of production was the greater utilization of the available land for crop growing as well as for livestock raising. The agricultural development program called in particular for the following changes.

(1) Land reclamation. The SKN territory contained extensive areas of uncultivated arable land.[3] Efforts could be made to reclaim such land in order to expand the crop area, as well as forest, pasture, and water land. Unfortunately, the practical reclamation possibilities were much more limited than the availability of land would suggest. Most of the land that could be reclaimed was located in the North, in Tingpien for instance, while most of the labor force which could be mobilized for the reclamation and subsequent cultivation of such land was located in the East, for example in Suite.[4] As additional efforts consisted primarily of increases in the number of workdays of persons occupied in farm work already,[5] this "surplus" of labor could not be moved easily from region to region. Reclamation work was further handicapped by the shortage of work animals.[6] Last, but by no means least, much of the virgin land was of inferior fertility and subject to poor climatic conditions, again especially in the North.[8]

In spite of such obstacles, reclamation work achieved dramatic results according to official claims, which are reproduced in table 6.1. The estimates of total cultivated land show an increase of 80 percent from 1936 to 1945 and one of 30 percent from 1940 to 1945. The average annual rate of growth during the latter period was 6.2 percent. Additions to cultivated land were especially large in 1939, 1940, 1943, and 1944. However, much of the increase from 1939 to 1940—about one million *mou*—appears to have been caused by the territorial changes of that time. Substantial as they were, the changes did not add up to the five-year total reported by Stein:

> During the last five years [1940-1944] reclamation has added 1,000,000 acres [6,000,000 *mou*] to the 1,500,000 acres [9,000,000 *mou*] of land that had formerly been under cultivation in the entire Border Region. The army alone with its 40,000 to 50,000 garrison troops has contributed about one-third to this new source of food and wealth.[9]

Table 6.1

LAND AND ITS USES, 1936-1945

Unit: Million mou

Year	Reclaimed land Plan	Reclaimed land Claim	Cultivated land	Irrigated land Plan	Irrigated land Claim	Cotton land Plan	Cotton land Claim
1936			8.431 g				
1937		0.195 d	8.626 b		0.0008 b		
1938		0.358 d	8.994 d				
1939	0.600 a	1.003 e	10.076 b		0.008 b		0.004 e
1940	1.000 b	0.699 e	11.742 c	0.010 b	0.024 f		0.015 c
1941	0.600 b	0.390 e	12.105 h				0.039 j
1942		0.281 e	12.487 g			0.150 k	0.094 g
1943		0.976 e	13.387 c			0.150 c	0.150 c
1944	1.000 c	1.288 f	14.675 i		0.041 f	0.200 l	0.315 j
1945			15.206 g			0.400 m	0.350 g

a. *Shan Kan Ning (1958)*, p. 32.
b. *Shan Kan Ning 1939-1941*, pp. 41-42.
c. *Shan Kan Ning pien ch'ü cheng-ts'e t'iao-li hui pien*, p. 26.
d. *Shan Kan Ning (1958)*, p. 21.
e. Mao Tse-tung, "Ching-chi wen-t'i," p. 10, plus Mao and others, *New Life in New China*, p. 123.
f. Inference: Reclamation during 1941-1944 minus reclamation during 1942 and 1943. See *Shan Kan Ning (1958)*, p. 285.
g. *Shan Kan Ning (1958)*, p. 283.
h. Land cultivated in 1942 minus land reclaimed in 1942.
i. Land cultivated in 1943 plus land reclaimed in 1944.
j. *Shan Kan Ning (1958)*, p. 212.
k. *Shan Kan Ning (1958)*, p. 97.
l. *Shan Kan Ning pien ch'ü cheng-ts'e t'iao-li hui pien*, p. 44.
m. Kao Kang, *1945 nien pien ch'ü ti chu-yao jen-wu ho tso-feng wen-t'i*, p. 4.

The reference to the reclamation work of the army cannot be confirmed in its entirety, either. The area of land cultivated by the garrison reached 830,000 *mou* in 1944 but was much smaller during the preceding years. Moreover, the annual data on land reclaimed by the army, which have been made public for selected years, do not suggest a total of two million *mou* for the five-year period.[10] The shares of the military and civilian contributions are thus uncertain. And the extraordinary magnitude of the increase in total cultivated land might even give rise to doubt about the feasibility of such an accomplishment, if the term "reclamation" were not so misleading. Since it usually meant not much more than the turning of relatively barren virgin loess in upland areas, both the initial cultivation of so much additional land and its repeated cropping during subsequent years appear to have been physically possible.[11]

(2) Afforestation. To diminish erosion, enlarge timber resources, improve diets, etc. the government promoted afforestation, especially in the beginning. Trees planted are said to have increased from 292,535 in 1937 to 482,852 in 1938 and to 1,392,160 in 1939. Data for subsequent years are missing. References to survival problems due to the lack of water and appropriate care suggest that the effort may have declined.[12] In any case, it probably affected a very small share of the total land.

(3) Expansion of pasture. To increase the supply of draft power and of various animal products, the government had to encourage animal husbandry, notably that of cattle, donkeys, and sheep. In the absence of changes in feeding methods, such increases required commensurate expansions of the area allocated to pasture land. Unfortunately, such a development cannot be demonstrated for lack of data, and questions concerning the actual changes in the animal stock pose problems of interpretation. If the government merely restored the stock to its "normal" size, little change in land use may have occurred. Whatever the result, pasture land also accounted for a small share of total cultivated land according to the findings of Buck.[13]

(4) Irrigation. Yields in crop growing, which remained the predominant land use in the region, could be increased substantially—even doubled—by changing from dry to wet cultivation.[14] Such a prospect provided the impetus for efforts to expand the irrigated area, however, the data of table 6.1 show that even though it grew relatively rapidly, irrigated land continued to account for only a tiny fraction of total cultivated land. Irrigation thus cannot have affected agricultural production greatly.[15]

(5) Multiple cropping. Land yields could also be raised notably by changing from the use of fallow to crop rotation and by moving from single to double cropping. The government promoted both changes, apparently with limited success. Data on the areas of fallow and of double-cropped land are lacking, but it has been reported that 6,400 persons practiced double cropping in 1943 and that 3,300 persons were converted to it subsequently.[16] Since the total number of double croppers constitu-

ted a mere 3 percent of the agricultural labor force according to table 5.2, the change cannot have affected yields and output greatly.[17]

(6) Crop shifting. Land yields could be increased further and the desired autarky could be approached as well by changes in the kinds of crops grown. The government supported several such shifts, but the effects are once again hard to determine. Buck's data for Hsunyi and Tingpien may be compared with a report of crop shares in 1943,[18] according to which various grains accounted for about 75 percent of all crops. The remainder consisted of beans (11.2 percent), potatoes (3.2 percent), flax (5.1 percent), cotton (1.4 percent), and vegetables (2.2 percent). The comparison points to increases in the production of legumes, tubers, and fibers relative to other crops. The shift to high-yielding potato crops is evident also in the production plans for 1944, but the plans indicate that merely 2 percent of the cultivated land was to be sown to potatoes.[19] The shift to autarky-enhancing cotton growing is depicted in table 6.1. It implies that even though cotton land expanded at a rapid rate, its share in cultivated land also remained rather small. During 1944-1945, it did not exceed 2 percent by much.[20]

In summary, it appears that whereas total cultivated land increased drastically due to reclamation, changes in the structure of land uses were less pronounced. This concentration on reclamation seems attributable to the interdependence of land uses which complicated modifications of an established pattern. The difficulties of restoring more fertility to the soil in response to its more intensive cultivation may account for the emphasis on exploiting the surface fertility of virgin lands—if only for a few years.

Changes in animal stock. Fertilizer is one by-product of animal husbandry. However, efforts to increase the animal stock were made primarily for other reasons. Oxen were the main source of tractive power, especially in agriculture, and expansion of cultivated land made increases in their number necessary. Donkeys served mostly as pack animals, notably in long-distance transportation, and the development of the salt trade as well as the provisioning of the border region garrison demanded the growth of their number. Sheep provided wool, and the interest in achieving autarky in clothing generated urgent appeals to increase their number. Oxen, donkeys, and sheep also supplied meat and skins, as did the other animals (camels, horses, mules, hogs), which were less numerous in the region.

Official estimates of the growth of the animal stock appear in table 6.2. The data depict very rapid increases in the numbers of oxen, donkeys, and sheep during the late thirties. The two sets of estimates for 1939 and 1940 may refer to different territories, but they also could point to uncertainty about the size of the stock. Buck's survey data, which appear in table 2.6, suggest a much more numerous livestock, especially in the cases of donkeys and sheep. Of course, estimates based on Buck are just as problematic.[21] An appropriately cautious interpretation, which is called for in such circumstances, seems to be that the growth until 1940 or even until 1942 reflected "normalization" in real as well as in statistical terms. In other words, the livestock of the region continued to recuperate from decimation by natural disaster and civil war, but it also was counted more and more completely by the government. The normaliza-

Table 6.2

ANIMAL STOCK, 1936-1945

Year	Oxen	plus	Donkeys	Mules	Camels	Sheep
1936 [a]		100,000				400,000 to 500,000
1937 [b]	70,000		50,000			500,000
1938 [c]	102,676		70,810	1,468	1,254	751,464
1939*	123,963[c] or 150,892[d]		97,407[c] or 124,935[d]	2,040[c]	1,329[c]	1,012,786[c] or 1,171,366[d]
1940*	148,408[c] or 193,238[de]		94,334[c] or 135,054[de]	1,817[c]	2,458[c]	1,625,170[c] or 1,723,037[de]
1941 [bd]	202,914		137,001			1,714,205
1942	209,684[f]	364,702[a]	161,966[f]			1,802,097[a]
1943*	214,000[g] or 220,781[e]		169,000[g] or 167,671[e]			1,923,000[g] or 2,013,868[f]
1944						
1945 [a]		403,920				1,954,756

* Note the existence of conflicting sets of numbers for oxen, donkeys, and sheep.
a. *Shan Kan Ning (1958)*, p. 283.
b. Chao Kuo-chun, *Agrarian Policy of the Chinese Communist Party, 1921-1959* (Bombay: Asia Publishing House, 1960), p. 60. Note that Chao's reference to 1,724,203 sheep in 1941 appears to be a printing mistake.
c. *Shan Kan Ning 1939-1941*, p. 43.
d. Mao Tse-tung, "Ching-chi wen-t'i," p. 10.
e. Mao and others, *New Life in New China*, p. 126.
f. Hsü, *A Survey*, Part 2, p. 77.
g. *Brief Account*, p. 11.

tion argument serves to focus the attention on changes in the
animal stock during the forties. The data of table 6.2 imply the
following developments:

Kind of Animal	Average Annual Rate of Increase		
	1940-1943	1942-1945	1940-1945
Oxen	4.5	3.5	4.4
Donkeys	7.5		
Sheep	3.7-5.3	2.8	2.6

The tabulation shows that the rates of growth declined substantially after 1942-1943, when the campaigns to increase transport capacity and wool production had achieved initial successes. Moreover, the actual rate of growth in the number of sheep
during 1940-1945 was surprisingly low. The size of the
flock in 1943 is uncertain. But it may well have been large
enough to entail the flock's stagnation or decline during 1944-
1945.

Changes in other inputs. Besides adding to cultivated land,
modifying its uses, and enlarging the animal stock, it was possible to increase production by improving various farm practices as well as other inputs. New methods of production were
to be introduced by a system of agricultural extension under
which instructors were sent to the countryside, classes on agriculture and animal husbandry were organized, how-to-do-it literature was circulated, and other propagandistic measures
were taken.[22] The impact of such activities is uncertain, in view
of the following statement in the government work report for
1943:

> A problem in the agricultural field that remains to be
> studied and promoted is that of deep furrowing and
> careful management. In matters of control, feeding,
> tending, and anti-plague work in the field of livestock
> raising, there are still serious shortcomings.[23]

Information on changes in the quantity and quality of other
inputs is almost completely lacking, presumably for two reasons. On the one hand, it was difficult to gather data of this type

because most of the items originated either as subsidiary products—mainly for own use—in peasant households or as primary products in traditional handicraft establishments. On the other hand, it was unnecessary to gather such data in the absence of a manifest need for production control. Short of it, the government could and did add to the private supply of inputs by establishing farm implement factories,[24] by producing feed and fertilizer as byproducts of bean and cotton-seed processing,[25] and by similar innovations. Moreover, it could and did increase the effective demand for agricultural inputs by offering agricultural loans on favorable terms.

The indications are that the government engaged in all of these activities to a very limited extent. Attempts to decrease the rate of interest are evident, but so are difficulties in achieving decreases, apparently for lack of loanable funds.[26] The amount of agricultural credit at current prices increased, but the prices of most goods seem to have increased similarly. As a result, the millet equivalent of such loans moved from 3,700 piculs in 1942 to 6,200 piculs in 1943 and to 4,250 piculs in 1944.[27] Data on producer goods prices, which have not been made available, may depict a somewhat different trend, but they are unlikely to change the impression that the volume of agricultural credit was extremely small, given a total grain output of 1.5 to 2.0 million piculs. In addition, there is evidence that the share of agricultural credit in total credit was quite small and that it benefited particular select groups.[28] The same may be suspected of the output of the state-operated farm implement factories.

Changes in factor proportions. In the absence of adequate information on changes in most inputs, it is impossible to reach firm opinions on the changes in their ratios. Merely two points appear to be worth making on the basis of the available evidence. First, the data on changes in cultivated land and in the stock of animals imply that the land-animal ratio did not vary greatly after 1940, when the process of recuperation seems to have come to its end. This implication is made explicit in table 6.4 for the relation between cultivated land and work animals (oxen plus donkeys), but it also is evident for the relation between land and all animals as recipients of feed and sources of manure. Second, and in combination with these data, the apparent constancy of the agricultural labor force may suggest increases in the land-labor and animal-labor ratios which were comparable in magnitude to those in the stocks of land and animals. However, since work efforts in agriculture could be increased substantially by adding to the number of workdays per person,[29] it also was possible that the land-effort ratio remained constant. Whether the labor mobilization policies had this effect is uncertain,[30] so it is impossible to form firm expectations in regard to yields as well as to labor productivity.

Changes in natural fortunes. Finally climatic variations could affect production significantly. The quality of successive agricultural seasons has not been discussed for the SKN border region in its entirety. However, estimates have been made available for one locality—Yang Chia K'ou of Michih Hsien—during the years 1937-1942. Table 6.4, which presents this information, shows that the season was probably poor in 1937, good in 1938 and in 1939, fair in 1940 and in 1941, and good again in 1942. Data for subsequent years could not be located, but the alleged decline in grain production from 1944 to 1945 suggests an adverse turn in the climate.

Changes in output. The effects of all changes in inputs and natural fortunes are difficult to determine because the information on changes in output is also incomplete. Table 6.3 lists the data which could be found plus a few personal estimates which could be made with a high degree of confidence. In appraising the significance of the limits to this evidence, one should recall Buck's data on the composition of the farm product in 1930-1931, which has been described in tables 2.7 and 2.8. In particular, table 6.3 accounts for five major components of the farm product:

(1) Grains. The output of grains, which apparently constituted almost all of the crop product and most of the farm product, is covered more comprehensively than the output of other products by two series of estimates. Both series depict substantial increases in grain production, in circumstances which the measures of table .4 indicate. Until 1945 the output of grains varied quite closely with the area of cultivated land and not so closely with the stock of work animals. Yields did not decline in

response to an apparently constant agricultural labor force, and—surprisingly—they also did not fluctuate with the natural fortunes. But they did fall in 1940, at the time when major territorial changes had occurred. Such a fall runs counter to the rise in yields which is to be expected on the basis of Buck's data, and it thus aggravates the discrepancy between the two sets of estimates for the initial territory.[31] Since the divergence could be attributed to the limitations of choice in our manipulation of Buck's data,[32] it might be ignored. However, if one compares the grain-product estimates of table 6.3 with the grain-consumption estimates which the rations of table 2.9 imply,[33] one finds that the revised data fail to meet this low standard of sustenance.[34] There are thus grounds for suspecting that the official data understate the actual yield and output levels, a suspicion that adds to uncertainty about the official trend estimates.

As a by-product of grain, the output of straw is increased. Estimates of total straw production could not be found, but since most straw was consumed on the farms, primarily as fodder and fuel, and since the grain-animal ratio remained rather stable during the 1940s, this lack of data is not very consequential.[35] However, the maintenance of a growing number of pack and draft animals for civilian and military transportation necessitated an increase in the transaction of straw, and this cannot be discussed in the appropriate detail.

(2) Cotton. The output of cotton, which constituted a small fraction of the total crop product, has been accounted for reasonably well. Data are lacking for the early years, when the quantity was negligibly small, but after the tightening of the economic blockade, cotton production increased with extraordinary rapidity. Still it did not grow as much as had been hoped. On the basis of earlier experiences, the SKN border region government envisaged yields of 15 to 20 catties of lint per *mou* of cotton land.[36] The data of tables 6.1 and 6.3 imply that an average yield of close to 15 catties per *mou* was reached in 1942. Contrary to expectation, the yield declined to 11.5 catties per *mou* in 1943 and 9.5 catties per *mou* in 1944, apparently due to late frosts.[37] As a consequence, actual production fell far short of planned production, especially in 1944 when 4.0 to 4.5 million catties of lint were to be produced.[38]

Table 6.3

FARM PRODUCT, 1937-1945

Farm Product	Unit	1937	1938	1939	1940	1941	1942	1943	1944	1945
Grains										
planned	Million piculs*						1.83[a]	1.76[b]	2.34[c]	
claimed	Million piculs*	1.49[d]	1.61[d]	1.75[d]	n.a.	1.63[e]	1.68[e]	1.84[e]	2.00[e]	
revised[f]	Million piculs*	1.26	1.27	1.37	1.43	1.47	1.50	1.60	1.75	1.60
Cotton										
lint	Million catties			0.06[g]	0.22[g]	0.58[g]	1.40[h]	1.73[h]	3.00[i]	
seed	Million catties			0.12	0.44	1.16	2.80	3.46	6.00	
Sheep										
additions[k]	Thousand heads					415	436	465		473
stock changes[l]	Thousand heads					-8	88	212		-59
subtractions	Thousand heads					423	348	275		532
skins	Thousand pieces							117[m]		
wool, data	Thousand catties			2,000[n]				1,005[m]		
estimates	Thousand catties		2,343		3,446	3,428	3,604	4,028		3,910
Oxen plus Donkeys										
additions[k]	Thousand heads					50.7	56.4	58.8		62.2[p]
stock changes[l]	Thousand heads					11.6	31.7	16.8		15.5
subtractions	Thousand heads					39.1	24.4	42.0		46.7
Cultivated land										
reclaimed[q]	Million mou	0.195	0.358	1.003	0.699	0.390	0.281	0.976	1.288	0.531

* One picul equals 300 catties.
a. *Shan Kan Ning (1958)*, p. 93.
b. *Shan Kan Ning pien ch'ü cheng-ts'e t'iao-li hui-pien*, p. 26.
c. *Ibid.*, p. 44.
d. *Shan Kan Ning 1939-1941*, p. 42. The estimates for 1937 and 1938, which were stated as 1.12 million piculs and 1.21 million piculs @ 400 catties, have been converted. See chapter 2, note 80.
e. *Shan Kan Ning (1958)*, p. 284.
f. *Ching-chi yen-chiu*, No. 2 (1956), p. 108.
g. Estimate: Cotton land according to table 6.1 times yield in 1942.
h. Van Slyke, *The Chinese Communist Movement*, p. 160.
i. *Chieh-fang jih pao*, No. 1295 (7 December 1944), p. 1.
j. Mao and others, *New Life in New China*, p. 47 (two catties of seed per catty of lint).
k. Estimate: Share of nonadult animals times animal stock. Derived from chapter 2, note 86, and table 6.2.
l. Derived from Table 6.2.
m.Mao and others, *New Life in New China*, p. 126.
n. *Shan Kan Ning 1939-1941*, p. 50.
o. Derived from *ibid.* and table 6.2 (two catties of wool per sheep).
p. Estimate: 15.4 percent of stock (extrapolation).
q. Derived from table 6.1.

Table 6.4

AGRICULTURAL PERFORMANCE INDICATORS, 1937-1945

Year	Year-to-year change in cultivated land [a] %	oxen plus donkeys [b] %	Area of land per oxen and donkey [c] Mou	Quality of the agricultural season [d]	Year-to-year change in total grain output [e] Original data %	1956 data %	Grain per mou of cultivated land [f] Original data kg	1956 data kg
1937	2.3	< 20.0	71.9	poor? [g]	n.a.	n.a.	25.9	21.9
1938	4.3	44.6	51.8	good	8.0	0.8	27.0	21.2
1939	12.0	27.6 [i]	36.5 [j]	good	8.7	7.9	26.1	20.4
1940	6.3 [h]	19.0 [j]	35.8 [j]	fair	n.a.	4.4	n.a.	18.3
1941	3.1	6.8	35.6	fair	n.a.	2.8	20.2	18.2
1942	3.2	7.3	34.3	good	3.1	2.0	20.2	18.0
1943	7.2	6.5	34.5	n.a.	9.5	6.7	20.6	18.0
1944	9.8	2.0 [k]	n.a.	n.a.	8.7	9.4	20.4	17.8
1945	3.6	2.0 [k]	37.6	n.a.	n.a.	-8.6	n.a.	15.8

a. Derived from table 6.1.
b. Derived from table 6.2.
c. Derived from tables 6.1 and 6.2.
d. Yen-an nung-ts'un tiao-ch'a tuan, *Mi-chih hsien,* pp. 140-142, 146, 148-149.
e. Derived from table 6.3.
f. Derived from tables 6.1 and 6.3.
g. Chapter 2, note 81.
h. Reclaimed land | 0.699/(11.742 − 0.699)|.
i. Table 6.2, note c.
j. *Ibid.,* note d.
k. Average rate of growth, 1943-1945.

The authorities noted at first that ". . . it will be difficult to attain complete self-sufficiency this year. . . ." for this reason, but they subsequently revised themselves to the extent of holding that 3.0 million catties would meet the autarky goal.[39] Such a total supplied two rather than three pounds of cotton lint per capita per annum.

In addition to lint, cotton contained seeds which could supply oil plus feed or fertilizer. Estimates of the output of cotton seed have not been published but can be inferred easily. The ratio of lint to seed was 1:2 according to SKN sources and 3:7 according to the National Agricultural Research Bureau.[40] The seed estimates of table 6.3 make use of the former ratio. On the assumption that the oil extraction rate from cotton seed was 15 percent,[41] the estimated oil equivalent of 420,000 catties in 1942 approximates the reported total production of 470,000 pounds (i.e., 427,000 catties) in that year.[42] The oil equivalent increased to 519,000 catties in 1943 and to 900,000 catties in 1944. The implied average per capita supplies were extremely small—in 1944 they barely exceeded half a pound per capita per annum.

(3) Animals and animal products. Of the few items in this category—Oxen, donkeys, sheep, and wool—most output must be estimated. The data of table 6.2 permit the derivation of stock changes, but determining the availability of livestock for slaughter or export also requires information on their reproduction rates. In the absence of official SKN data on animal reproduction, Buck's findings may be used once again.[43] Because of uncertainty about the growth of the animal stock during the late 1930s, calculations are limited to the years 1941-1945. The results, which appear in table 6.3, show that the number of sheep disposed of in 1943 is more than twice the official estimate of sheep skins produced in that year. Data on the production of donkey and ox hides have not been made available.

The estimates of how many animals were disposed of during 1941-1945 imply the following potential supplies of meat, on the assumptions that all animals could be eaten and that their carcass weights were 15 kg per sheep[44] and 100 kg per oxen or donkey.[45] The output was—in million catties of 500 grams:

Animal	1941	1942	1943	1945
Sheep	12.69	10.44	8.25	15.96
Oxen and donkeys	7.82	4.88	8.40	9.34
Both categories	20.51	15.32	16.65	25.30

These totals imply average per capita supplies of ten to sixteen catties per annum or of about one pound per month, exclusive of other kinds of meat, notably of pork. Such quantities are far in excess of Buck's findings for the rations of the farm population,[46] but they fall short of the rations other sources attribute to soldiers and workers.[47] The decline in the supply of meat from 1941 to 1942/3 is consistent with the effort to build up herds rapidly, but it runs counter to changes in the level of living of troops.[48]

The output of wool has not been reported systematically, but it can be estimated on the basis of 1939 data which imply an average of two catties per sheep per annum. Such an average, which is also indicated by other sources,[49] yields a total output of wool for 1943 which is four times as large as the one reported for that year. The estimated output of wool increased slowly during the 1940s in proportion to the stock of sheep. As a consequence, the per capita supply of wool must have remained close to constant. Moreover, since dirt and grease accounted for 30 to 40 percent of the weight of unprocessed wool,[50] the per capita supply of clean wool cannot have been much more than 1.5 pounds per annum.

(4) Additions to cultivated land. Various basic construction activities and reclamation work have already been discussed as inputs which could account for increases in agricultural output. However, such changes must be listed also as part of the sector product, together with changes in the animal stock, which likewise appeared among the inputs. Tables 6.3 and 6.4 present the available information on changes in the area of cultivated land. Other kinds of intrasectoral capital formation cannot be measured as well, and the valuation of all such additions to capital is, of course, precarious. Nevertheless, the estimate of near-constant returns to land, which is inherent in the official data on cultivated land and on grain output, suggests that land reclamation in particular contributed a substantial share of the sector product.[51] The production of producer goods for own use thus appears to have had a significant effect on the production of consumer goods by agriculture.

Salt Extraction

The strategy which apparently met with considerable success in agriculture was practiced also in the extraction of salt. The output of salt was to be increased especially by additional efforts in producer goods production and by limited improvements in production techniques. Such changes were to be brought about in particular by cooperative organization. In comparison to agriculture, however, this development could not be as exclusively intrasectoral a phenomenon.

Table 6.5

SALT PRODUCTION AND DISPOSAL, 1937-1944

Item	Unit	1937	1938	1939	1940	1941	1942	1943	1944
Salt production potential	Loads [a]			740,000 [b]					1,000,000 [c]
Salt fields									
Kaochih	Fields [d]	461 [e]			600 [f]			882 [g]	
Laochih	Fields [h]	none [e]						801 [g]	
Nanmichih	Fields [h]	few [e]						445 [g]	
Lienhuachih	Fields [h]	few [e]						564 [g]	
Four other ponds	Fields [i]	few [e]						142 [g]	
Total	Fields [i]	500?						2,834	
Salt production									
planned	Loads [a]							400,000 [j]	600,000 [k]
realized	Loads [a]	"several 10,000" [e]				700,000 [l]	271,617 [m]	600,000 [j]	
Salt sales									
planned	Loads [a]			190,000 [l]				max. 360,000 [j]	400,000 [k]
realized	Loads [a]		70,000 [l]		230,000 [l]	299,068 [l]		329,893 [n]	
Salt transport	Loads [a]		70,000 [n]					349,893 [n]	
Pack animals									
private	Heads						15,280 [o]	21,337 [o]	
cooperative	Heads						246 [o]	3,706 [o]	10,000 [p]

a. One load equals 150 "big" catties of 24 ounces or 225 regular catties of 500 grams.
b. Derived from Ch'i Li, *Shan Kan Ning pien ch'ü shih-lu*, p. 1.
c. *Salt Production*, p. 8.
d. Fields on the average equal 0.25 *mou. Ibid.*, p. 2.
e. *Ibid.*, p. 1.
f. Fields in 1943 minus fields built by soldiers since 1941. *Ibid.*, pp. 1-2.
g. *Ibid.*, p. 2.
h. Fields on the average equal somewhat more than one *mou. Ibid.*
i. Size of field unspecified.
j. *Shan Kan Ning pien ch'ü cheng-ts'e t'iao-li hui-pien*, p. 26.
k. *Ibid.*, p. 44.
l. Mao, "Ching-chi wen-t'i," pp. 71-72.
m. *Salt Production*, p. 3.
n. *Ibid.*, p. 7.
o. Mao and others, *New Life*, pp. 128-129.
p. Planned. *Shan Kan Ning pien ch'ü cheng-ts'e t'iao-li hui-pien*, p. 45.

Productive potential and productive capacity. Table 6.5 shows that according to official estimates, the region contained substantial salt deposits which were being exploited to a minor degree in the beginning of the period. In addition, there is evidence that salt production had declined during preceding years and that salt producers had shifted to farming. As a consequence, not only the productive potential, but also the productive capacity of the salt-producing district may have been under utilized initially. It thus seemed possible to increase production to some extent simply by inducing peasants to shift back to salt-making as a form of subsidiary work.[52] However, the likely deterioration of idle salt production facilities must have set fairly narrow limits to the existing excess capacity.

Changes in salt fields. Salt production could be increased more substantially by increases in capacity through capital construction. Table 6.5 indicates that the number of salt fields increased nearly five times from 1937 to 1943. The sizes of these fields were not standardized, and the data on average field sizes are incomplete. However, the available information suggests that the area enclosed in salt fields increased perhaps as much as ten times.[53] Most of the additions seem to have been made in 1941, and many appear to have been attributable to the three or four thousand soldiers who were sent at that time to participate in salt production. They constructed close to one-half and possibly more of the additional salt fields.[54]

Changes in techniques. The output of salt could also be increased by technical changes which served to free the production process from natural fortunes. To yield the greatest amount of salt, the fields had to be inundated at appropriate intervals with appropriate amounts of water. By substituting for irregular rainfalls man-made water works, it was not only possible to control to some extent the ill effects of floods and droughts, but through water conservancy as well as by pumping underground brine to the surface, it was also possible to lengthen the salt-producing season. Attempts to regularize salt production in this manner, which required additional construction efforts, were evidently made, allegedly with positive results[55] Other conceivable changes, which necessitated substantial resource commitments in addition to labor, were not made.[56]

Changes in factor proportions. The available data do not permit any firm statement, but the indication that the number of persons engaging in salt extraction also may have grown close to ten times from 1937 to 1942[57] lends support to the guess that the salt field area per laborer remained fairly constant. The construction of water works to help regularize salt production may have raised the capital labor ratio in salt production, but in the absence of data on such construction, this development cannot be quantified.

Changes in output. In response to all input changes, the output of salt according to table 6.5 increased from several 10,000 loads in 1937 to 700,000 loads in 1941 and—after a drastic decline in 1942—to 600,000 loads in 1943. The salt transportation and sales data for 1938 suggest that the output in 1937/1938 may not have been much more than 70,000 loads, notably because a portion of the transported salt could have come from adjacent locations in Inner Mongolia.[58] It therefore seems that the output of salt increased close to ten times during the period, so that the yield per unit of salt field area as well as the output per salt worker may have remained fairly constant over time.[59] However, several qualifications should be made in this connection.

A portion of the salt output in 1941 and again in 1943, which was much larger than the output target for that year, consisted of inferior salt produced by inadequate methods.[60] The salable portion of output, which would be a more appropriate measure for achievement in production, has not been reported, but it may not have differed much from the amount of salt sold (exported) plus the quantity consumed within the SKN border region.

Salt sales increased substantially from 1938 to 1940 and 1941, i.e., before the major effort at capital construction was made. This phenomenon, too, may be statistical as well as real. In either case, however, the contribution of the new salt fields seems to have been more limited than the comparison of data for 1937/8 and 1943 suggests. To explain this unexpected finding, one may note that the newly created productive potential probably remained underutilized. Salt exports, which constituted the greater share of total sales, could have reached 600,000 to

700,000 loads in the opinion of SKN officials if they had not been restricted by the national government.[61] Such restrictions apparently imposed effective constraints on salt production during earlier years, too.[62]

The actual quantities of salt exported have not been reported, but they may be approximated by an estimation of internal consumption. To meet a ration of 500 grams per month, the amount apparently allotted to members of the institutional households during the early 1940s, required for the entire population 75,000 loads in 1936, 80,000 loads in 1940, and more than 85,000 loads in 1944. Exports therefore are likely to have risen from practically zero in 1938 to 250,000 in 1943.

There are indications that the export price of salt decreased from 1943 to 1944,[63] during a period when all other prices and especially the internal price of salt increased several times![64] This development, which was attributable to policies of the national government, must have had negative effects on salt extraction within the SKN border region. The lack of references to salt production and salt sales in the government reports for subsequent years points to this conclusion, and it suggests in particular that the targets for 1944 may not have been met.

In summary, salt production must have grown enormously but not, probably, at the phenomenal rate the official data tend to intimate. Whatever the real magnitude of change may have been, it was affected by the capital construction activities of the army which must be included as part of the sector product. Although the value added by the construction of new salt fields, water works, and tools cannot be quantified properly, it appears to have been very substantial,[65] but external limits prevented full exploitation of the productive potential and apparently even of the newly created capacity. As a consequence, however, the labor shortage in salt production, which loomed so large in 1943, was probably less pressing than anticipated.[66]

Manufacturing and Mining

The constraints which limited the choice in agriculture and in salt extraction to a development strategy of nearly complete self-reliance, had a similar effect on manufacturing and mining.

If various products were to be produced at all within the SKN border region, they had to be produced for the most part by indigenous means and methods. Not only numerous consumer goods for the civilian and military sectors, but also the producer goods for their production had to be created internally. The Chinese communists could organize the production of both kinds of goods in comparatively modern social forms, but the backwardness of the area plus its separation from the rest of the world limited them in the main to an outmoded handicraft technology which had already begun to vanish from the area under conditions of unrestricted trade. Adding some more modern expertise and equipment could ameliorate this situation.

Changes in production. Most of the available information on changes in the number of enterprises, their organizational forms, their branches of industry, and their employment has been presented in tables 4.1 to 4.4 and 5.2 to 5.4. Although this evidence leaves some questions unanswered, it points to a rapid expansion of nonagricultural production in response to the renewed blockade. Unfortunately, information on the means and methods of production which were used in these enterprises is much more incomplete. As a consequence, one must discuss production process changes in a much more impressionistic fashion on the basis of the observations of a few foreign visitors.

(1) Initial state. Prior to the completion of the Long March, nonagricultural production was carried on primarily by a relatively small number of handicraftsmen. The data of table 2.4 appear to indicate the nature and range of such activities. In addition, there seem to have operated a few manufactories, especially in rug-making. The only "truly" modern enterprise was an oil field plus refinery which had been an unprofitable undertaking to the national government for the preceding twenty years.[67] ". . . Even a small machine industry was almost entirely absent before the Soviets were set up. . . ."[68] Coal was mined to an uncertain extent, mostly for use as a domestic fuel,[69] and spinning as well as weaving almost had succumbed to external competition.[70]

The capital which had been invested in these few manufacturing and mining ventures has not been reported, but there is no doubt that it consisted mostly of the few traditional hand tools. In particular, there remained merely ". . . a trifling number of antiquated spindles and looms. . . ." in the area according to Stein.[71] Even the oil-drilling and oil-refining equipment was far from satisfactory in Forman's opinion:

> The few steel drilling bits left by Socony [in 1916!] are almost at the limit of their usefulness. The worn-out pistons in the suction pump have been covered with cloth and leather to prevent leakage. For lack of steel, sheets of slate, quarried from the river bank, are used for lining the oil storage tanks. As a matter of fact, improvisation and substitution are the rule here, also. The steam engine is the one installed by the Japanese engineer in 1906; the unit brought in by Socony is unusable for lack of spare parts. The kerosene and crude oil are transported from the oil fields in bamboo-and-lime casks. . . .[72]

Tables 5.3 and 5.4 suggest that the number of persons possessing nonagricultural production skills was correspondingly small. In particular, spinning and weaving had become something of a lost art in the area. And there was ". . . no one who really knows anything about scientific oil-drilling. Some of the old workmen are still on the job. Of these, Chen Tsun-hsia, who manages the fields, confesses that he is no oil engineer, but merely a man with some years of practical experience in working in the oil fields under foreign supervision. . . ."[73] The initial productive capacity of the area was thus extremely limited.

(2) *Importation of producer goods and skills.* The minute stocks of nonagricultural tools and talents within the area could be augmented to some extent by inflows of skilled producers and producer goods from the outside. Such inflows occurred on several occasions. To begin with, Snow notes that the immigrating Red Army brought along ". . . many lathes, turning machines, stampers, dies, etc. . . ." as well as other machinery and materials.[74] Their total quantity has not been made public, but Snow's reference to "dozens" of Singer sewing machines suggests that "many" cannot have been a large number. This impression is supported by Nym Wales who observed that hand

sewing was common, for ". . . the Red Army had had to bury or give away most of its machinery during the March. . . ."[75] Snow noted further that:

> Battles have been fought by the Red Army just to get a few lathes, weaving machines, engines or scrap iron. Nearly everything they had in the category of machinery while I was there had been "captured"! During their expedition to Shansi province in 1936, for example, they seized machines, tools and raw materials, which were carried by mule all the way across the mountains of Shensi, to their fantastic cliff-dwelling factories.[76]

Apparently, this practice continued after 1937 in Japanese-occupied territory. Forman and Stein learned in 1944 that the Chinese communists tore up steel rails and captured wire as well as other items for use as industrial raw materials,[77] but because it was difficult to obtain and transport such "imports," their quantities seem to have been quite small. Similarly limited in number appear to have been the imports Stein records of various ". . . ancient lathes, planing, drilling, rolling and stamping machines made in China, the United States, England, and Germany which were bought second-, third-, or probably tenth-hand in Sian before the Kuomintang blockade . . ."[78] Forman noted that the enterprise to which Stein referred in this statement, i.e., the agricultural implement factory founded in 1938 which had been converted into an arsenal at the beginning of the blockade, ". . . then had only two lathes, one casting machine, and a single experienced gunsmith."[79] Smuggling during subsequent years cannot have added greatly to the stock.[80]

In summary, all observers agree that the import of modern machinery and materials was highly restricted at most times. Information on the inflow of more traditional inputs is limited chiefly to cotton, which apparently could be obtained more readily, but at prohibitive prices.[81] In combination, prohibitions and tariffs kept producer goods imports so small that they could not bring about the expansion of industry at the desired pace. Obstacles to the immigration of skilled personnel tended to impose similar constraints. Although detailed information is lacking, there are indications that workers and even technicians could enter more easily than machinery and equipment did,[82] so that the latter remained the more stringent bottleneck.[83] This did not mean, however, that the immigrating workers were sufficiently numerous to sustain the growth of manufacturing and mining at the desired speed.[84]

(3) Technique of import substitution. The limited accumulations of modern producer goods and skills within the SKN border region made it impossible to produce internal substitutes by other than traditional handicraft technology. However, modern expertise could improve outmoded tools and practices in many instances as could mass ingenuity, both of which were to be activated by the educational and production campaigns.[85] Efforts to develop manufacturing on the basis of an improved handicraft technology are evident for the more important branches.

a. *Textile manufacturing* became the most prominent example for the implementation of this strategy. Practically every visitor to the area felt compelled to comment on its development. When Snow visited in 1936, he discovered that:

> ... the Reds had established a spinning-school at An Ting, with 100 women students. The workers were given three hours' general education daily and five hours' instruction in spinning and weaving. Upon completion of their course, after three months, students were sent to various districts to open textile factories. . . .[86]

Snow did not explain how the newly trained spinners and weavers obtained equipment for these ventures. However, Stein discussed this aspect on the basis of information gained in 1944:

> ... simple wooden looms were designed for production by industrial cooperatives, army workshops, and village carpenters; ...
> ... hand spindles ... were produced locally on patterns provided by the government and industrial cooperatives.[87]

Most of the looms as well as the spindles were used in home industry, by private and public households. The remainder were installed in state, CIC, and capitalist manufactories, where they were operated not only by hand, but also by animal and water power. Both Stein and Forman visited such a mill and described its techniques of production. To Stein,

> . . . it seemed like a reproduction of a big medieval manufacturing enterprise. Its large halls were crowded with hundreds of noisily clattering looms, entirely of wood with scarcely a piece of iron visible, driven by a large water wheel over woolen transmitter belts. In a carpenter's shop, wooden machinery for the constant expansion of the mill is made by hand with the most primitive tools. The few old lathes in the small mechanical workshop are kept in motion by an old mule trotting in a circle in the courtyard and turning a big wheel.[88]

Forman commented in particular on the additional technical problems which the use of such power sources posed. He was impressed by the ". . . considerable native ingenuity in compensating for the lack of proper machines,"[89] and his examples of innovation in the production of transmitter belts and of springs are indeed striking.[90] Manufactories specialized in weaving rather than in spinning and obtained their yarn from home spinners. To secure yarn supplies, they tended to coordinate both production processes by similarly "medieval" putting-out systems. The Bands observed and described such a system for processing wool:

> Three sets of machines, that had been manufactured at the science college machine shop, were powered each by one mule. After shaking and combing by these machines, the wool was farmed out to private individuals for homespinning through a home-spinners' co-operative. Four grades of product were accepted. The factory then combined the homespun strands into knitting wool, or wove it into material on their hand-operated looms. . . .[91]

b. *Paper manufacturing* developed on the same pattern as textile manufacturing did. Paper had been made by handicraft methods since time immemorial. The paper makers in the SKN border region in 1941 included two private plants plus fifty household enterprises in addition to the twelve state enterprises listed in table 4.4.[92] At least within the state sector, persons were trained to make the implements for its production as well as the paper itself. Stein reported:

> I saw a good-sized paper mill standing over a stream. Large wooden water wheels drove giant grindstones set in a complicated-looking wooden superstructure, milling grass from the near-by hillsides into pulp. This factory, within the few years of its existence, has become the parent of more than a dozen other paper mills which were set up all over the Border Region with a few of its experienced hands as the *nuclei* of their new, farm-recruited personnel.[93]

c. *Printing,* a prime user of paper, tended to operate with somewhat more modern machinery and equipment due to the fact that much of it had been brought along on the Long March. However, replacements and additions had to be produced locally by similarly traditional techniques, and a great deal depended on the innovative ingenuity of the labor force. Stein observed:

> The primitive printing shops at press headquarters are safely housed in the beautiful, thousand-year-old Caves of the Ten Thousand Buddhas at the bottom of the hill. Long rows of carved Buddhas on the walls of the tall, ancient caves and some huge statues look down on an odd assortment of busy machinery—old-fashioned pedal-driven printing presses, some of which were made in Yenan with remodeled Japanese "dud" bombs as rollers, and all kinds of improvised equipment of which even men who once worked in Shanghai's modern printing plants are extremely proud.[94]

d. *Metal processing* in general and *armaments manufacturing* in particular also developed on this pattern, as Stein did not fail to point out:

> The armament industry in the Border Region and the war areas grew mainly in similar ways—on the basis of primitive handwork. Blacksmiths were mobilized everywhere. They had to train ever-increasing numbers of apprentices. Army units in the rear and at the front had soldiers trained, and established their own blacksmith shops. No iron deposits in the hills and plains were considered too poor for use. Farmers were asked to help exploit them. And new forges were set up next to primitive mines.[95]

However, the production of iron apparently posed serious problems, ". . . due principally to the fact that the workers and directors know very little about running an iron foundry. . . ." according to Forman.[96] Moreover, these technological constraints also prohibited the production of steel, and the absence of appropriate deposits prevented the mining of most nonferrous metals. For steel and copper therefore the region depended entirely on imports and scrap, as most visitors noted. A reference to rails as an outside source of steel has been made already. In addition to wire, which likewise was captured from the Japanese, ". . . all the copper used in the plant is from copper cash or odd pieces of old dragons and Buddhas, collected by the peasants on scrap drives. . . ."[97]

Whereas a great deal of blacksmithing and coppersmithing continued to be carried on in small shops, which tended to remain individual household enterprises, most of the armaments manufacturing was concentrated in a few manufactories, some of which were institutional household enterprises. In comparison with the small shops, manufactories had more equipment as well as additional sources of power. In the previously mentioned arsenal, Stein found besides the imported machinery

> . . . simple new machines of various kinds made in the arsenal itself or in one of the Border Region's new engineering workshops. All the machines are

well kept. And they run—driven by an old truck engine with a home-produced charcoal-burning attachment.[98]

Such production methods as the foregoing indicate the class of solutions applied to all production problems in manufacturing and mining. All branches used handicraft techniques for familiar as well as for unfamiliar purposes. Where the product itself was not a traditional one, handicraft techniques yielded ". . . primitive substitutes for every essential that is lacking in its conventional shape."[99]

The extent of this producer goods production cannot be measured appropriately. In his report on "Economic Problems and Financial Problems," Mao Tse-tung noted merely that the tool-making industry had been formed to produce spinning wheels, weaving looms, cotton bows, cotton gins, paper-making equipment, large carts, wood-working tools, agricultural implements and other items, most of which were handicraft tools.[100] Other sources remained similarly imprecise.[101] A reasonably complete enumeration could be found only in the case of looms for the years 1938-1943. The data of table 6.6 indicate that the total number of looms (exclusive of hand looms) grew from about 4,500 to about 25,000 during this period. Hand looms are said to have numbered 68,000 in 1941,[102] and spinning wheels 120,255 in 1943.[103] Almost all items of both kinds of implements appear to have been manufactured within the region during the course of the import-substitution campaign.

Changes in capital. Data on the value of the industrial capital stock have appeared in somewhat greater number. However, inadequate specification, conceptual heterogeneity, and problems of valuation under conditions of inflation make it impossible to integrate all of these bits of information into a coherent picture. The most revealing item is a report on the value of the capital (tzu-chin) of the sixty-two state-operated industrial enterprises which existed at the end of 1942. Table 6.7 shows that at fall 1942 prices, their cash value seems to have been equivalent to 43,000 piculs of millet in *toto* and to 10.8 piculs of millet per employed person. At an average wage rate of about six piculs of millet per worker per annum, these quantities were

Table 6.6

WEAVING INDUSTRY, 1938-1943 [a]

Sector	Year	Shops	Workers	Looms	Bolts*
State	1938	1	96	16	125
	1939	1	210	23	1,426
	1940	11	850	160	14,740
	1941	29	1,845	354	18,750
	1942	16	1,083	370	14,565
	1943	23	1,357	449	32,968
CIC	1938	—	— —	—	— — —
	1939	2	25	8	400
	1940	4	82	20	850
	1941	22	352	132	4,600
	1942	27	385	179	4,500
	1943	38	374	179	6,000
Capitalist	1938	5	34	18	1,620
	1939	16	154	52	5,690
	1940	20	185	64	4,500
	1941	40	205	121	8,460
	1942	50	310	150	12,000
	1943	?	702	196 [b]	19,634
Home	1938		5,000	4,500	5,625
industry	1939		8,000	6,850	8,750
	1940		10,000	10,000	12,500
	1941		13,000	11,875	14,500
	1942		13,500	12,000	14,158
	1943		41,540	24,547 [c]	45,700
All	1938		5,130	4,534	7,370
sectors	1939		8,389	6,933	16,266
	1940		11,117	10,244	32,590
	1941		15,402	12,482	46,310
	1942		15,278	12,699	45,223
	1943		43,973	25,371	104,302

* One bolt measures 32.3 m x 0.78 m. See note 135.
a. Hsü, *A Survey,* Part 2, p. 93.
b. Residual.
c. *Wei kung-yeh p'in,* p. 59.

Table 6.7

**CAPITAL (TZU-CHIN) OF SIXTY-TWO
STATE-OPERATED ENTERPRISES IN DECEMBER 1942**

Branch of industry	Money value of total capital [a] SKN yuan	Millet equivalent of capital in *toto* [b] Piculs	per employee [c] Piculs
Textile	29,900,000	20,550	14.4
Garment	1,001,100	688	1.7
Paper	4,100,000	2,818	6.4
Printing	5,200,000	3,574	9.4
Chemical	17,030,000	11,704	17.4
Tools	3,662,792	2,517	10.6
Coal mining	1,777,070	1,221	2.8
All branches	62,670,962	43,072	10.8

a. See Mao, "Ching-chi wen-t'i," p. 92.
b. Derived from *ibid.* and table 7.3. Price of millet: 1,455 yuan per picul of 300 catties.
c. Derived from *ibid.* and table 5.3.

equivalent to 7,200 man-years of work in *toto* and to 1.8 man-years of work per employed person.[104] Such magnitudes do not seem unreasonable, and they are consistent with the following information which Stein obtained:

> We gave our army units and our various government and educational institutions capital in the form of notes and ordered them to provide for their future needs out of their own production. As a rule, they

were given the equivalent of two years' current expenditure to finance their new production enterprises . . . .[105]

Yet table 6.7 indicates in addition that the capital-labor ratio fluctuated substantially from industry to industry. Its extreme variation may reflect differences in technology as well as problems of valuation under conditions of inflation. Using the December 1942 price of grain as a deflator may also serve to exaggerate the predominance of investments in textiles and especially in various branches of chemical manufacturing.

Changes in the capital of state-operated industrial enterprises can be approximated for the years 1940-1943 with data on government investments in and border region bank loans to industry.[106] These data, which appear in table 6.8, indicate that almost all of the stock of 1942 was accumulated during the first two years of "blind expansion." The absence of bank loan data for the following years entails understatements of the actual additions to capital thereafter. However, during the rationalization campaign, increases in the capital stock were probably relatively small. Later on, internal capital formation, which cannot be accounted for, became a major source of its growth, and the emphasis tended to shift from state enterprises to cooperative home handicrafts.

Changes in the capital invested in CIC enterprises cannot be reconstructed in a fully satisfactory manner, either. However, several bits of information could be found which appear in table 6.9. These data indicate that the contributions of the cooperators accounted for a small share of the total capital until 1944, when the millet equivalent of the share capital is in doubt due to uncertainty about the millet price. In 1942 the share capital seems to have been equivalent to about 400 man-years of work in *toto* and thus to less than one man-year of work per cooperator.[107] These small own contributions were supplemented drastically at first by outside contributions, most of which came from overseas Chinese.[108] Such inflows probably were equivalent to nearly 4,700 man-years of work, thus allowing for unusually high capital-labor ratios.[109] When outside contributions diminished to a trickle with the imposition of the blockade, the border region government assumed financial responsibility to a more limited degree by lending the equivalent of more than 1,200 man-years of work during the years 1941-1943. During 1942 and 1943 these loans were much larger than those made to state-operated industry.[110]

Data on the other producer cooperatives are so incomplete that they suffice merely to make one point: the capital invested in such ventures was clearly of secondary magnitude.[111] Information on the value of capitalist holdings of manufacturing and mining assets is lacking.

Changes in factor proportions. The evident limits to the information on changes in most inputs make it impossible to observe significant tendencies of change in their proportions. In particular, little can be said about the development of the capital-labor ratio in manufacturing and in mining. The data of tables 5.2, 6.8, and 6.9 suggest that this ratio apparently fell during the first phase of "blind expansion," that it rose again during the rationalization campaign of 1942, and that it declined once more during the subsequent phase of "conscious expansion." Unfortunately, these alternating tendencies of short-run change do not suffice to identify a long-run trend. In the absence of such evidence, Stein's report that ". . . industrial production seems to have increased more than the number of workers. . . ."[112] could be interpreted to mean that the capital-labor ratio tended to increase. However, gains in labor productivity of this kind could have been brought about by technological progress as well or by unmeasured increases in work effort.

Table 6.6 poses the same problems of identification and attribution in cross-section perspective. Differences between the ratios of looms to employed persons in state, CIC, regular capitalist and peasant sideline enterprises could be related to differences between the types of looms used in these organizations of production, but they also could indicate differences between the patterns and degrees of manpower utilization in capitalist and socialist enterprises, in full-time and part-time ventures, etc. And both explanations—alone or in combination—could account for productivity differentials among these organizations which are apparent in table 6.6. In the absence of more refined measurements of all inputs, one cannot say more than that.

Table 6.8

ADDITIONS TO CAPITAL IN STATE-OPERATED INDUSTRY, 1940-1943

Year	Government investments Yuan	Border Region bank loans Yuan	Investments plus loans Yuan	Millet price Yuan per picul	Millet equivalent of total additions Piculs
1940	700,000 [a]	1,000,000 [e]	1,700,000	60 [f]	28,441 [g]
1941	500,000 [b]	3,000,000 [b]	3,500,000	278 [h]	12,590
1942	1,700,000 [c]	n.a.	1,700,000	973 [i]	1,747
1943*	2,600,000 [d]	n.a.	2,600,000	1,455 [j]	1,787

* Planned.

a. Winter 1940 and spring 1941. See Mao, "Ching-chi wen-'ti," pp. 140-141.

b. *Ibid.*, p. 89.

c. *Ibid.*, p. 90.

d. *Ibid.*, pp. 48-49.

e. *Ibid.*, p. 88.

f. 1,700,000/28,441.

g. 1,000,000/52 (June 1940 price) plus 700,000/76 (December 1940 price). Table 7.3.

h. June 1941 price. Table 7.3.

i. June 1942 price. Table 7.3.

j. December 1942 price. Table 7.3.

Table 6.9

SHARE CAPITAL AND CONTRIBUTIONS RECEIVED BY CIC, 1939-1944. [a]

Year	Millet price [b] Yuan per picul	CIC share capital Money value Yuan	Millet equivalent Piculs	Outside contributions Money value [d] Yuan	Millet equivalent Piculs	Government loans Money value Yuan	Millet equivalent Piculs
1939	37	11,130 [c]	301	503,232	13,601		
1940	52			698,190	13,427		
1941	278			204,280	735	200,000 [e]	719
1942	973	2,491,600 [c]	2,561	93,567	96	18,800,000 [f]	3,342 [g]
1943	4,488			1,330,000	296		3,342 [g]
1944	23,500	1,398,994,518 [d]	59,532				
1939-43				2,829,269		19,000,000	7,403

a. Not including contributions toward CIC Yenan office expenses.
b. Table 7.3. June data.
c. Mao, "Ching-chi wen-t'i," p. 50.
d. Nym Wales. Notes, pp. 63-64.
e. Ibid., p. 60.
f. 19,000,000 minus 200,000. See notes d and e.
g. Estimate: contributions in terms of millet equivalent were the same in 1942 and 1943.

Changes in output. The increases and improvements of labor and capital in manufacturing and mining yielded increases in the variety, quantity, and quality of output. Like the changes in inputs, however, changes in output have not been reported systematically. As a consequence, it is impossible to verify the ultimate success of import substitution in a comprehensive form. The available evidence may be presented under three headings.

(1) Variety. The reason for making a growing number of new tools and implements, many of which have been enumerated, was to produce an increasing variety of private and public consumer goods, many of which were in demand due to the presence of the Chinese communists. To name but a few, tables 4.4, 5.3 and 6.7, as well as other listings, indicate that the government emphasized the production of textiles—cotton, woolen, and linen yarn, cloth and knitwear plus rugs. In addition, these sources also point to the emergence of a chemical industry which produced soap, refined salt, alkaline tooth powder, chalk, matches, porcelain, glass, alcohol, printing ink, pharmaceuticals, tan, dyes, etc.[113] Other commodities—e.g., paper and coal—have been mentioned already. The oil refinery put out gasoline, kerosene, diesel oil, lubricating oils, and candles.[114] The Yenan science college machine shop manufactured in addition to various producer goods items of daily use such as spoons, buttons, and belt buckles,[115] and the arsenal which once had been an agricultural implement factory made

> . . . cast iron, neat-looking trench mortars, cartridges, bayonets, Very pistols, and—since the farmer enjoys a high priority everywhere—copper syringes for veterinary use in the campaign against cattle epidemics. Other shops repair rifles and light and heavy machine guns and refill Chinese and Japanes rifle cartridges.[116]

Of course, these items do not exhaust the list of newly manufactured products, and there certainly is no doubt that a wide variety of them was being produced.

(2) Quality. Information about the quality of these new products is hard to come by, but the indications are that at least in

the beginning many items tended to be inferior to products manufactured on the outside. For many of the producer goods, such an appraisal can be inferred from the quotations describing the methods of import substitution. The primitive nature of the producer goods accounted in turn for the primitive quality of the consumer goods which they served to manufacture. Inferior quality of course appeared in a wide range of variants, as the following two examples may illustrate.

a. *Textiles*. The primary shortcoming in textile manufacturing was the inferiority of home spinning. It yielded a coarse and uneven yarn which could not be woven as well as machine-spun yarn. Moreover, cloth made of homespun yarn was thick and heavy. It embodied several times the quantity of textile fiber[117] and was less comfortable to wear than the other cloth. Homespun, therefore, was not so popular at first and had to be protected against imported cloth so long as the latter could be obtained.[118] Yet however people felt about wearing it, homespun evidently served its principal purpose quite well. It kept people clothed.

b. *Weapons*. Similar shortcomings appeared in armaments production, but the inferiority of locally made weapons was much more consequential. In Snow's words: ". . . the arsenal's output was crude work, and most of its products equipped the Red partisans, the regular Red forces being supplied almost entirely with guns and munitions captured from enemy troops!"[119] Allocations from the nationalist government added to the stock of superior weapons during the period of truce and some arsenals in the base areas behind Japanese lines could meet higher standards of product quality.[120] In spite of such improvements, the production of inferior arms continued to limit the military capacities of most base areas severely, even though it kept people armed.

The significance of quality differentials between internally and externally manufactured goods thus varied greatly, yet apparently irrespective of such variations, the SKN border region government tried to diminish all of them. As part of the autarky campaign, efforts were made to increase the quality of output generally.[121] This endeavor necessitated especially an upgrading of the work of many state-operated enterprises, which was attempted in the context of the rationalization campaign.[122] How successful this policy was has not been reported systematically, but several Western visitors commented on the attributes of specific products. The Bands, for instance, who lived in the base areas for two years, noted:[123]

> . . .General Hsiao provided us with ample bedding (cotton-wool padded blankets), padded winter uniforms and cloth-soled marching shoes. It took us a long time to get used to ourselves in this outfit, especially the padded trousers, but they were light and warm, and completely eliminated the need for wearing our overcoats while marching.
>
> . . . Within five minutes we were fitted with excellently made cloth shoes. . . .
>
> The [CIC soap] factory was turning out two grades of soap, for toilet use and laundry purposes; also an alkaline toothpowder and purified table salt. For the soap they were using ox fat; the free samples they gave us proved quite good for Bill's bi-weekly shave.
>
> . . . We still [in 1948?] have the excellent woolen blankets as a memento of Yenan's home products. . . .

Similarly, Forman found that ". . . the candles made from the by-products [of local oil] are of a fairly high quality, much better than any obtainable in Chungking or other places in the Big Rear. . . ."[124] Stein learned that locally manufactured gunpowder was "fairly effective."[125] Informants of the US government reported that the area produced ". . . a rough but rather good quality paper . . ." and that the production of some pharmaceuticals was "fairly efficient," but they also described locally made iron, which was especially important for arms production, as "of a poor quality." And they implied a similar opinion of locally made steel, which could be produced only in minute quantity.[126] In summary, such statements suggest that by 1943/1944, when the autarky campaign could be expected to have had some success, the SKN border region was able to substitute local products of acceptable quality for some of the more important imported commodities.

(3) Quantity. Unfortunately, quantity is impossible to determine satisfactorily. Changes in the quantity of manufactured output were not reported systematically by the SKN border region government. Data not only are lacking in the cases of ferrous metallurgy and of arms production, where strategic considerations could have called for secrecy, but they also are incomplete in the cases of textile, soap, and paper production, where the civilian use predominated and where propagandistic considerations favored publicity. Moreover, the few data which have been made available may not be accurate. Like the inadequate reporting on changes in employment, these shortcomings seem to indicate the border region government's limited control. Such a constraint in turn may be due not only to the region's backwardness *per se* but also to the autarky strategy of stressing self-sufficiency on the smallest possible scale and especially within the scope of the familial or institutional household. The available evidence, which is listed in table 6.10, warrants the following comments.

a. *Yarn.* An estimate of yarn output could be found for merely one year, 1943. On the assumption that the output per spinner remained constant at the implicit six catties per annum,[127] one could infer from the employment data of table 5.2 that the total output of yarn reached 450,000 catties in 1941 and 900,000 catties in 1945. A norm of eight catties, which in 1941 was considered feasible as well as adequate for the achievement of autarky,[128] would have yielded 1,200,000 catties in 1945. This achievement is all the more remarkable in view of the indication that prior to the communist presence there home spinning appears to have been almost extinct in the area.

However, there are also reasons to doubt this pattern of development. Producer cooperatives' total sales, which probably consisted mostly of yarn, have been reported for the years 1939-1943. If one deflates their current value with the price index for homespun, one arrives at values in 1937 prices of 288,462 yuan in 1939, of 1,032,875 yuan in 1940, of 779,615 yuan in 1941, of 209,483 yuan in 1942, and of 859,130 yuan in 1943.[129] The use of other price indices as deflators yields similar patterns of fluctuation, all of which suggest that the production of yarn increased dramatically in the early period, that it suffered setbacks when the blockade was imposed, and that these were overcome at least in part by the production campaign of 1943.

More generally, it seems evident that the inferred outputs of yarn would not have exhausted the inputs of cotton and wool which were being produced locally during those years.[130] In addition, the region imported substantial though unspecified quantities of cotton without exporting similar quantities of cotton or wool.[131] The resulting total supply of textile fibers may well have been large enough during the years 1943-1945 to approach autarky, which was said to require three million catties of yarn for weaving, plus yarn for knitwear, wool for rugs, waste cotton for padding, etc.[132] The discrepancy between this potential output and the output claimed for 1943 cannot be resolved definitively. Most plausible appears to be the explanation that the claim for 1943 and its implicit productivity estimate are partial data. Both probably refer to yarn produced under putting-out arrangements by peasant households which may or may not have been affiliated with cooperative putting-out systems. Because own consumed yarn could have accounted for 50 percent or more of the total yarn output,[133] most of the difference between claimed output and potential output would be explained. Of course, the SKN border region's accomplishments in yarn production tend to be aggrandized by this argument.

b. *Cloth.* Estimates of the cloth output can be located for more years and in greater detail. They also depict a remarkable development from very small beginnings. But they, too, should be questioned, in view of the conflicting output claims for 1941 and 1942 in table 6.10.[134] In addition, it must be noted that autarky required the production of 250,000 or 310,000 bolts of cloth, respectively, according to estimates of 1942 and of 1944.[135] The estimated supply of textile fibers apparently sufficed to produce that much cloth annually during the years 1943-1945,[136] especially if it was augmented by imports of machine-made yarn in unknown yet possibly substantial quantity. The discrepancies between this potential and the cloth output claims for 1943 and 1945 cannot be resolved any more convincingly than the discrepancy in the case of yarn. However, the same explanation seems to make sense. Much if not most of the yarn

spun for own use must have been used in weaving. It is therefore likely that the cloth output of home industry is underestimated, perhaps grossly so.[137] By implication, the achievements in cloth production, too, probably were more impressive
than claimed. Of course, these greater achievements had to
depend less on state- and CIC-operated enterprises, which probably contributed 15 rather than 30 percent or more of the total
cloth output. However, the larger total also could not account
for an ample supply of clothing. The autarky goal of 1944 called
for the production of about five square meters of cloth per
capita per annum.

c. *Paper and soap.* Like the production of yarn and cloth, the
output of paper and soap grew very rapidly from very small
beginnings. It thus appeared as a noteworthy achievement, too.
But it also provided for only small average per capita supplies — a bit more than one-third of a piece of soap in 1943
and less than ten sheets of paper in 1945. Because both products were consumed primarily by the army, organs, and
schools, these averages are of course misleading. However,
most of the paper and much of the soap were produced in
state-operated enterprises, so the output estimates are probably
fairly accurate. Self-sufficiency required the production of
more than 8,000 reams of paper according to a 1941 estimate
and of more than 20,000 reams of paper according to a 1944
estimate.[138]

d. *Oil, coal, and iron.* The output estimates for oil, coal, and
iron are of very limited use. Most of the data refer to the state
of affairs prior to the "hightide" of the import-substitution campaign, and most of them had to be derived by generalizing
partial data. Particularly questionable is the extraordinary increase in oil production by 1943, even though new oil wells
were being developed. The same is true for the iron output
claim for 1941. Because it antedates the operation of the first
state-run iron foundry by one and one-half years, it must be
attributed to more traditional forms of iron-making. Yet such
ventures apparently came close to meeting the iron requirements of the border region, which were estimated as 2,350 tons
in the aggregate and by implication as somewhat more than
three catties per capita per annum.[139] Output estimates for later

Table 6.10

SELECTED MANUFACTURING AND MINING PRODUCTS, 1938-1945

Product	Unit	1938	1939	1940	1941	1942	1943	1945
Yarn, total	catties						835,704[a]	
Cloth, total	{ large				61,239[b]	100,000[c]		150,000[c]
	bolts	7,370[d]	16,266[d]	32,590[d]	46,310[d]	45,223[d]	104,302[d]	
Carpets, total state factories	pieces			420[e]	7,661[e]	18,800[e]		
Paper, total state factories	{ 1,000 sheets				3,000[f]	6,900[c]		15,000[c]
Soap, total	cakes	50[g]	637[g]	833[g]	1,981[g]	4,983[g]	5,671[g]	
Hsin Hua factory	cakes				150,000[f]	300,000[f]	546,855[h]	
Crude oil	tons	(200)[i]	90[j]				482,588[h]	(400)[n]
Coal	tons				90,000[m]		91,200[l]	
Iron	tons				2,000[m]		511[k]	
Hoes, total	pieces							
Plow shares, total	pieces				8,400[o]			
agric. factory	pieces							

a   *Wei kung-yeh p'in*, pp. 58-59.
b. Nym Wales, *Notes*, p. 61.
c. *Shan Kan Ning (1958)*, p. 283.
d. Table 6.6.
e. Mao and others, *New Life*, pp. 49-50.
f. *Ibid.*, p. 51-52. 1942 estimate: 6,006,000 sheets.
g. Hsü, *A Survey*, Part 2, p. 95.
h. *Wei kung-yeh p'in*, p. 49.
i. 1936 data. Derived from Snow, *Red Star*, p. 269.
j. Estimate: 360 x 500 catties per day. Ch'i Li, *Shan Kan Ning*, p. 1.
k. Estimate: 360 x 70-80 five gallon casks x 3.7853 litres per day. Van Slyke, *The Chinese Communist Movement*, p. 163.
l. Hsü, *A Survey*, Part 2, p. 104.
m. *Chieh-fang jih pao* (12 November 1941), p. 1.
n. 1944 data. Hsü, *A Survey*, Part 2, p. 102.
o. Derived from Mao and others, *New Life*, p. 52.

years are lacking not only for iron, but also for coal. The coal output in 1941 averaged less than 25 catties per person and admittedly could ". . . not even meet the needs of Yenan municipality. . . ."[140]

e. *Selected implements.* The estimates of agricultural implement output in 1941 are evidently very rough guesses, nor can they be indicative of the development of producer goods production during the import-substitution campaign. More significant information on the changes in the stock of the textile industry has been presented in table 6.6. In the aggregate, the increase in the number of looms seems to parallel the increase in the output of cloth. Handlooms, however, which characterized side-line weaving in home industry, are not covered by this enumeration, and reference to them or to the number of spinning wheels may be as inadequate as estimates of the output of homemade yarn and cloth.[141]

f. *Other products.* Table 6.10 does not contain mentions of other products, e.g., the number of characters set in 1942 (51,600,000),[142] the numbers of knee mortars and projectiles produced by border region arsenals during inadequately specified periods of time,[143] and the like. Of interest in this connection is the report that the production of knee mortars seems to have declined due to steel shortage.[144]

In summary, the output data of tables 6.6 and 6.10 tend to support the impressions which could be gained from the evidence on changes in the numbers of industrial establishments and employees. However, these product estimates are not any firmer nor any more complete than the information on the producers. Even in assessing changes in the quantity of output, it therefore becomes necessary in the end to refer to the observations of visitors and to their comments about the apparent level of living in the SKN border region.

Road Construction and Transportation

The importation of cotton in the beginning, the exportation of salt during subsequent years, and the movement of many other products within the border region required transport facilities which were extremely limited at first. Since time immemorial, salt and most other products had been carried by donkey or mule over roads which often were not much more than footpaths. Famine and insecurity had affected the number of pack animals as well as the condition of the roads. As a consequence, it was possible to enlarge the regional transport capacity substantially simply by restoring the traditional facilities in the traditional way, by using corvée labor, indigenous materials, and a growing animal stock. In order to increase the flow even more, these means and methods of transportation could be improved in various ways.

Road construction. The border region government not only could repair the existing roads, it also could widen, plane grade, and even relocate stretches of them. In addition, it was feasible to connect existing routes and extend them into previously neglected parts of the territory, thereby closing gaps in the network. The indications are that all of these steps were taken in the development of the four major highways listed in table 6.11. The Fuhsien-Michih highway, which was completed very early, facilitated all external trade and at first did much to ease the import problems of the region.

Most important for the salt trade was the construction of the Tingpien-Yenan highway and of the Yenchih-Tingpien section of the Tingpien-Chingyang highway. The Yenchih-Chingyang section of the latter, which ran along the western border of the SKN territory, provided another outlet for salt. The Chingchien-Chingpien highway was built primarily to serve the region's internal trade.[145]

Most of the 750 miles of road which were part of this network were considered usable by motor vehicles. They were dirt roads which had not been surfaced. Indeed, table 6.11 indicates that the outlay for road construction materials was extraordinarily limited in most instances. It appeared comparatively large in the case of the Fuhsien-Michih highway only because this project involved the construction and repair of several bridges.[146] In general, road building made use of the same primitive techniques as the reclamation of land and the construction of salt fields did. Laborers moved rock and soil by hand or with very simple tools. Since little could be done to reinforce the road bed, the highways doubtlessly were very vulnerable to

Table 6.11

HIGHWAY CONSTRUCTION, 1937-1942 [a]

Period of construction	Line of communication	Length of line Km	Number of corvée laborers	Cost of materials SKN yuan	Millet equivalent of material cost Piculs
-1937	Fuhsien-Michih	385	12,800	300,000	15,000 [b]
1940-1942	Tingpien-Yenan	325	83,300	400,000	1,439 [c]
1940-1942	Tingpien-Chingyang	330	2,800 [f]	14,000 [f]	50 [c]
1941-1942	Chingchien-Chingpien	165	36,000	7,000	12 [d]
1942	Total construction		45,400	800,000	822 [e]

a. Derived from Mao and others, *New Life*, pp. 53-55.
b. Cost of materials divided by twenty SKN yuan (average price of millet in 1936). See Yen-an nung-ts'un tiao-ch'a t'uan, *Mi-chih hsien*, p. 149.
c. Cost of materials divided by price of millet in June 1941. See table 7.3.
d. Cost of materials divided by price of millet in December 1941. See table 7.3.
e. Cost of materials divided by price of millet in June 1942. See table 7.3.
f. Repair of Yenchih-Huanhsien section of this highway.

wear and tear, which had to retard the flow of traffic and cause constant repair.[147]

Because laborers were conscripted to perform road work in corvée, they did not receive wages, room, or board and apparently had to provide even their own tools and work animals if they owned them.[148] Those liable to render corvée could be conscripted for at most thirty-six days per annum.[149] The numbers of mobilized laborers listed in table 6.11—as well as those listed in table 5.2—therefore overstate the actual man-years of road work by a factor of at least ten. By implication, the average man-years of road work per annum during the years 1940-1942 seem to have reached 4,500 at most. In 1942 and in 1943 they were evidently much smaller, viz. 340 and 75 man-years, respectively.[150] It is difficult to value these exertions, yet whatever its imputed worth, road construction during the years until 1943 apparently sufficed to remove an important bottleneck.[151] Maintenance of the network during subsequent years may have required still smaller inputs of labor and materials; in any event the lack of references in later government reports suggests that road maintenance posed few problems.

Transport vehicles. To move goods, especially salt, in increasing quantities over improved highways required appropriate numbers and types of vehicles. In addition to the time-honored human carrier, the border region made use of pack animals, carts, and trucks. Trucks, as the most modern vehicles, were exceedingly rare. Forman had heard of "twenty-odd dilapidated" specimens in and around Yenan,[152] and his information may well have exaggerated the actual stock. Moreover, there are indications that motor vehicles could not be serviced easily and that their number may have decreased due to cannibalizing.[153] At the very least, the fleet of trucks did not grow, and it evidently did not suffice to meet a substantial share of the region's transport requirements.[154] Carts or wagons, which one source called "the basis of transportation in the Border District,"[155] constituted a highly elusive phenomenon. References to their number are lacking. Their output is said to have decreased in quantity while it improved in quality from 1941 to 1942.[156] And they do not figure prominently in descriptions of road scenes. Pack animals, i.e., mostly donkeys and mules, appear to have been the prevailing means of transportation. By tradition, they carried most of the salt. In addition, they moved a substantial share of most other goods, especially some of the newly produced commodities. For example,[157]

> Long mule-trains move over the roads, loaded with solid chunks of good anthracite . . . .
> The kerosene and crude oil are transported from the oil fields in bamboo-and-lime casks loaded on mules and donkeys.

The number of pack animals used in transportation has not been specified. At the risk of overstating their total, one may choose as the upper limit the number of all adult animals, i.e., about 80 percent of all mules and donkeys.[158] The data of table 6.2, which may exaggerate the growth of the animal stock, suggest maxima of 110,000 donkeys in 1941, 135,000 in 1943, and, perhaps 150,000 in 1945. The intensity of their use in transportation cannot be determined, but there are indications that carrying capacity remained a bottleneck at least until 1944.[159] The assortment of loads has not been reported either. Table 6.5 merely contains information on the number of pack animals used full time in salt transport. Although their number rose from 15,526 in 1942 to 25,043 in 1943, it still did not suffice to meet the estimated requirement of 27,000 animals.[160] The remaining gap was to be closed by the formation of additional transport cooperatives and by the use of corvée animal labor.[161]

Road services. In order to increase the volume of traffic along the roads, it also was necessary to expand various auxiliary services. To be specific, a greater flow of official and especially of military personnel required the establishment of a network of public rest houses or hostels,[162] and the growing volume of animal traffic necessitated the building of new fodder inns and watering places in addition to warehouses and trade posts. The development of such facilities was particularly important for the desired increase in salt transportation—according to a report on the difficulties encountered in this trade in 1941.[163] With the probable exception of veterinary care, such problems had been alleviated substantially by 1943:

Along the highway for salt transportation from San-
pien to Yenan, Fuhsien, Chingyang and other Hsiens,
there are fodder inns run by the Government. They
sell fodder to transporters at a fair price and have
abolished the exploitation of transporters by some
inn-keepers in the past.[164]

Road facilities were established not only by branches of the
border region government, but also by cooperatives. Table 4.2
lists ninety-two cooperative hostels for June 1944. In view of
the fact that the South Ch'ü cooperative of Yenan Hsien pioneered also in salt transportation,[165] it seems likely that such
ventures were undertaken by the newly integrated cooperatives
in response to the needs of their transport brigades. More comprehensive data on the provision of road services are lacking.

Transport volume. The effects of changes in road construction, transport vehicles, and road services have not been publicized comprehensively. Only the salt traffic, which was of
extreme importance for the external trade of the SKN border
region, has been reported in its entirety and with some regular-
ity. Table 6.5 depicts very rapid increases in the transportation
and sale of salt during the years 1938-1941. Since the traffic
in salt appears to have expanded more speedily during this
period than the highway mileage, animal stock, and road facilities did, it may well have infringed upon the traffic in other
commodities. During the following period, these relations
changed. The stock of pack animals grew more rapidly than
the number of salt loads did, thereby easing transport problems.
Nevertheless, even in December 1942 Mao Tse-tung considered it very difficult to find private carriers for 210,000 to
250,000 loads of salt in 1943.[166]

Summary

The available information on the development of production
in the SKN border region is not only incomplete, but also of
questionable quality. Many specific assertions—notably those
of a quantitative nature—are therefore more or less problematic. In combination, however, numerous bits of such evidence

do convey the impression that the border region government made significant progress in developing production within its territory, especially after the reimposition of the blockade in 1940/1. They further show that most advances were achieved by outmoded methods, some of which had to be reintroduced into the area. Of course, such results tended to be inferior to those which modern technology would have produced, but they also could be and may well have been the best possible outcomes in circumstances which distorted previous patterns and terms of trade with the rest of the world.

In agriculture, the output of food crops probably increased at least moderately, primarily due to large-scale land reclamation for the purpose of grain cropping. The output of clothing materials certainly increased strongly after the reactivation and promotion of cotton growing. The additions to the animal stock, too, seem to have been relatively large, at least until 1941/1942. As a consequence, the output of many animal products showed particular growth after 1942.

Additional efforts in extraction, plus the construction of salt fields and of irrigation facilities, accounted for very substantial increases in salt output. Constraints to its expansion appeared first in the form of labor shortage, inferior technical capability, and limited transport capacity. During later years, trade restrictions imposed by the nationalist authorities are said to have prevented the full exploitation of the area's productive potential.

For manufacturing and mining, there appeared numerous indications of rapid progress in import substitution. Not only increasingly many goods for private and public consumption, but also more and more tools for their production were being put out in growing quantity and improving quality. A great deal of emphasis was placed on the development of spinning, weaving, paper, and soap-making—both because expansion of these activities was necessary to attain autarky and because it was feasible from the beginning in a technically backward form. The development of metal-processing and armaments-manufacturing lagged because it was so much more difficult to accomplish with the available resources and skills.

To develop traffic capacities which would match the growing production capacities of the territory, the SKN border region government relied mostly on traditional means and methods. Primitive roads were built and repaired by corvée labor with few tools, and a growing volume of freight was carried primarily by pack animals which also had to render corvée. The development of transportation may have lagged until 1941/ 1942 but could have caught up with the growth of production thereafter, so that traffic bottlenecks diminished during the final phase of the war.

The rapid expansion which appears to have been characteristic of many import-substituting and export-oriented industries seems to have affected other activities as well. Travellers reported a great deal of housing construction, especially in the form of cave digging, and a mushrooming of trade and service establishments in centers such as Yenan. In many ways, it thus appears that the government was rather successful with its efforts to develop production. As a result of such advances, the border region may well have been able to meet the autarky targets for food, clothing, and shelter during 1943-1945. Of course, these goals reflected standards of severe austerity in consumption, and they were being met due to the activism of the army, organs, and schools in most lines of production. This contribution of the institutional households has yet to be discussed systematically.

VII

External Relations and
Public Finance

The development of production in the SKN border region
was meant to solve problems of external trade as well as of
public finance. Natural disasters and political instability had
rendered trade with the outside world and fiscal relations
within the area precarious long before the advent of the Red
Army, but its immigration into the area aggravated and complicated these difficulties. In its initial state, the border region
economy was both too specialized and too unproductive to
provide the means for the two immediate ends of the Chinese
communists. That is to say, it could not maintain the institutional households of the immigrants and at the same time
sustain the social reforms which they advocated. The immediate realization of both objectives required outside aid, which
entailed dependence on the nationalists and thus vulnerability
in case of the renewal of economic warfare. Such dependence
could be transformed into interdependence by the development of trade as an alternative to aid, making economic
warfare costly for the nationalists, too, but the border region
economy would not cease to be vulnerable. To achieve invul-
nerability autarky was necessary. The development of import-
substituting as well as of export-oriented production, which
served this purpose, therefore became a special task of the
institutional households.

External Relations

Perhaps because they concerned delicate political issues,
even fragmentary data on exports and imports as well as on
other external receipts and disbursements of the SKN border

region are extraordinarily hard to come by, so the region's balance of trade and balance of payments cannot be reconstructed with any precision. A more impressionistic treatment suitably begins with Snow's description of the *status quo ante* Sian.

Soviet period. Until the united front was formed, the Northwest Soviet experienced a blockade to which the Chinese communists reacted as in Kiangsi. On the one hand, they reenforced their segregation from Kuomintang territory by introducing a currency of their own, while on the other, they promoted substantial smuggling in order to overcome the effects of their isolation. The difficulties of blockade-running aggravated the basic problems of the area's external trade and currency exchange. In Snow's words:

> In practice, this of course, meant that all "foreign" imports had to be paid for in "foreign" exchange. But as the value of imported manufactures (meagre enough) greatly exceeded the value of Soviet exports (which were chiefly raw materials, and were all sold in a depressed market as smuggled goods), there was always a tendency towards a heavy unfavorable balance of payments. In other words, bankruptcy. How was it overcome?
>
> It was not, entirely. . . .[1]

The government tried to decrease the deficit in the balance of trade with Kuomintang territory by regulating trade as well as by depreciating the soviet currency to a minor degree, so that one nationalist yuan exchanged for 1.21 soviet yuan.[2] But the government also financed a residual excess of imports over exports with other receipts. In addition to the nonsoviet currency which had circulated in the area initially, it obtained contributions from supporters on the outside and confiscations of liquid assets from "exploiters" (mainly landlords and usurers) on the inside.[3] Finally, there was a reserve of specie which the Red Army had brought along on its Long March.[4]

United front. The agreements with the Kuomintang changed this pattern of external relations drastically. The transformation of the Northwest Soviet into a special region of the Republic of China did away with the blockade as well as with soviet currency. Stein was told by the manager of the Border Region Bank that:

> When the United Front was formed at the beginning of the war, . . . we withdrew all our former 'Soviet' notes from circulation and replaced them with the national currency we received from the National Government for part of the upkeep of the Eighth Route Army. From 1937 to 1941 the official medium of circulation in our areas was national currency.[5]

The exchange of currencies may have posed temporary payment problems which could be eased by the spending of national currency reserves;[6] otherwise, however, the financial situation of the SKN border region improved immensely. Besides arms and equipment, the Eighth Route Army received from the national government at first 500,000 yuan and later 600,000 yuan per month, i.e., about twice as much as it had been able to raise previously.[7] Such an amount should have sufficed to cover all expenditures of the SKN border region government at previously established levels;[8] yet whatever its contribution to the budget, it certainly enabled the area to sustain a large balance of trade deficit. Snow noted that it was used effectively for this purpose:

> The first payment to the Reds ($500,000) was delivered shortly after Chiang Kai-shek's return to Nanking. Some of the Kuomintang money was used to convert Soviet currency, to buy manufactures for their cooperatives—now well stocked—and some to purchase needed equipment. None of it was wasted on salaries . . . .[9]

The deterioration of this very favorable initial position during the years 1937-1940 has not been reported systematically. Nevertheless, a few guesses can be wagered on the basis of partial evidence. Data on imports, which apparently consisted primarily of cotton goods, are lacking. Table 6.5 shows that the sale of salt increased rapidly, from only 70,000 loads in 1938 to 230,000 loads in 1940, most of which left the SKN border region. At the same time, however, the terms of trade with the outside appear to have changed to the disadvantage of SKN. The price data for Yenan imply such a turn to the extent that the region exchanged salt for cotton cloth rather than for cotton fiber.[10] Moreover, outside price data indicate the same development for the sale of raw materials in exchange for manufactured goods generally.[11] Increases in the quantity of exports therefore may have served mostly to compensate for increases in the (relative) prices of imports. Support payments to the Eighth Route Army continued to be made until the end of 1940. Further adjustments in the amount of the grant have not been announced, and the value of the original amount must have diminished greatly due to the progressing inflation.[12] Moreover, supplies of munitions are said to have stopped in October 1939.[13] One positive addition appeared in the form of CIC contributions, which have been listed in table 6.9 net of 10,800 yuan for office expense. Yet since the annual receipts on CIC account in 1939 and in 1940 did not exceed the monthly receipts from the national government, it was impossible for them to affect the balance of payments situation greatly.

The impact of these developments cannot be specified precisely, but there are two claims which illuminate the situation to some extent. In his report of November 1941 on the work of the government, Chairman Lin Pai-ch'ü noted that because of the contributions to the Eighth Route Army, the SKN border region government had been able to balance its budget in the past and had even run surpluses in 1939 and in 1940.[14] He thereby intimated that the area did not suffer payments problems until 1941. Nevertheless, Forman learned in 1944 that "...taking as a base (100%) the level of living in December 1939, the army's standard of living dropped to 88% by 1940, and to 84.2% by 1941—all as a definite consequence of the blockade...."[15] which must have been instituted gradually. The choice of base period suggests that the turning point coincided with the winter campaign of 1939, but it does not preclude the more gradual and prolonged deterioration which the price data of table 7.3 support. Mao Tse-tung in 1945 looked back upon these events as follows:

The War of Resistance has been going on for eight
years. When it began we had food and clothing. But
things got *steadily* worse until we were in *great* difficulty, running short of grain, short of cooking oil and
salt, short of bedding and clothing, short of funds.
This *great* difficulty, this *great* contradiction, came
in the wake of the big Japanese offensives and the
Kuomintang government's three large-scale attacks
on the people (the "anti-communist onslaughts") in
1940-1943. . . .[16]

Needless to say, such consequences of worsening external
relations affected not only the army and the other institutional
households, but the entire population of the base area.

Economic warfare. Besides terminating the payments of support to the Eighth Route Army by the end of 1940, the national
government not only imposed a partial blockade on the SKN
border region, but also apparently began to levy taxes on the
remaining imports and exports, thereby aggravating the payments problems of the area greatly. And it seemingly obstruc-
ted the flow of CIC contributions into the SKN border region,
which diminished to a trickle in real terms according to table
6.9.[17] In response to this renewed isolation, the SKN border
region government reintroduced under new names several important institutions and policies of the soviet period. In particular, the border region bank was authorized again to issue a
separate currency for the territory,[18] so that the interregional
payments problem appeared once more as a conversion problem. The trade bureau was reestablished in order to regulate
exports and imports, and many separate trading companies
were incorporated into this organization. Moreover, trade restrictions as well as taxes were levied for the purpose of promoting territorial autarky. As a consequence, the external trade of
the region changed as follows.

(1) Commodity restrictions. Limitations affecting the trade
in both directions were imposed by both sides. In the case of
border region imports, the national government prohibited the
sale of equipment and materials for war industry as well as that
of drugs and medical instruments. It apparently complicated

the sale of necessities and of many manufactured goods, but it permitted the sale of luxury goods, nonessentials, and inferior products.[19] The border region government objected to the last category of goods and apparently prohibited their importation.[20] However, "the peculiarities of the smuggling trade" according to Stein accounted for some flows contrary to the interests of both sides. In 1943, the imports of the SKN border region consisted to 70 percent of cotton and cotton products, to 8 percent of wine, tobacco, and cigarettes, to 5 percent of firecrackers and incense, to 3 percent of metals and metal products, and to 1/3 percent of drugs. The remaining 13.7 percent have not been identified.[21]

In the case of border region exports, the national government was interested primarily in salt, which accounted for 90 percent of all the exports in 1941[22] and for similarly large relative shares in subsequent years. Second in importance ranked petroleum products, followed by foods, animals, hides and furs, and medicinal herbs, in that order.[23] In view of the fact that the border region had little else to offer in trade, it appears that outside restrictions concerned less the variety and more the quantity of goods to be exported. The border region government at times may have prohibited the exportation of foods[24] as well as of other items.[25] The effect of smuggling on the composition of exports has not been made public.

(2) Tax restrictions. For a variety of reasons, both sides chose to levy taxes on some or all of the commodities which continued to be traded. The sequence of events is hard to untangle. The Chinese communists modified the national system of taxation enormously during the soviet period and did not revert to it under united-front auspices. The national government accepted this deviation for some time, but objected to the failure to reestablish the prerevolutionary *status quo* in this as in so many other respects. Eventually, it responded by collecting "its" taxes at the boundary. More generally, the national government must have wished to handicap the Chinese communists, and it even could have attempted to serve its need for revenue by taxing imports as well as exports, also apparently at high rates. Details have not been reported systematically, but the SKN border region government publicized the following

December 1943 prices for Yaohsien in KMT territory and for Liu Lin in SKN territory, which were located about fifteen miles apart from each other:[26]

100 catties of	Yaohsien	Liu Lin
Cotton, import price	6,960 yuan	12,180 yuan
Salt, export price	3,030 yuan	1,800 yuan
Ratio of prices	2.3 : 1	6.8 : 1

In 1944 the export price of salt is said to have been 15.52 yuan per catty, to which the national government added salt tax in the amount of 14.03 yuan per catty.[27] In contrast with the apparent fall of the export price of salt from 1943 to 1944, the prices of most imported goods are likely to have risen several times during the same period,[28] causing the region's terms of interregional trade to deteriorate grossly once more, after they had developed very adversely during the preceding years. Information on year-to-year changes has not been reported, but it has been noted that from 1937 to 1943, import prices on the average rose more than five times as much as export prices did. For the more important commodities, the changes were as follows:[29]

Commodity	Price	Increase, 1937-1943
Salt	Export	411 times
Kerosene	Export	777 times
Cotton	Import	2,725 times
Cloth	Import	2,667 times
Cast iron	Import	1,800 times
Matches	Import	5,308 times

By aggravating changes in the price structure through taxation, the national government greatly diminished the border region's ability to pay for imports, yet it thereby also "protected" many import-substituting activities which the border region government promoted. The increase in the price of cotton fiber, which exceeded the increase in the price of millet by three to six times,[30] must have provided strong incentive for shifts to cotton production whenever such shifts were technically feasible. Nevertheless, the SKN border region government deemed it necessary to provide additional inducements, in particular land tax exemptions.[31] Nor did even larger increases in the price of cotton cloth favor local spinning and weaving sufficiently in the government's opinion. So it provided added protection by taxing imported cotton fiber and cotton yarn at 1 percent but imported cotton cloth at 15 percent *ad valorem*.[32]

More generally, the SKN border region government modified the impact of outside restrictions by taxing luxuries heavily but necessities lightly or not at all. Educational materials and paper, which were viewed as necessities, were burdened with 2 percent and 5 percent rates, respectively,[33] while liquor, plus tobacco and religious supplies, which were considered luxuries, carried 80 percent and 100 percent rates, respectively.[34] In the case of salt, the government at first collected relatively little, and that in an absolute form. Later, responding to inflation, it imposed an ad valorem tax which amounted to 5 to 7 percent of the sales value in 1943.[35]

(3) Trade deficit. The fragmentary data on changes in the volume and value of salt exports, on their share in total exports, on the development of export prices and import prices, and on other constraints combine to depict a grim situation. Increases in exports at most sufficed to offset the adverse changes in the terms of interregional trade. The quantity of imports which could be bought with these exports at best remained constant. The support payments of the national government as well as the CIC contributions had added substantially to the border region's ability to pay for imports, so the termination of these transfers could be expected to result in a decline of total imports—unless new forms of payment could be found.

Data on changes in the volume of imports have not been made public. However, even a cursory calculation and comparison of a few relations indicates that imports must have decreased considerably. Salt sales, which apparently accounted for most of the exports then as well as later, seem to have yielded about 420,000 yuan in 1937.[36] In comparison, the national government was committed to supply 7,200,000 yuan support for the Eighth Route Army, not counting deliveries in kind.[37] Imports could thus exceed exports perhaps by as much as twenty times, and they actually may have come close to doing it. In 1943, on the other hand, the border region imported goods worth 4,455 million SKN yuan, exported goods worth 3,581 million SKN yuan, and thus incurred a deficit in the balance of trade of 874 million SKN yuan which appears to have been equivalent to about 150 million KMT yuan.[38] The ratio of imports to exports therefore fell from perhaps as much as 20 in 1937 to 1.24 in 1943, and it even may have come close to unit value in 1941.[39] This meant that if the import equivalent of exports did not increase, total imports decreased to an extraordinary degree.

(4) Payments problems. Whatever the decline in imports may have been, the appearance of even the smallest deficit in the balance of trade meant that the SKN border region government had to have other means of payment. The renewed hostility between nationalists and communists resulted also in a controversy over the sources of such funds. The national government charged that the SKN border region government promoted the production and illegal exportation of opium,[40] a charge the US government seconded:

> In an effort to redress this unfavorable balance and obtain sufficient currency to acquire the imports desired, the cultivation of opium was carried on and some of it smuggled into Chungking territory. . . .[41]

Border region officials denied these allegations and insisted that they had ". . . always enforced a strict ban on the production, use, and smuggling of opium. . . ."[42] The Bands reported seeing poppy fields behind Japanese lines and mentioned Japanese interest in opium production, but they also described the active opposition of the Chinese communist guerrillas in Japanese-held territory against this land use and did not refer to it in their travelog for the SKN border region.[43] Forman and Stein, who kept looking for poppy fields there, could not find any, yet a Chinese member of their press party, who had not parted company with them during their journey, reported seeing poppy fields everywhere on their way to Yenan.[44] Forman suggested as a possible explanation that:

> The cotton fields were spotted with bright red and white blossoms—and here is perhaps the origin of the charge that the Communists were growing opium, for cotton plantations in bloom look from a distance much like poppy fields.[45]

Whatever the origin, the border region government apparently did not intend to incur nor anticipate a deficit in the balance of trade in 1943. An overestimation of the increase in cotton production and apparently an underestimation of the deterioration in the terms of interregional trade accounted for the unexpected import surplus.[46] To pay for it, the border region bank ". . . had to spend large amounts of its national currency reserves . . .," Stein was told.[47] Because of the rapid inflation, notes left from the budget surplus years of the united-front interlude probably could not cover more than a small fraction of the deficit. The residual holdings of national currency by SKN citizens, which might have been sold to the border region bank after 1941, apparently could not do much more. It is therefore likely that the bank had to draw on the hoard of silver yuan which it had kept since the days of the national currency reform of 1935.[48] But there is conflicting evidence.

The use of external exchange reserves to pay for the import surplus should have had deflationary effects on the SKN border region economy. In fact, of course, the region experienced a much more rapid inflation than the nationalist area did,[49] and SKN officials attributed this phenomenon repeatedly not to internal budget problems, but to external payments problems. Thus, Stein learned from the manager of the border region bank that:

> All these imports through the blockade lines have in the last analysis to be financed against the issue of notes. This upsets our own price level, in spite of the fact that the finances of our administration have long been in good shape.[50]

Table 7.1

RATE OF EXCHANGE: SKN YUAN PER KMT YUAN, 1941-44.

Month	1941	1942	1943	1944
January	— — —	2.58	1.98	11.00
February	1.08	2.58	2.10	11.00
March	1.15	2.90	2.28	8.01
April	1.23	3.00	3.10	8.50
May	1.40	3.50	3.32	8.00
June	1.57	3.54	3.49	8.00
July	2.00	3.42	3.50	8.97
August	2.22	2.94	3.60	8.50
September	2.00	2.29	5.50	8.50
October	2.35	2.16	6.53	
November	2.30	2.19	8.00	
December	2.50	2.57	9.03	

a. Hsü, *A Survey,* Part 2, p. 7. Note that these rates were quoted in Yenan.

The statement seems to indicate that the bank was able to obtain, at worsening rates, substantial amounts of national currency (or silver) in exchange for its notes which then became effective demand within the SKN territory. Information on the rate of exchange between KMT yuan and SKN yuan, which appears in table 7.1, points to the sudden emergence of the payments crisis in the autumn of 1943, after a more limited deterioration of the payments situation during the preceding two years. Table 7.1 also shows a minor improvement in the rate of exchange during 1944. SKN officials related this event to their increasing success in import-substitution.[51] The magnitude of the remaining import surplus has not been reported, but the rates of price increase within the region decreased again to magnitudes which had been common before the crisis.[52]

Public Finance

The succession of changes in external relations evidently affected the finances of the SKN border region government greatly and caused it to revise its revenue policies drastically on two occasions. Fortunately, there are data to demonstrate both consequences—probably because the government took pride in its eventual ability to make ends meet. In the beginning, of course, the government experienced a highly beneficial windfall, as the contrast between the soviet period and the united-front period shows.

Soviet period. Until the Sian Incident was settled, the Northwest Soviet continued the revolutionary fiscal practices which had evolved in Kiangsi and on the Long March. The existing tax system, which had burdened the rural classes inequitably, was modified beyond recognition. As Lin Pai-ch'ü told Edgar Snow:

> We say we do not tax the masses, and this is true. But we do heavily tax the exploiting classes, confiscating their surplus cash and goods. Thus, all our taxation is direct. This is just the opposite of the Kuomintang practice, under which ultimately the workers and the poor peasants have to carry most of the tax burden. Here we tax less than 10 percent of the population— the landlords and usurers. We also levy a small tax on a few big merchants, but none on small merchants. Later on we may impose a small progressive tax on the peasantry, but at the present moment all mass taxes have been completely abolished.[53]

Lin, then in charge of the soviet's finances, may have generalized unduly on this occasion, yet whatever the specific changes that were instituted, any massive redress in favor of the lower classes had to have predictable effects on total revenue. The findings of chapter 2 suggest that landlords, usurers, and big merchants together controlled relatively little wealth in the area. Moreover, much of it was land which was redistributed without yielding revenue to the government. The limitation of taxation to the confiscation of other assets therefore could be

Table 7.2

SKN BUDGETS, 1936-1944

Revenue and Expenditure	A. Percentage and Yuan Values				B. Grain Equivalents in Piculs of 150 kg.			
	1936[a]	1938*	1943	1944	1936[i]	1938*[k]	1943[l]	1944
Contributions	15-20%	7,200,000[c]			34,500[j]	255,900		
Confiscations	40-50%				88,600[j]			
Public straw			422,000[d] 6/6[f]				15,000[m]	15,000[m]
Public grain			591,000[d] 1/6 = 20%[g]	} 30%[h]		15,000	180,000	160,000[n]
Other taxes			18%[g]			21,000	30,000	} 64,000[o]
Bank loans			62%[g]	} 70%[h]			27,000	
Public Production#	} 30-45%		180,000[d]		73,900[j]	6,400	93,000	150,000[o]
Total	3,840,000[b]	8,393,000?		7.8 bill.[g]	197,000	298,300?	325,000	389,000
Army	60%	7,200,000?			118,200	255,900?		
Civilian	40%	1,182,000[d]			78,800	42,000		
Surplus		11,000[e]				400[e]		

* October 1937 to September 1938.
# Including profits of public enterprises.
a. Snow, *Red Star*, pp. 250, 284.
b. Derived from monthly data *ibid.*
c. Hsü, *A Survey*, Part 2, p. 18.
d. Ch'i Li, *Shan Kan Ning pien ch'ü shih-lu*, p. 29.
e. On civilian account.
f. *Brief Account*, p. 13.
g. Stein. *The Challenge*, p. 207.
h. Van Slyke, *The Chinese Communist Movement*, p. 167.
i. Derived from note a and Yenan nung-ts'un tiao-ch'a t'uan, *Mi-chih hsien*, p. 149. One picul costs 19.50 yuan.
j. Average of range in section A.
k. Derived from notes c plus d and table 7.5. Estimate: 422,000 yuan buy 15,000 piculs of grain (approximate average of collections in 1937 and 1938).
l. Derived from notes f plus g and table 7.5. Other taxes equal one-sixth of public grain levy.
m. Note 77.
n. Table 7.5.
o. Derived from note h and Kao Kang, *1945 nien pien ch'ü chu-yao jen-wu ho tso-feng wen-t'i* (9 January 1945), p. 6. Total production by public institutions is equivalent to 150,000 piculs of grain.

expected to result in a substantial decline of tax receipts. Such a development seems evident. Lin himself reported that the revenue of a sample of five *ch'ü* fell from 35,460 yuan in prerevolutionary times to 14,754 yuan in postrevolutionary years.[54] Estimates for the entire SKN border region have not been made public, but the elimination of hsien tax alone probably involved a revenue loss of 146,000 piculs of grain or its equivalent, according to Buck's data.[55] In contrast, all confiscations apparently produced less than two-thirds of this amount in 1936 — according to Snow's information and other data referred to in table 7.2.

Because receipts from confiscations failed to meet total expenditures, which were equivalent to close to 200,000 piculs of millet, the government had to find additional sources of revenue. Table 7.2 reveals that external and internal contributions provided a minor share of the difference, that a major share was accounted for by bank loans and public production. Information on the earnings of institutional households and state enterprises has not been made public for 1936, but it seems likely that they were comparable in magnitude to the value of public production in 1938, which appears to have been equivalent to 6,400 piculs of grain. By implication, bank loans probably financed a residual of about one-third of total public expenditures in 1936. In the absence of commensurate sales of long-term debt to the private sector, which are not in evidence, such loans had to be met by note issue.

The issuing of bank notes on a comparatively large scale could be expected to generate inflationary pressures and thus affect the private sector much like the indirect taxes had done. However, this pressure did not have to materialize so long as the government had the opportunity to replace previously circulating national currency, which now could be used to pay for imports, with soviet currency as the new internal medium of exchange. The quantity of money required for the latter purpose is not known. There is reason to believe that it may have accounted for a large share of the total note issue during the soviet period,[56] but there also are grounds for the suspicion that deficit-financing had inflationary effects, too. The government's decision to depreciate soviet currency could have been related to this as well as to other causes of external payments problems. Snow apparently negated such a possibility with his observation that soviet money "... had full buying power, prices being generally slightly lower than in the White districts . . ."[57] In contrast with his intimation of price stability, however, the records for Yang Chia K'ou in Michih Hsien depict rather drastic increases in the prices of millet, black beans, and wheat from fall 1935 to spring 1937.[58]

In the absence of more conclusive evidence, one may summarize the experience of the soviet period as follows. The poverty of the Northwest seems to have set rather narrow limits to the practice of revolutionary public finance, but the brevity of the revolutionary period in the Northwest made it unnecessary to face the consequences of this constraint fully at once. In other words, before more permanent internal solutions had to be found, the united front was formed.

United front. The agreements with the Kuomintang committed the Chinese communists to change their fiscal and monetary policies enormously. They had to terminate their confiscations and give up their separate currency. In exchange, they were to receive payments of 700,000 yuan per month, in addition to arms and equipment for the Eighth Route Army.[59] There are indications that the actual monthly payments were less than that amount, viz. 600,000 yuan.[60] However, table 7.2 shows that even this smaller sum sufficed in 1938 to meet more than the entire public expenditures of 1936.[61] It thus appears that the alliance relieved the SKN border region government of all previous financial difficulties for a period of nearly two years.

The windfall apparently diminished after 1938 when wartime inflation made itself felt. There is no indication that the amount of the grant from the national government was adjusted in response to price changes. If the millet prices of table 7.3 are used as a deflator, the grain equivalent of 600,000 yuan declined from 24,000 piculs in June 1937 to 7,900 piculs in December 1940. In terms of the basket of all commodities bought in Yenan, the fall in purchasing power during the same interval was more than twice as large, from 600,000 yuan to 83,700 yuan (in June 1937 prices). Moreover, with the beginning of 1941 the

Table 7.3

PRICE INDICES FOR SELECTED COMMODITIES, YENAN, 1937-44.

Year	All commodities[a]	Month	All commodities	Fine cloth[b]	Home-spun[b]	Cotton fiber[b]	Pork[b]	Salt[b]	Millet[b]	Millet, per picul[*]
1937	100[c]	June	100	100	100	100	100	100	100	25 Yuan[d]
		Dec.								
1938	143	June	161	235	199	110	231	164	128	32 "
		Dec.								
1939	237	June	202	377	208	150	309	171	149	37 "
		Dec.	377	613	293	246	323	301	168	42 "
1940	500	June	421	1,250	400	369	308	352	208	52 "
		Dec.	717	1,890	778	796	614	1,200	304	76 "
1941	2,200	June	1,900	5,080	1,820	1,830	1,790	2,240	1,110	278 "
		Dec.	4,400	15,500	4,580	4,990	6,650	2,880	2,270	568 "
1942	9,900	June	10,100	34,200	11,100	11,400	11,200	9,790	3,890	973 "
		Dec.	13,800	45,600	13,700	16,900	16,100	12,700	5,820	1,455 "
1943	119,900	June	64,700	193,000	57,500	76,600	58,900	40,100	17,952	4,488 Yuan[e]
		Dec.	344,000	960,000	279,000	476,000	277,000	193,000	90,500	22,600 "
1944	564,700[f]	June	556,300	1,770,000	397,000	581,000	299,000	216,000	94,000	23,500 "
		Aug.	677,700	2,160,000	549,000	776,000	409,000	252,000	170,000	42,500 "

* One picul equals 150 kg.
a. Hsü, A Survey, Part 2, pp. 8-9.
b. Derived from ibid. and table 4.8.
c. Average, January to June.
d. Hsü, A Survey, Part 2, p. 18.
e. Ibid. p. 6.
f. Average, January to September.

payments themselves stopped. The SKN border region government thus lost most of its previous cash revenue within a period of two years. The deliveries of military goods to the Eighth Route Army terminated even earlier. As a consequence, the government now had to revert to internal sources of revenue—in a hurry.

Self-sufficiency. The SKN border region government apparently was prepared for this challenge. Indeed, it probably anticipated such a contingency practically from the beginning of its cooperation with the KMT government. In 1937, at the time when its expenditures first were met by transfers from the outside, the government began to regularize its imposition on its territory. And in January 1939, well before relations with the outside had deteriorated badly, it instituted a development program which aimed at increasing the self-sufficiency not only of the SKN border region as a whole, but also of the institutional households within it. Public revenue was thus to increase in the form of taxes on growing private production as well as from developing public production. All such efforts to mobilize internal sources were intensified in 1941 and thereafter, in response to the renewal of economic warfare with the nationalists. Public revenue changed specifically as follows.

(1) Public grain. As Lin Pai-ch'ü had forecast in his conversation with Edgar Snow,[62] the government in 1937 imposed a tax on the peasantry. It was progressive and therefore a tax on income rather than on land. It also was collected in kind, as "patriotic public grain," rather than in cash. Table 7.4 shows that in the beginning, the tax rates were quite low. They were raised slightly in 1939 and greatly in 1941. The reform of 1941 also reduced the progression of the tax rate schedule and lowered the amount of tax exempt income. A further revision in 1943 served to adapt the tax rates more closely to local particularities and modified previous changes. It once more increased both the progression of the tax rate schedule and the amount of tax exempt income—slightly.

Table 7.4

TAXATION OF AGRICULTURAL INCOME, 1937-1945

Per capita income in millet catties*	Percent of income collected as public grain					
	1937 [a]	1939 [b]	1941 [c]	(A) [d]	(B) [d]	(C) [d]
- 150	0	0	0	0	0	0
150 - 300	0	0	5-10	0-9 [e]	0-8 [f]	3-9
300 - 450	1	0-1 [g]	10-15	9-16	8-15	9-15
450 - 750	2	1-3	15-25	16-28	15-27	15-27
750 - 1,050	3	3-5	25-30	28-34	27-33	27-33
1,050 - 1,500	4	5-7	30	34-35	33-35	33-35
1,500 -	5	7	30	35	35	35

* One catty is equal to 500 grams.
a. *Ching-chi yen-chiu,* No. 2 (1956), p. 102.
b. Ch'i Li, *Shan Kan Ning pien ch'ü shih-lu,* p. 30.
c. *Chieh-fang jih pao,* (20 November 1941), p. 4.
d. *Ching-chi yen-chiu,* No. 2 (1956), p. 105.
   (A) Including the Yenshu Region, plus Huach'ih Hsien and Huan Hsien of the Lungtung Region.
   (B) Including the Kuanchung Region, plus Chingyang Hsien, Ch'ützu, Hoshui Hsien, Chenyuan Hsien of the Lungtung Region.
   (C) Suite Region.
e. Beginning with 4 percent of 180 catties.
f. Beginning with 6 percent of 240 catties.
g. Beginning with 1 percent of 351 catties.

The implementation of the unified tax, especially in its 1941 version, appears to have posed considerable problems.[63] Nevertheless, in response to the succession of reforms and improvements in tax administration, total receipts of public grain increased greatly according to table 7.5. Public grain initially accounted for little more than 5 percent of the entire budget.[64] The growth of receipts from 1938 to 1940 by about 80,000 piculs compensated for at least half of the loss in real transfer payments during these two years, but it did not suffice to prevent a major deficiency in the public sector during spring 1941, which was aggravated by the termination of outside support at the beginning of that year.[65] The borrowing of about 50,000 piculs of grain prior to the harvest closed the gap temporarily,[66] and the collection of an additional 100,000 to 110,000 piculs of public grain in the fall made up for the deficiency permanently, at the price of creating hardship in the private sector. During the following three years, the burden on the private sector was 10 or 20 percent less than in 1941, apparently due to the exemption of 21 percent of the peasant households from taxation.[67] Further relief in 1945 may have been related to a bad harvest as well as to the decline in the size of the public sector.[68]

A comparison of the grain collection data of table 7.5 with the grain production data of table 6.3 yields two interesting observations. The tax share increased from less than 1 percent of the product in 1937 to 12 or 13 percent of it in 1941 and ranged near 10 percent during the following three years. Such changing impositions apparently made it possible for the amount of grain retained by the private sector to continue growing until 1940. It probably fell in 1941 but increased again thereafter even after the production of the institutional households has been deducted. In 1945 it once more decreased. Doubts about the accuracy of the official grain production estimates lead one to question the 1937-1940 trend as well as the magnitudes of all the changes in grain retention.[69]

Table 7.5

TAX COLLECTIONS IN KIND, 1937-1945

Year	Grain Planned	Grain Realized Claimed	Grain Realized Revised[g]	Straw Realized	Wool Estimate
	Piculs*	Piculs*	Piculs*	1,000 catties	Catties
1937	10,000 [a]	13,859 [a]	10,000		
1938	10,000 [a]	15,972 [a]	10,000		
1939	50,000 [a]	52,250 [a]	50,000		
1940	90,000 [a]	97,354 [a]	90,000		
1941	200,000 [b]	200,000 [d]	200,000	27,000 [d]	380,000 [j]
1942	160,000 [b]	165,000 [e]	160,000	16,800 [e]	
1943	180,000 [b]	180,000 [f]	180,000	18,000 [h]	
1944	160,000 [c]	160,000 [f]	160,000	18,000 [i]	
1945		120,000 [f]	125,000		

* One picul equals 300 catties at 500 grams.
a. *Shan Kan Ning 1939-1941,* p. 54.
b. Mao Tse-tung, "Ching-chi wen-t'i," pp. 166-167, 178.
c. *Brief Account,* p. 13.
d. *Chieh-fang jih pao* (1 June 1942), p. 1.
e. *Chieh-fang jih pao* (26 October 1942), p. 2.
f. *Shan Kan Ning (1958),* p. 284 (reprint).
g. *Ching-chi yen-chiu,* No. 2 (1956), p. 108.
h. Hsü, *A Survey,* Part 2, p. 27.
i. Van Slyke, *The Chinese Communist Movement,* p. 167.
j. *Shan Kan Ning 1939-1941,* pp. 55-56.

The significance of the changes in burden can be assessed further by comparing the receipts of public grain according to table 7.5 with the hsien tax revenue estimates for 1930/1931.[70] The grain equivalent of the latter was comparable to the average receipts during the years 1942-1944. The 1941 levy exceeded this standard by about 15 percent. It thus appears that due to the renewal of economic warfare, the Chinese communists were forced to impose as heavily on the area's farm sector as prerevolutionary governments had done. Because they adopted a progressive income tax in lieu of the old land tax, however, this heavy burden was distributed very differently on the various peasant classes, so that it was more easy to bear.[71]

(2) Other taxes in kind. In addition to "public grain" the SKN border region government imposed taxes in kind on straw and on wool. Both appear to have been introduced in 1940/1941, in response to the renewed blockade. Levies of "public straw," which served to feed the transport animals of the institutional households and especially those of the army, seem to have been assessed in conjunction with and on the basis of levies of "public grain." Table 7.5 suggests that like the grain levy, the tax on straw may have been excessively burdensome in 1941.[72] However, information on the total output of straw is lacking. The more limited receipts of tax straw during later years were supplemented with uncertain amounts of publicly produced straw.[73]

A head tax on sheep, which had yielded the equivalent of one catty of wool per sheep per annum according to communist sources, had been done away with during the revolutionary period. It was reintroduced in the winter of 1940/1941, but with lower rates. The government now collected four ounces of wool per white sheep and two ounces of wool per black sheep, at a time when sheep were expected to yield an average of two catties of wool per annum. The anticipated receipt of three ounces per sheep accounted for close to 10 percent of this total. It thus constituted a burden which was comparable to that of the grain levy. Table 7.5 presents the total receipts predicted for 1941, which were valued at 760,000 yuan.[74] Subsequent references to this tax could not be found.[75]

The importance of both taxes in the budget may be indicated by the grain equivalents of their yields. The receipts of straw, which appear to have been omitted from the "other taxes" in table 7.2, seem to have been equivalent to millet in the amounts of 22,500 piculs in 1941, of 14,000 piculs in 1942, and of 15,000 piculs in 1944.[76] Their share in total revenue fell from less than 10 percent in 1941 to about 4 percent in 1944. The receipts of wool in 1941 probably were equivalent to 2,700 piculs of millet, which accounted for less than 1 percent of the total revenue.[77] Both taxes thus were minor sources of revenue for the government, even though they may have contributed critically to the maintenance of the institutional households in the region.[78]

In addition to these strategic goods, the government requisitioned strategic services through a system of corvée, which has been outlined in chapter 5. The contribution to "public work" in road construction has been recorded in tables 5.2 and 6.11. Other information makes it possible to derive the following total values.[79]

Year	Persons mobilized for work	Average days of corvée	Man-year equivalent of work	Millet equivalent of work
1942	64,923	1.9	340	2,040
1943	45,643	0.6	75	450

The data suggest that at least during the years 1942 and 1943, the requisitioning of people for construction work also added relatively little to total public revenue.

The contributions of men and work animals to "public transportation," notably of grain and salt, which could be commuted by cash payments, have not been reported in detail. The transportation of "public grain" required 32,500 animal days for 15,000 piculs in 1942 and 31,622 animal days for 13,737 piculs in 1944, with uncertain costs in terms of millet. The transportation of public as well apparently as of private salt probably imposed much more heavily, since both the quantities carried and the distances moved were greater. However, information on man years and animal years has not been made public. The government paid 30 percent of the load carried for the transportation of salt. Corvée or its cash substitute had to cover the residual.[80]

(3) Other taxes in cash. The Chinese communists had abolished most taxes during the soviet period, a total of "42 petty, special, miscellaneous taxes" according to Chairman Lin.[81] But they had preserved sales taxes on the major exports of the area—edible salt, skins and wool, and medicinal herbs—which they now collected at the uniformly low rate of two yuan per donkey load.[82] In order to promote exports, at least those of salt, the charge appears to have been reduced further to 1.2 yuan per load. Taxes were raised subsequently in response to inflationary price changes,[83] and eventually they were imposed differently. The tax on skins and wool became part of the agricultural income tax, and the tax on salt was made a fraction of the sales price—5 to 7 percent in 1943.[84]

In reaction to the renewal of economic warfare, the SKN border region government added to these taxes in an attempt to promote austerity and autarky. As previously mentioned, necessities such as educational materials and paper were taxed lightly at 2 and 5 percent rates, whereas luxuries such as liquor and tobacco as well as religious supplies were taxed heavily at 80 and 100 percent of the sales value. Correspondingly, cotton fiber and cotton yarn, which had to be imported to some extent, were burdened with 1 percent duties, while cotton cloth, which could be manufactured internally, experienced an impost of 15 percent *ad valorem*.[85]

In addition to these indirect taxes, the SKN border region government imposed a direct tax on business, which replaced the earlier, less regular levies. In the winter of 1940 the government collected 400,000 yuan in contributions for winter clothing from this source. In 1941 it enacted a progressive profit tax for business. Technical difficulties such as inadequate record keeping precluded its implementation in a bureaucratic form. As an alternative, the government relied on semiannual assessments of all merchants by their local chambers of commerce. Such levies were more arbitrary and yielded relatively little in the beginning,[86] but the procedures soon improved. By 1943 the government is said to have collected from 4 to 19.6 percent of the net profit of merchants in this manner.[87] The average taxation rate has been reported as 13 percent.[88] The

burden placed on commerce was thus comparable to that imposed on agriculture.

The contribution of the sales and business profit taxes to the
budget cannot be discussed in great detail. If the tax on salt
increased proportionately to the price of salt, it had to yield the
following revenues.[89]

Year	Cash	Millet equivalent
1938	137,760 yuan	4,305 piculs
1939	389,880 yuan	10,537 piculs
1940	971,520 yuan	18,683 piculs
1941	8,064,000 yuan	29,007 piculs

In contrast, the millet equivalent of the salt tax probably came
close to only 18,000 piculs in 1943[90] and apparently fell thereafter.[91] The 400,000 yuan contributed by the merchants for
winter clothing should have bought more than 5,000 piculs of
millet in winter 1940,[92] while subsequent levies may have been
worth more. However, the business profit tax apparently did
not become a major source of revenue for the government. The
same may be said of all the other taxes even though specific
information is lacking for them. Table 7.2 indicates that all
taxes other than "public grain" and "public straw" (i.e., salt tax
included) together yielded less than 10 percent of the total
revenue in 1938 as well as in 1943. As a consequence, they did
not contribute much to the closing of the gap which the termination of outside support in 1941 and the reduction of the
"public grain" levy in 1942 had left. Nevertheless, the likely
increase in salt tax revenue until 1941 may have eased the
transition from outside support to self-reliance considerably.[93]

(4) Public production. Besides imposing much more heavily
on the base area population, the SKN border region government tried to make its army, organs, and schools less of a
burden. To this end, it urged the economizing of expenditure as
well as the production of income by the public sector in two
forms. State-operated enterprises, including those run by the
institutional households, were encouraged to earn profit as a
source of public revenue, and the institutional households themselves were induced to engage in subsistence production. Such
activities soon became the movement's "glory" according to

Mao Tse-tung. Unfortunately, this and other laudations did not lead to a more systematic accounting of the development of public production. Table 7.6 provides highly incomplete information on the results.

Until the beginning of 1939 the public sector apparently met a tiny fraction—2 to 3 percent—of its total requirements by its own production, but the call for a production campaign by the institutional households, which was made at the beginning of that year, found a strongly positive response according to the available data. Army, organs, and schools reclaimed and cultivated extensive areas of land. In addition to the grain listed in table 7.6, they produced straw and grass, 1.2 million catties of vegetables, numerous hogs,[94] and cloth to meet part of their requirements.[95] The total value of public production, which has been placed at two million yuan,[96] appears to have been equivalent to 54,000 piculs of grain. The increase raised the share of own produced income to about 20 percent of the likely total expenditure, and it served to offset most of the estimated loss of transfer payments due to inflation since 1937.

The initial production campaign generated only a limited momentum. Government organs and schools did not reclaim additional land in 1940, and they produced less grain as well as few vegetables than in the preceding year.[97] The activities of the army have not been detailed, but the estimated value of all public production tends to imply that they cannot have increased greatly. A total of "more than three million yuan" was equivalent at best to 58,000 piculs of millet in 1940.[98] During the following two years, such production is said to have been increased considerably, especially by the army.[99] Yet the failure to report accomplishments in the aggregate, the emphasis on exemplary achievements such as the Nanniwan project, and the promulgation of the policy of "better troops and simpler administration" in the fall of 1942 suggest also that the progress may not have been so significant.[100] Most important appears to have been the undertaking of salt-mining by a few thousand soldiers, which resulted in the output of 60,000 loads of public salt in 1941. The output planned for 1942, i.e., 127,500 loads,[101] was approximated with difficulty, but a reduced target of 100,000 loads, which was envisaged for 1943,[102] was realized in that year and surpassed in 1944.

Table 7.6

PUBLIC PRODUCTION, 1938-1944

Item	Unit	1938	1939	1940	1941	1942	1943	1944
Land reclaimed								
army units	Mou		25,136 [a]		14,794 [a]		215,000 [b]	
organs + schools	Mou		113,414 [c]					
Land cultivated								
army units	Mou		same				306,000 [d]	830,000 [a]
organs + schools	Mou		same					
Grain produced								
army units	Piculs		2,590 [b]				31,000 [b]	} 80,000 [e] / 90,000 [a]
organs + schools	Piculs		11,325 [c]	6,000 [c]				20,000 [e]
Salt production	Loads				60,000 [f]	120,000 [g]	100,000 [g]	105,000 [g]
Transport cost: 30% [h]	Loads				18,000	36,000	30,000	31,500
Salt income [h]	Loads				42,000	84,000	70,000	73,500
Millet equivalent [i]	Piculs				34,300	85,700	63,200	68,400
Total product: Grain plus its equivalent*	Piculs	6,400 [j]	54,000 [k]	57,700 [l]			93,000 [j]	} 150,000 [e] / 290,000 [a]

* Including byproducts of grain, other agricultural products, products of other occupations, plus· the profits of public enterprises.

a. *Shan Kan Ning (1958)*, pp. 281-282.

b. Forman, *Report*, p. 74.

c. Mao, "Ching-chi wen-t'i," pp. 138-139.

d. *Shan Kan Ning pien ch'ü cheng-ts'e t'iao-li hui-pien*, p. 32.

e. Kao Kang, *1945 nien pien ch'ü ti chu-yao jen-wu ho tso-feng wen-t'i* (9 January 1945), p. 6.

f. *Wei kung-yeh p'in*, pp. 56-57.

g. Hsü, *A Survey*, Part 2, p. 32.

h. Derived from *ibid.*

i. Derived from *ibid.* and table 20 (June data). Price of salt in 1943: 18 yuan per catty and thus 4,050 yuan per load. See note f. Price of millet: 4,488 yuan per picul. See table 7.3.

j. Table 7.2.

k. 2,000,000 yuan/37 yuan per picul. See *Shan Kan Ning 1939-1941*, pp. 56-57, and Table 7.3.

l. 3,000,000 yuan/52 yuan per picul. See *ibid.*

The effects of the renewed production campaign became apparent in 1943 and even more so in 1944. The army was especially active in reclamation and cultivated land on a very large scale, according to official claims; in the end, soldiers on the average worked nearly as much land as the peasants did. The yield per *mou* of army land seems to have been relatively low,[103] perhaps because it was marginal land, but the total output grew enormously, especially in the case of grain. The organs and schools did not increase their production of grain proportionately. Nevertheless, table 7.6 shows that the institutional households together reaped at least 100,000 piculs of grain in 1944, i.e., 5 or more percent of the area's total output of grain in that year and as much as or more than the levy of public grain had yielded in 1940.[104]

In addition to grain, the institutional households continued to produce supplementary foods and fodder, assertedly in increasing though unspecified quantities. Soldiers also continued to participate in salt extraction. The planned output of 100,000 loads of public salt in 1943, which appears to have been accomplished, should have been equivalent to 63,000 piculs of millet net of transport cost.[105] Soldiers further engaged in coal and iron mining as well as in metal processing, and all institutional households undertook home handicraft production for both subsistence and transaction, especially in textile manufacturing. The results of all these efforts have not been enumerated, but their total contribution to public revenue has been reported indirectly for 1943 and directly for 1944. The 1943 estimate may be an understatement,[106] and the 1944 estimates allow for a large number of possibilities.[107] Nevertheless, table 7.6 implies that in the official opinion, the value of nongrain production by the institutional households was equivalent to at least 42,000 piculs of grain in 1943 and to at least 50,000 piculs of grain in 1944.

The grain equivalent of the total value of public production grew correspondingly by at least 35,000 piculs from 1940 to 1943 and by at least 57,000 piculs from 1943 to 1944. As a result, public production not only compensated for the decrease in agricultural taxation,[108] but it even began to rival the latter as the primary source of revenue. A comparison of Tables 7.5 and

7.6 reveals this change in relations which may have become even more pronounced in 1945 up to the moment when a large part of the SKN garrison departed.[109] As a consequence, table 7.2 indicates further that public production by 1944 contributed close to 40 percent of the region's entire public revenue. The SKN border region government thus had become self-supporting to an extraordinary degree.

(5) Extrabudgetary transfers. The official budgets as well as the data of table 7.2 omit in addition to the value of corvée various transfers of goods and services which the population was required or encouraged to make. Almost from the beginning of their presence in the countryside, the Chinese communists followed the practice of allotting land to their veterans and active soldiers with families.[110] To the extent that these dependents of the movements were unable to provide for themselves, local communities were called upon to help out by cultivating the allotted land as well as by doing other chores for them. The value of these services, which apparently could be commuted by gifts of grain and of other products, has rarely ever been estimated. In the SKN border region, with 20,000 soldiers' and veterans' families totalling 90,000 members, this contribution was reported to have been equivalent to 60,000 piculs of grain in 1943.[111] One may guess that it rose to this level gradually over the years, in response to both the recruitment of new soldiers and the settlement of old soldiers in the areas,[112] and that it did not change much during the final two years of the war.

Besides providing in this manner for the dependents of their movement, the Chinese communists mobilized additional support for its activists by initiating in 1943 a campaign of pledging the giving gifts to the army on the occasion of the lunar new year. The large variety of gifts given during 1943 were said to be equivalent to 60,000 piculs of millet.[113] Information on the overall value of similar contributions in 1944 and 1945 is lacking. However, aid in this form during all three years cannot be viewed as a simple transfer payment because the army units were called upon to reciprocate with gifts of their own.[114] The worth of such reciprocal services—from ceasing to impose on the people for transport services and other forms of corvée to providing medical care for them with army medics — cannot be determined either, however great it may have been.

(6) Budget deficits, note issue, and inflation. In spite of the very large increases in receipts first from agricultural taxation, then from public production, and finally perhaps even from extrabudgetary gifts, the government continued to experience payments problems. Table 7.7 lists the available information on the state of the budget and note issue. Imprecise and incomplete as they are, the data show that surpluses have been claimed for 1939 and 1940, even though outside support declined and internal sources failed to offset the loss during this period. The balance changed in 1941, when the external payments had stopped. Budget deficits were incurred and the note issue grew for this reason at least until 1943 and probably also in 1944. The last development is in question.[115] More fundamentally, however, the entire process of deficit-financing and its repercussions are somewhat obscure, for lack of comprehensive information.

Budget deficits resulted initially from the government's immediate inability to make up for the loss of external resources. As a consequence the government borrowed from the SKN border region bank at first mostly to close the gap by developing the production of the institutional households. This is what the manager of the border region bank told Stein in 1944:

> We had to issue notes to develop production in every possible way. And we did. These first issues of our own bank notes were used mainly as capital funds for new enterprises like the army farm project you saw in Nanniwan. We gave our army units and our various government and educational institutions capital in the form of notes and ordered them to provide for their future needs out of their own production. As a rule, they were given the equivalent of two years' current expenditure to finance their new production enterprises.... [116]

The actual amounts of these advances have not been reported. In addition, notes were issued to finance imports into the SKN border region.[117] The extent of note issue for this purpose has not been announced, either. And it is also uncertain whether public expenditure on imported goods necessitated budget deficits. But it may be noted that due to the adverse changes in the terms of external trade, the cotton equivalent or the iron equivalent of public revenue did not grow nearly as much as the grain equivalent or the salt equivalent

Table 7.7

BUDGET BALANCE AND NOTE ISSUE, 1936-1944

Year	Budget balance	Date	Note issue SKN yuan
1936	deficit [a]		n.a.
1937 ⎱ 1938 ⎰	surplus [b]		90,000 [c]
1939	surplus [d]		
1940	surplus [d]	year-end	3,500,000 [e]
1941	deficit [d]	⎰ Feb. 18 ⎱ November ⎰ year-end	5,000,000 [e] 12,000,000 [f] 25,000,000 [e]
1942	deficit [g]	May	52,000,000 [e]
1943	deficit [g]	year-end	350,000,000 [h]
1944	deficit [i]	May	1,600,000,000 [j]

a. Snow, *Red Star,* p. 250.
b. October 1937 to September 1938. Ch'i Li, *Shan Kan Ning pien ch'ü shih-lu,* p. 29.
c. Stein, *The Challenge,* p. 197.
d. *Shan Kan Ning (1958),* p. 94.
e. Hsü, *A Survey,* Part 2, p. 6.
f. *Chieh-fang jih pao* (9 November 1941), p. 4.
g. Stein, *The Challenge,* p. 207.
h. Van Slyke, *The Chinese Communist Movement,* p. 155.
i. *Ibid.,* p. 167.
j. Stein, *The Challenge,* p. 198.

did. More specifically, it is evident that 1 catty of cotton exchanged for 1 catty of salt in 1937 but for 6.8 catties of salt in 1943.[118] It seems doubtful that the growth of public revenue sufficed to offset such a decline in purchasing power.

However, public production was being developed in particular for the purpose of providing import substitutes. Progress in this direction, which has been made evident, had to diminish the dependence on budget deficits and note issue as means of financing investments as well as imports. The continuing excess of expenditure over revenue therefore had to be related to other causes as well. The official explanation attributed it primarily to the very success of the production campaign. As soon as subsistence seemed secured, the government mounted a campaign to stockpile provisions until the reserves would amount to one year's harvest.[119] Stein was told that in the absence of such inventory accumulation, the budget would have shown a surplus:

> The hidden surpluses of the last two years are partly contained in the fast expanding grain reserve which the government has accumulated in order to provide against the possibility of a crop failure and the special needs of the final counteroffensive. For the all-out attack on Japan in the last stage of the war will necessitate the withdrawal of troops at present engaged in production, as well as the mobilization of many militiamen in the villages where lack of labor power may then affect production. . . .[120]

In any case, the excess of expenditure over revenue appears to have been comparatively small. Table 7.2 implies that the bank loans in 1943 accounted for less than 10 percent of total public expenditure, inclusive of taxes in kind.[121] The share of the deficit may have been similarly large in 1942,[122] and it probably was smaller in 1944.[123] In contrast, the KMT government financed two-thirds to three-fourths of its entire expenditure by borrowing and note issue.[124] In view of such relations, it seems surprising that the SKN border region experienced rates of price inflation which were not only extremely high according to table 7.3 but also far in excess of those evident for nationalist territory.[125]

Both paradoxes appear to be attributable to the fact that the extent of private money economy was extraordinarily limited in the border region. The private sector consisted mainly of farm households which produced mostly for their own consumption rather than for the market. Moreover, a part of their trading continued to be carried on in the form of barter. In spite of such restrictions, the cash transactions sphere generated close to 10 percent of the total public revenue in the form of sales and commercial profit taxes. However, any additional demand of the government in this market apparently encountered private supply constraints.[126] In such circumstances, even a series of seemingly small budget deficits could be expected to induce a rapidly progressing inflation.

In fact, of course, the government tended to double its imposition in the cash transaction sphere by means of its note issue.[127] The population did not show significant inertia or willingness to retain cash for any other reason, so prices appear to have risen in proportion to the note issue without much delay, and the note issue had to grow extremely fast in order to assure the government of its desired share in total cash transactions. Table 7.3 and 7.7 imply the following indices of note issue, millet price, and all prices:

Year	Date	Note issue	Date	Millet price	All prices
1940	End	1.0	Dec.	1.0	1.0
1941	End	7.1	Dec.	7.5	6.1
1942	May	14.9	June	12.8	14.1
1943	End	100.0	Dec.	298	480
1944	May	457	June	309	776

Assuming that the reported note issue for 1943 is correct,[128] the available information does not explain fully the extraordinary increase in prices relative to the note issue. It seems to have been related to the deterioration in the exchange rate, which is evident in table 7.1. Since the decline in the exchange rate was in turn attributed to the note issue,[129] one has to look for additional reasons to account for both price changes in 1943. A rapid escalation of economic warfare by the national government, which is frequently mentioned officially, as well as the sudden internal stockpiling for the final offensive may explain much of the discrepancy. Whatever its full explanation, 1944 saw a return to "normalcy" in the sense of a closer correspondence between evident changes in money supply and in prices, but it did not bring an end to deficit-financing and inflation, contrary to some expectations.[130]

Summary

In their relations with the outside world, the Chinese communists experienced an initial nationalist blockade prior to the formation of the SKN border region, then a period of gradually diminishing free trade plus nationalist aid which lasted from 1937 to 1940, and a final period of renewed economic warfare. The initial liberalization as well as the eventual restriction of external trade affected the border region's public finance in the extreme. Data problems make it impossible to explore the consequences of these events in full detail, but the available information does reveal the major developments clearly.

At first the pattern of external trade and internal finance reflected the fundamental conflict between nationalists and communists in several respects. The nationalists blockaded the Northwest Soviet, thereby raising the cost and probably reducing the volume of external trade of an area which was not self-sufficient. The communists redistributed public burdens within the soviet by abolishing most taxes and by confiscating the wealth of the rich, yet these assets failed to yield enough to pay for public expenditures and imports. As a consequence, the communists could not avoid imposing on the people again. In lieu of taxation, they resorted to note issue and currency devaluation. Apparently before the effects of these measures could manifest themselves fully, the united front was formed.

The united-front agreement of 1937 brought two very important changes. Termination of the blockade made external trade for the region less costly relative to internal production, and financial support for the Eighth Route Army helped balance the border region's trade deficit as well as its budget deficit, in spite of the fact that confiscations ceased. In combination, these changes enabled the Chinese communists both to meet local needs and to sustain themselves better than ever before without imposing more heavily on the local population. Because they had these positive effects, however, the changes also tended to impede advances in import-substitution as well as in exportation.

The experience of economic security through external support lasted for perhaps two years, after which the situation deteriorated rapidly. Wartime inflation eroded the value of the monthly cash payments to the Eighth Route Army, which apparently remained unadjusted for changes in the cost of living, and the disintegration of the united front manifested itself further in the termination first of aid in kind, then of aid in cash, and eventually of much of the trade between the two territories. This renewal of economic warfare forced the Chinese communists to confront once more the principal economic and financial problems that they had encountered during the soviet period.

The production campaigns, which the Chinese communists had promoted as part of an autarky strategy at least since early 1939, aimed at solving these problems in several ways. The deficit in the balance of trade was to be eliminated by the development of import-substituting and of export-oriented industries. Substantial progress was made in this direction, but the gap could not be closed entirely, appparently because the terms of external trade deteriorated so badly. The SKN border region government attributed the extraordinary magnitude of this change for the worse to nationalist machinations.

The deficit in the budget was to be reduced immediately by increasing the taxation of agricultural production and of commerce, and it was to be offset eventually by developing in addition the public production of import substitutes as well as of exportable commodities. In terms of grain or its equivalent, the collection of tax revenues and the output of public enterprises grew remarkably, compensating for the loss in outside support by 1941/42. However, autarky was not in sight at that early date, and the deterioration of the terms of external trade precluded a balanced budget in terms of cotton or iron equivalent.

To finance the deficits which it had incurred and to start public enterprises and stockpile provisions, the SKN border region government had to borrow from the border region bank. The bank in turn had to issue notes, and the increase in the money supply led to an increase in the price level. The inflation progressed at an extraordinarily rapid speed, probably because the money economy was extremely limited in scope.

VIII
Income and Expenditure

In the end, the strategy of the Chinese communists changed the structures of income and expenditure within the SKN border region in several important respects. The initial land reform, confiscatory public finance, and equalitarian public spending all had contributed to a less pronounced social differentiation during the soviet period. The receipt of outside support made it possible to preserve this postrevolutionary status quo during the first phase of the united-front period. Its subsequent loss tended to be offset by increasing taxation and developing production. Moreover, the introduction of a progressive income tax further helped to reduce income differentials, while the attempt to achieve self-sufficiency aimed at improving the level of living in the area as well. Development was also to manifest itself in growing amounts of surplus in various forms, which was to be invested in the war against Japan and in China's liberation.

Living in the Public Sector

Public revenue—whether from confiscation, contribution, taxation, or own production—had to provide first of all for the members of the army, organs, and schools, plus their dependents, most of whom lived in institutional households and received supplies plus allowances rather than wages in the usual sense.

Total expenditure. Public expenditure for the sustenance of public employees has not been reported systematically or in detail.[1] In 1941 the government stated that food rations for the party, government, and army members, plus their dependents,

required 120,000 piculs of grain.[2] In the same year it was estimated that their clothing rations called for 44,000 to 49,400
bolts of cloth.[3] Their clothing expenditures plus other expenses
at that time were to be met by an outlay of thirteen million
yuan, which appears to have been equivalent to 47,000 piculs of
millet at June 1941 prices.[4] To provide for this group thus
necessitated close to 170,000 piculs of grain or its equivalent in
1941. The total bill may have been somewhat smaller during
the united-front period, prior to the reinforcement of the border region garrison, but it seems to have grown in later years,
due both to changing price relations and rising living standards
brought about by increasing public production. According to
Mao Tse-tung:

> The annual requirements of the army units and the
> government and other organizations [in 1944] total
> 260,000 *tan* [i.e., piculs] . . . of husked grain (millet),
> of which they get 160,000 from the people and pro-
> duce the rest themselves; . . .[5]

The revenue estimates of table 7.2 suggest that the soviet
government was barely able to commit the necessary expenditures in 1936. Problems of supply had disappeared by 1938,
but they recurred when economic warfare recommenced and
continued so long as the increases in taxation and public production failed to make up for the decreases in outside support.
Tables 7.2, 7.3, 7.5, and 7.6 imply the following major changes
from year to year, in piculs of grain or its equivalent.

Year	Change in outside con- tributions	Change in public grain receipts	Change in public pro- duction	Balance of year-to-year changes
1939	− 61,300	+ 36,278	+ 47,600	+ 22,578
1940	− 56,100	+ 45,104	+ 3,700	− 7,296
1941	− 138,500	+ 102,646	n.a.	(− 35,854)

More specifically, tables 7.5 and 7.6 show that prior to 1941
the collection plus own production of public grain did not suffice to supply the public sector with basic food. Moreover, the
1941 increase in the public grain levy occurred after the govern-

ment in the spring of that year had encountered sales resistance when it attempted to buy additional grain.[6] Correspondingly, table 6.10 suggests that prior to 1942 the production of state, CIC, plus private factories could not meet the public demand for cloth. Such observations indicate that during the years 1940 and 1941 in particular, the government may have been unable to maintain the previous standard of living in the public sector.[7]

Average expenditure and level of living. The available information on wages and the values of rations plus allowances in the public sector tends to confirm this indication, even though the data are far from complete. Table 8.1 presents the most important bit of evidence in this connection, an index of the level of living of the army in the SKN border region for the years 1939-1943. Elsewhere this index is described as a measure of the supply of food and clothing per soldier.[8] Because its base period is uncertain,[9] it is impossible to say when exactly the shortage of supplies became pressing. By the end of 1939 at the latest, however, the supplies per soldier were 20 percent less than in 1943. They fell in 1940 and again in 1941 to barely more than two-thirds of the 1943 level. Moreover, in 1942 they only began to approach the initial 1939 level. The decline in the army's level of living during 1939-1942 and especially during 1940-1941 thus appears to have been severe.

Comparable data for other occupational groups are lacking,[10] but it seems reasonable to assume that cadres, students, and even factory workers did not fare any better than the soldiers did. Table 8.1 probably depicts the magnitude of the crisis generally. Its impact on the living conditions in the public sector can be specified further by linking the index of table 8.1 to information on real wages and on values of rations in this sector. Table 8.2 presents the few data that could be found, all of which pertain to noncrisis years. It suggests that in 1943-1944 most persons in the public sector received the equivalents of 900 to 1,200 kg of millet per annum. In relation to this base, the index yields the following series of millet equivalents of average supplies:

| 1942 | 690-920 kg | 1940 | 631-841 kg |
| 1941 | 604-805 kg | 1939 | 717-956 kg |

Table 8.1

INDEX OF THE LEVEL OF LIVING OF SOLDIERS OF THE SKN BORDER REGION GARRISON, 1939-1943. [a]

Year	1939 = 100.0 [b]	1943 = 100.0 [c]
1939 [b]	100.0	79.7
1940	88.0	70.1
1941	84.2	67.1
1942	96.3	76.7
1943	125.5	100.0

a. *Shan Kan Ning (1958)*, p. 282, and Forman, *Report*, p. 74.
b. Annual average or December average? *Ibid.*
c. Derived from note a.

Table 8.2

ANNUAL WAGES AND VALUES OF SUPPLIES IN THE PUBLIC SECTOR, 1938 and 1943-1944.

Year	Occupation, type of payment	Kg of millet
1938	Soldiers, office workers, rations [a]	900-1,200
1943	Teachers, millet standard wage [b]	630- 900
1943	Communications workers, millet	1,170-1,770
1943	standard wage [c]	
1943	Factory workers, average wage [d]	1,200
1944	Factory workers, average wage, planned [e]	> 1,200
1944	Public employees, students, rations [f]	900

a. *Ching-chi yen-chiu,* No. 2 (1956), p. 101.
b. *General Survey of National Education,* p. 6 (referring to the Suite and Kuanchung subregions).
c. *Shan Kan Ning pien ch'ü cheng-ts'e t'iao-li hui-pien,* p. 175.
d. *Brief Account,* p. 15 (apparently equivalent of rations).
e. *Ibid.*
f. *Shan Kan Ning (1958),* p. 214 (equivalent of food and clothing).

Table 8.2 also indicates that in 1938 the millet equivalents of most rations fell within the 900-1,200 kg range. It thus intimates that most persons in the public sector regained their 1938 living standard during 1943. Table 8.2 shows further that factory workers received relatively high incomes at that time, thus pointing to the possibility that changes in the sector's occupational structure, which followed the rapid development of state-operated industry, also produced increases in average expenditure per member of the public sector.

A comparison of the above estimates with the data of tables 2.11 and 2.12 finally yields two important points. First, even though the grain equivalent of the expenditure per soldier, office worker, and student had fallen drastically by 1940-1941, it apparently still exceeded the amount of grain which the wages of farm laborers and soldiers had bought during the presoviet period. Second, the grain equivalent of the average supplies in 1938 and in 1943 seems to have come close to that of the net value added per person employed in public service during presoviet times. Of course, this apparent maintenance of the income level was associated with an extreme change of the income structure in the public sector—for instance the pay of common soldiers doubled whereas that of most officials halved!

Rations and allowances. The relatively high level of living as well as the high degree of income equalization in the public sector are evident most specifically in information on rations and allowances. Table 8.3 presents the available reports of actual supplies received in 1938-1939 and in 1943-1944 by members of selected occupations. Table 8.4 adds to these data the official food rations of 1944, in a form which makes them comparable to the estimates of table 2.9. The data of table 8.3 unfortunately are incomplete as well as in need of interpretation.

(1) Grains. So far as the supply of grains is concerned, most sources suggest the absence of a major change from precrisis to postcrisis years. Only Forman's report implies a substantial improvement. But his findings conflict with the simultaneous observations of Stein as well as with the regulations of table 8.4. The discrepancy, which is substantial, could be attributable to

Table 8.3

SUPPLIES AND ALLOWANCES, 1938-1944

Item	Unit	Soldiers, Employees 1938 [a]	Hsien chief 1939 [b]	Cadres 1943 [c]	Teachers 1943 [d]	Soldiers 1943 [e]	Workers 1944 [f]	Workers 1944 [g]
Food								
Millet	Catties per month	30-45	37.5	33.25	45	60	40	30
Wheat flour	"						20	15
Vegetables	"			37.5		48	36	30
Meat	"	0.9-1.5 Yuan	1.2 Yuan	1.5	1,200 Yuan	4.6	4	3
Oil	"			0.94				1
Salt	"							1
Clothing								
Summer suit	Suites per year	1-2			1	2		2
Winter suit	"	1/3-1/2			1	2		1
Overcoat	Coats per year					1/4		
Summer shoes	Pairs per year				1	1		⎫
Winter shoes	"				1	1		⎬ 3
Sandals	"					1		⎭
Quilt	Pieces per year					1/2		

Table 8.3 (*continued*)

Item	Unit	Soldiers, Employees 1938 [a]	Hsien chief 1939 [b]	Cadres 1943 [c]	Teachers 1943 [d]	Soldiers 1943 [e]	Workers 1944 [f]	Workers 1944 [g]
Towels	"				2	2		2
Soap	"				6			12
Allowance								
Soldiers	Yuan per month	1						
Students	"	1						
Cadres	"	1-5	2					
Teachers	"	2-7						
Workers	Catties of				40-50			-100
Apprentices	Millet per month							10-20

a. *Ching-chi yen-chiu*, No. 2 (1956), p. 101, and Ch'i Li, *Shan Kan Ning pien ch'ü shih-lu*, pp. 126-127, 155, 158, 169.

b. *Shan Kan Ning (1958)*, p. 19.

c. Band, *Two Years*, p. 260.

d. *General Survey of National Education*, pp. 6-7 (referring to Kulin, Yenan City, and Chinchang).

e. Forman, *Report*, pp. 74-75. In addition, each soldier received per annum 1/2 putties, 1/3 bandolier, 1/3 rice bag, and 3 catties of wool for spinning.

f. *Ibid.*, p. 75.

g. Stein, *The Challenge*, p. 178, and *Wei kung-yeh p'in*, p. 23.

Table 8.4

FOOD RATIONS, 1944 [a]

Recipient	Item	Grams per day	Kilograms per year	Percent supplied
Grains				
Organs + Schools [b]	Millet	593	217	100 ?
Army units [c]	Millet	750	274	100 ?
Transport workers	Millet	1,000	365	100 ?
Hospital patients	Millet	656	240	100 ?
Children, 0-1	Wheat	375	137	100 ?
1-3	Wheat	500	183	100 ?
3-5	Wheat	624	228	100 ?
5-	Millet	593	217	100 ?
Supplementary foods				
Normal diet (ta tsao)	Meat	33	12	50
	Oil	16	5.6	80
	Vegetables	500	180	0 ?
	Salt	17	6	75
	Coal	750	270	67

Table 8.4 (continued)

Recipient / Item	Grams per day	Kilograms per year	Percent supplied
Special diet (hsiao tsao)			
Meat	67	24	50
Oil	25	9	38
Vegetables	500	180	0 ?
Salt	17	6	0 ?
Coal	1,167	420	36

a. *Shan Kan Ning pien ch'ü cheng-ts'e t'iao-li hui pien*, pp. 241, 244-245.
b. Including civilian and military administrators, teachers, and students.
c. Including soldiers, students of military schools, and armament workers.

an unusual degree of additional provisioning by own production in specific cases.

(2) Supplementary foods. The supply of supplementary foods may have increased considerably over the same time interval. Table 7.3 indicates that the cash payments per soldier or employee in 1938 were equivalent to eleven to fifteen catties of millet per month whereas those per teacher in 1943 were worth eighty catties of millet per month. However, other price data[11] imply that the rations of vegetables, meat, oil, and salt per worker in 1944 as listed by Stein exchanged for a much smaller quantity of grain. The same may be said of the normal rations of supplementary foods which appear in table 8.4.

(3) Clothing. Although the information on clothing is most sketchy, it suggests that the rations increased from the time when the Eighth Route Army was supplied by the national government in accordance with its norms, to the time when clothing for the public sector in the SKN border region was mostly own produced. Such a development seems to be indicated in particular for winter clothing, due to the fact that Chu Teh initiated in 1940 the production of woolen cloth by the public sector.

(4) Allowances. In contrast with some other items, most allowances may not have changed in real terms from 1938-1939 to 1943-1944. The payments of one to seven yuan pocket money per month in 1938 were equivalent to 10 to 70 catties of millet, according to table 7.3. They thus did not differ greatly from the 10-20 to 100 catties of millet per month which were paid as wages in public enterprises in 1944. Again, however, the data are too few for a firm impression.

In summary, information on the rations of supplementary foods and clothing tends to suggest improvements in living from 1938-1939 to 1943-1944 which the data of table 8.2 fail to indicate. However, both sets of materials are imprecise and incomplete. Ration changes during the crisis years have not been made public. On the assumption that all items of consumption were affected in equal proportion by the renewal of economic warfare, one may guess that the grain rations of soldiers declined to a minimum of thirty catties per month, that their clothing rations fell to two uniforms per year, etc. In spite of such reductions, the army probably continued to provide more food per soldier than the farm households used to consume per capita during 1930-31. However, the administrative organs and schools may have failed to meet this standard during 1940-1941.[12] By 1944, of course, all institutional households maintained their members at much higher levels. A comparison of tables 2.9 and 8.4 shows that supplementary foods were consumed in much larger quantities, in part due to institutional own production.

Tables 8.1 to 8.4 do not account for "noncommodity expenditures." The institutional households provided many cultural, educational, health care and other services collectively for their members—and often also for the private residents in their proximity.[13] Changes in the extent and the quality of such provisions have not been reported, but their development may be inferred from the cumulative effects of education which improved the capabilities of institutional household members in particular. A study of tables 4.6 and 4.7 suggests that these effects were substantial. As an important limitation to the provision of services, one must note the difficulties of obtaining—by importation or substitute production—the drugs and medicines essential to the successful practice of modern (western) medicine.[14]

Living in the Private Sector

While the level of living in the institutional households was to be maintained, regained, or improved, this objective was to be accomplished with a minimum of ill effects on the private sector. Indeed, the level of living in private households was to be raised as well, and the promotion of both private and public production served this purpose, too. According to Mao Tsetung:

> . . . if they [the institutional households] did not engage in production themselves, either they or the people would go hungry. Thanks to our production campaigns, we are free from hunger, and in fact the troops and the people are quite well fed.[15]

Mao's statement may well have described the situation in the SKN border region. However, in the case of the people, the supporting evidence is so incomplete and so problematic that the adequacy of their living conditions cannot be established satisfactorily.

Availability of essentials. There is little information that applies to the private population as a whole. In the absence of a more comprehensive measure, it is possible to discuss the availability of the most important consumer goods.

(1) Grains. By subtracting from the grain output estimates of table 6.3 the cost of production, estimated as 10 percent, plus the consumption of the public sector, reported as 120,000 piculs, one arrives at residuals which could be exported, accumulated, or consumed privately. The division of these residuals by the estimated private population yields potential per capita supplies of grain which appear in table 8.5.

The exportation of grain appears to have been a minor final use,[16] while the accumulation of grain reserves seems to have been an important objective, especially after 1943.[17] However, table 8.5 suggests that the estimated per capita residuals did not suffice to serve either end. Indeed, the potential per capita supplies were so limited that they failed to meet the standards of tables 2.9 and 8.4 by wide margins. The original grain production estimates account for potential intakes of from 75 to 80 percent of the 1930-31 average. The 1956 data allow for even less, viz., for from 60 to 75 percent of this bench mark. The reported consumption of 1,620,000 piculs of grain in 1943 and the accumulation of a surplus of 220,000 piculs implies similar relations.[18] The supposed surplus covered little more than the estimated cost of production, and the estimated consumption provided for less than one picul per capita in the private sector, after allowance has been made for the consumption of the public sector.

People who received grain in such limited quantities could not appear to have been "quite well fed," yet independent observers, too, gained the impression that the SKN border region did not experience food shortages during 1943-1944.[19] In the evident absence of food imports,[20] it is therefore likely that the authorities underestimated the output of grain, and substantially so. The probability of such errors in turn detracts from the significance of the pattern of change in the per capita residual which is in question by itself. The original grain production data imply that the potential per capita supplies declined during the crisis years, but much less than the rations in the public sector did. In contrast, the 1956 data imply that the grain available per capita of the private population increased continuously from 1938 to 1944. Interestingly, the seemingly plausible presence of a supply crisis according to the former data is traceable to a questionable decline in yield, and the seemingly surprising absence of a supply crisis according to the latter data is attributable to increases in cultivated land due to reclamation.[21]

(2) Supplementary foods. In the absence of systematic information on the production of supplementary foods, it was possible to estimate the output of two such items. Table 6.3 implied that the extraction of cotton oil increased rapidly with the development of cotton production.[22] Until 1944, however, the product did not suffice to meet the vegetable oil rations of the public sector.[23] As a consequence, nothing can be inferred in regard to the availability of cotton oil for private consumption.

Table 6.3 also allowed for guesses concerning the potential supplies of meat.[24] The consumption of the public sector, estimated as 2.4 million catties per annum,[25] may be subtracted from these totals. The residuals, which could be consumed as well as exported or disposed of otherwise,[26] may be divided by the population of the private sector. The results of these operations: 5.9 kg in 1941, 4.2 kg in 1942, 4.5 kg in 1943, and 7.2 kg in 1945, account for about half of the per capita consumption in the public sector,[27] but they exceed by far the 2.1 kg which table 2.9 shows a member of a farm household to consume on the average in 1930-31.

(3) Clothing. The availability of clothing materials cannot be determined because the imports of textiles and of textile fibers have not been reported. It is possible, however, to study the asserted autarky requirements of the region which may or may not have been met in fact. In 1941 it was estimated that the people's needs would be met by 150,000 to 200,000 bolts of

GUERRILLA ECONOMY

Table 8.5

AVAILABILITY OF GRAIN PER CAPITA OF THE PRIVATE POPULATION, 1937-1945

Unit: Kg of grain

Item	1937	1938	1939	1940	1941	1942	1943	1944	1945
Total population in million persons[a]	1.424	1.449	1.474	1.500	1.524	1.549	1.574	1.600	1.626
Grain available per capita[b]									
Original data	128.6	137.6	144.4		132.6	134.8	146.4	157.5	
1956 data	106.8	105.9	113.3	116.7	118.4	119.1	125.8	'136.4	121.8

a. Derived from chapter 2, note 20, by interpolation.
b. Estimate: 150 times (0.9 x output in piculs − 120,000 piculs)/total population. Derived from note a and table 6.3.

cloth. Underlying this calculation was the assumption that the people would make do with at most 0.3 bolt of local cloth per capita per annum.[28] On the premise that the requirements of the public sector did not change greatly, those of the private sector must have increased to somewhere near 250,000 bolts by 1944.[29] Much of the increase appears to have been attributable to a correction of the population estimate and to the growth of population rather than to a change in the clothing ration. In terms of 0.78 m wide cloth, the per capita requirement was placed at 0.15 bolts (4.85m) in 1941 and near 0.156 bolt (5.05 m) in 1944.[30] It thus approximated one-third of the per capita requirement in the public sector, which seems to have been 0.5 bolt.

According to the estimates of table 6.6, home industry in the SKN border region failed to supply such rations. Indeed, as late as in 1943 it was thought to produce merely 25 percent of the cloth requirements of the private sector. Of course, there is reason to believe that the output of home industry has been understated by the authorities, perhaps grossly so.[31] Moreover, its production was augmented by the importation of cotton and cotton products on a large, though unspecified, scale. As a result, the above standard may have been met during 1943-1944. It is also likely, however, that the supply problems of the crisis years affected both the public and the private sector. Information on the supply of clothing prior to the resumption of economic warfare is lacking, as are bench-mark data for the presoviet period.

In summary, then, it seems fair to say that the evidence on the provisioning of the private sector with grain, supplementary food, and clothing is too limited and too problematic to substantiate any specific impression or claim. The same appears to be true of the evidence on the availability of most services. The obvious exception to this rule is education, as tables 4.6 and 4.7 demonstrate, yet even its notable development seems to have had a very limited impact in the short run.[32]

Cooperative sales. Our estimates of per capita residuals of essentials may be supplemented with information on the value of sales by consumer cooperatives per member of the organization. Total cooperative sales are the most comprehensive meas-

ure known of the supply of goods other than basic foods (which
tended to be self-provided), and membership of consumer cooperatives has been reported. However, cooperators constituted an uncertain, though growing, fraction of the total private-
sector population, according to table 4.5, and the applicability
of the Yenan price indices of table 7.3 is in question. As a
consequence, one cannot be certain that the deflated sales per
cooperator are representative of real per capita change.

Sales by consumer cooperatives increased rapidly in current
prices, according to table 8.6, not only in *toto* but also per
cooperator. Yet most, if not all, of this expansion was inflationary. The sales per member deflated by the price index for
millet, which are more likely to indicate the member's "real"
cash income from agricultural production than any expenditure, remained almost constant from 1937 until 1941, when they
fell by about 8 percent, perhaps because agricultural taxation
increased during that year. Subsequent growth of sales in terms
of millet is so great that it must reflect not only probable increases in production and evident problems of deflation,[33] but
also efforts on the part of the government to stabilize the price
of the most basic good, which had been made the standard of
value in the region.

The sales per cooperator developed on a different pattern if
they are deflated by price indices for commodities which are
likely to have been items of expenditure. In all cases, "real"
sales per member declined drastically during the united front
period and rose again during the years of the production mass
campaign. However, both the magnitudes of change and the
turning points varied with the commodities considered. Table
8.6 indicates abrupt decreases in the value of sales in terms of
most commodities for which prices have been listed in table
7.3. The decline was least sudden in terms of salt, which was
being produced locally, and there was actually a temporary rise
in the cotton-fiber equivalent, perhaps because the region
could not at first make adequate use of the available cotton
supply. In terms of all commodities which could be produced
internally, cooperative sales per member fell by by 45 to 55
percent from 1937 to 1941/42. Their fine-cloth equivalent
dropped even more dramatically to 16 percent of the base year

amount in 1942. Their power to purchase other imports must have declined similarly, because average sales deflated by the price index for all commodities had their minimum already in 1940, i.e., before many goods became unavailable.

The "real" value of sales per member increased from 1942 to 1943 by all measures, but whereas it came to exceed the base year value in terms of all internally produced goods, and substantially so, it rose to less than half of that standard in terms of imported fine cloth. Divided by the annual average price index for all commodities, which solves problems of deflation but poses questions of weighting, sales per cooperator reached 74 percent of the 1937 value in 1943. Relative to 1939, of course, even this limited improvement was comparable to the change in the level of living which the soldiers of the SKN border region garrison experienced according to table 8.1. Subsequent developments could not be inferred.

Income by occupation. The data on the earnings of various occupational groups within the private sector are similarly incomplete and problematic. Nevertheless, they yield a number of insights which add to the picture of living conditions in the area.

(1) Income from farming. Comprehensive reports on the income of farm households (which accounted for close to 85 percent of the population in the private sector) could not be found, but estimates of their income from the production of grain may be formed in analogy to table 2.8. By subtracting from the total product the product of the institutional households, the cost of private production, and the public grain levy, one arrives at the sum of the factor incomes from the production of grain. The results of these operations appear in table 8.7, per capita of the estimated farm population.

A comparison of tables 2.8 and 8.7 suggests first of all that again both series of output estimates for the years 1937-1945 are deficient. The original data depict less progress in land reclamation than the 1956 data do, but the latter indicate the quality of the agricultural season even more inadequately than the former. As a consequence, both estimates fail to reach the output that had been produced most frequently according to Buck—a bench mark which production might be expected to have surpassed in the circumstances.

Table 8.6

SALES BY CONSUMER COOPERATIVES, 1937-1943

Unit: Yuan

| Year | Sales at current prices | | Sales per member deflated by price index for[c] | | | | | | | Millet equivalent[f] |
	Total[a]	Per member[b]	All commodities[d]	Fine cloth[e]	Home-spun[e]	Cotton fiber[e]	Pork[e]	Salt[e]	Millet[e]	
1937	261,689	4.52	4.52	4.52	4.52	4.52	4.52	4.52	4.52	27.1 kg
1938	391,282	5.87	4.10	2.50	2.95	5.34	2.54	3.58	4.59	27.5 kg
1939	552,249	6.66	2.81	1.77	3.20	4.44	2.16	3.89	4.47	26.8 kg
1940	1,156,435	9.38	1.88	0.75	2.35	2.66	3.05	2.66	4.51	27.1 kg
1941	6,493,399	46.31	2.11	0.91	2.54	2.53	2.59	2.07	4.17	25.0 kg
1942	34,932,109	243.06	2.46	0.71	2.19	2.13	2.17	2.48	6.25	37.5 kg
1943	600,000,000	4,000.00	3.34	2.07	6.96	5.22	6.79	9.98	22.28	133.7 kg

a. Hsü, A Survey, Part 2, p. 122.
b. Derived from note a and table 4.1.
c. Derived from note b and table 7.3.
d. Annual price average.
e. 1937, 1939-1943: June price average; 1938: December price average.
f. Sales of millet x 150 kg/25 yuan.

The comparison reveals also the impact of the changes in agricultural taxation. Contrasting table 2.8 to the original estimates for the years 1937-1939 in table 8.7 indicates the farm population's gain from the initial tax reduction. The 1956 data show in addition that the small increases in the potential per capita supply of grain to the private sector, which appeared in table 8.5, were associated during 1940 and 1941 with more substantial decreases in the farm sector's per capita income from grain production. The negation of a more general food crisis is thus compatible with the assertion of added hardship for the farm population. The subsequent tax reduction diminished this burden somewhat, and the growing public production of grain made its renewed imposition unnecessary.

The comparison of tables 2.8 and 8.7 fails to account for the likely influence of the land reform and rent reduction movements which—surprisingly—have not been reported in detail. It may be acceptable to ignore the payment of land rent during 1937-1939, even though it is evident that not all of the rental land in the original territory had been redistributed during soviet times.[34] After the territorial adjustments of 1939-1940, however, the area evidently contained such land in the newly incorporated hsien.[35] For lack of more specific information, one may guess that at most half of the original rental land within the new territorial limits had not been redistributed[36] and that rental land therefore accounted for 8.3 percent of the cultivated land. After the rent reduction campaign of 1943, the rental apparently averaged 35 percent of the grain product of the rental land.[38] Agriculture tax claimed 35 percent of the rental receipts.[39] By 1944, therefore, net rental income accounted for close to 23 percent of the grain product of the rented land and for 1.9 percent of the total output of grain. Its shares may have been somewhat higher prior to the rent reduction and tax revision of 1943.[40] In contrast, net rental income according to table 2.8 approximated 7.5 percent of the entire crop product in 1930-1931.

Because of the conflicting product estimates of tables 2.8 and 8.7, the comparison suggests unlikely changes in per capita grain income from 1930-1931 to 1937-1945. Even the original data for the years 1937-1939 may well understate the actual

Table 8.7

PRODUCTION AND DISTRIBUTION OF GRAIN PER CAPITA OF THE FARM POPULATION, 1937-1945

Unit: Kg of grain

Item	1937	1938	1939	1940	1941	1942	1943	1944	1945
Farm population in million persons [a]	1.179	1.200	1.220	1.282	1.303	1.324	1.346	1.368	1.390
Original grain data									
Product [b]	189.6	201.2	210.2		187.6	190.3	205.0	219.3	
public sector	0.0?	0.0?	1.7 [c]		1.8 [d]	3.1 [e]	4.3 [f]	11.0 [c]	
private sector [g]	189.6	201.2	208.5		185.8	187.2	200.7	208.3	
cost [h]	19.0	20.1	20.8		18.6	18.7	20.1	20.8	
tax [i]	1.8	2.0	6.4		23.0	18.7	20.0	17.5	
income [g]	168.8	179.1	181.3		144.2	149.8	160.6	170.0	

1956 grain data

Item	1937	1938	1939	1940	1941	1942	1943	1944	1945
Product [b]	160.3	158.8	168.4	167.3	169.2	169.9	178.3	191.9	172.7
public sector	0.0	0.0	1.7[c]	1.6	1.8[d]	3.1[e]	4.3[f]	11.0[c]	10.8[k]
private sector [g]	160.3	158.8	166.7	165.7	167.4	166.8	174.0	180.9	161.9
cost [h]	16.0	15.9	16.7	16.6	16.7	16.7	17.4	18.1	16.2
tax [i]	1.3	1.3	6.1	10.5	23.0	18.1	20.0	17.5	13.5
income [g]	143.0	141.6	143.9	138.6	127.7	132.0	136.6	145.3	132.2

a. Estimate. 1937-1939: 0.828 times total population; 1940-1945: 0.855 times total population. Derived from tables 2.3 and 8.5.

b. Derived from note a and table 6.3.

c. Derived from note a and table 7.6.

d. Derived from *ibid.* Estimate: total production in 1941 equals total production in 1939 plus 0.1 times land newly reclaimed by army.

e. Estimate: average, 1941 plus 1943.

f. Derived from note a and table 7.6. Estimate: total production in 1943 equals 31,000 times 100,000/80,000 piculs.

g. Residual.

h. Estimate: 0.1 times private sector product.

i. Derived from note a and table 7.5.

j. Estimate: total product the same as in 1939.

k. Estimate: total product the same as in 1944.

improvement,[41] but they at least place the income in kind near 500 grams per capita per diem, i.e., the average daily intake of grain during the poor year 1930-1931, according to Table 2.9. The per capita income falls drastically thereafter and approaches this level once more in 1944 according to the original data. Yet it fails to come anywhere near it at any time according to the 1956 data. Instead, the latter imply averages which are less than or equal to the disastrously low income from grain production in 1930-1931. The implicit potential intakes of 350 to 400 grams of grain per capita per diem fall 20 to 30 percent short of the minimum consistent with a state of being "quite well fed." It thus appears again that the official output estimates understate the actual production of grain considerably.[42]

Of course, income from grain production does not account for all of the farm income. Other crops and animal husbandry added to it substantially. In the absence of adequate data, it is merely possible to reiterate the bench-mark relations and to suggest likely changes in proportions. In 1930-1931, grains contributed 97.1 percent of the total crop product, and income from cropping provided 77.0 or 78.6 percent of the income from farming, depending on whether reference is made to the original or the adjusted territory. By either measure, close to three-fourths of the income from farming were attributable to grain production. Its relative share appears to have been greater yet during the late thirties, due to both the decrease in taxation and the decimation of the animal stock. The share probably declined during the early forties to its "normal" level because of the increase in taxation as well as the rehabilitation of the animal stock. And it may have fallen below this level by 1943-1944 in response to the development of cotton production.

In summary, it must be stressed that the actual income changes remain uncertain. In order to appear quite well fed, the farm population surely had to consume at least 180 kg of grain and earn at least 240 kg of grain equivalent per capita per annum. The latter required an income near 500 kg of grain or its equivalent per employed person per annum. One may assume such an income level for 1944, for instance. One also may use this level as a base and relate to it the index of per capita income from grain production which can be derived from the 1956 data in table 8.7. One even may suspect that the income from farming is understated by this procedure, but one should remember, too, that these are merely guesses.

(2) Income from subsidiary activities. According to table 2.8 subsidiary activities contributed close to 25 percent of the total income of farm households in 1930-1931. Comparable reports for the years 1937-1945 are lacking. In their absence, a review of the changes in the major kinds of subsidiary work and income may suggest the directions of change. Table 2.3 lists as the predominant subsidiary occupations in the order of their numerical importance in 1930-1931 those of merchant, home industry worker, and farm laborer. Other skilled and unskilled workers, which come next in the enumeration, were clearly less numerous.

It has been noted previously that the development of marketing as a subsidiary activity remains somewhat uncertain. On the one hand, increases in agricultural production could be expected to result in increasing sales of agricultural products, but increasing agricultural taxation in kind plus the growing subsistence production in the public sector tended to offset and perhaps even reverse this development. Cooperative marketing systems, which grew in scope, also attempted to limit commercial profits. In addition, however, these organizations tried to economize efforts in marketing and to facilitate shifts to nonagricultural production activities such as home spinning and weaving. It has been shown that this promotion was quite effective. As a consequence, it is reasonable to assume that the income from subsidiary work increased with the output of subsidiary products, such as yarn and cloth, but the magnitude of this gain cannot be guessed with confidence.[43] In the case of marketing, even the direction of change in income is not clear.[44]

Income from farm work as a subsidiary occupation seems to have fallen for two reasons. First, both the need and the opportunity for such employment must have declined due to the initial land reform and because of the subsequent formation of labor aid groups. Second, the stickiness of wages, which accounted for unusually high earnings during the deflationary period 1931-1936, may have reflected itself in rapidly declining real wages during the subsequent period of wartime inflation. Tables 8.8A and 8.8B indicate this development not for farm laborers but for common household laborers and for one location, Yang Chia K'ou in Michih Hsien.[45] There the real wages of laborers on annual contracts fell drastically—in the case of female laborers so much that they hardly provided pocket money.[46] Moreover, the annual lump-sum payments for laundering, which apparently did not involve board, dropped similarly, according to the records of Ma Wei-hsin. The following payments in kind were made for it (in kg per annum).[47]

Year	Millet	Black Beans	Millet Equivalent of black beans[a]	Millet plus equivalent
1937	30	15	6.56	36.56
1938	30	15	7.06	37.06
1939	30	15	7.67	37.67
1940	30	15	10.43	40.43
1941	15	15	8.33	23.33
1942	7.5	15	5.79	13.29

a. Derived from Yenan nung-ts'un tiao-ch'a t'uan, *Mi-chih hsien*, p. 149.

The real wages of laborers on daily contracts did not decrease correspondingly but fluctuated instead. As a consequence, there occurred a shift from annual contracts to daily contracts which tended to benefit the laborers per diem but not necessarily per annum. Indeed, Ma Wei-hsin's wages bill appears to have declined for this reason as well as because there was a shift from male to female labor which even allowed for an increase in the number of workdays.[48]

The real wages of craftsmen (carpenters, masons, and blacksmiths) in Yang Chia K'ou, all of whom appear to have been paid by the day, changed as the real wages of common day laborers did. They fell strongly from the deflationary period 1931-1936 to the following inflationary period, but they also fluctuated rather than declined during the latter years. Estimates of craftsmen's annual earnings require guesses concerning the number of days of employment. In the extreme, one may assume that the craftsmen worked 360 days per annum. In addition, one may hold that they received supplementary payments in kind as the farm laborers did in 1930-1931 according to table 11. Such premises yield income estimates for the years 1937-1941 which come close to the net value added in handicraft production during the early 1930s according to table 2.12. In contrast, the earnings data for urban craftsmen and tradesmen suggest that the incomes may have been much lower.[49] Reports for the years 1942-1945 are lacking, but it seems reasonable to assume that the import-substitution campaigns affected handicraft employment and income positively.

In summary, it is difficult to weigh the effects of the diverse developments that could be noted, none of which is quite certain by itself. There appears to have been a shift from marketing and agricultural wage-laboring to nonagricultural production, but the balance of the employment effect must be guessed. There also seems to have been a high degree of constancy in the trend of daily wages for skilled and unskilled labor in one location, but the annual wages of unskilled labor *ibidem* tended to fall. Information on the returns to marketing could not be found. Only the income from home spinning and weaving increased without doubt. On the basis of such evidence, one may guess that the contribution of subsidiary activities to the income of farm households remained at least as great as in 1930-1931, when it had been equivalent to 58 kg of grain per capita according to our estimate.[50] One may also guess that the income from this source increased, perhaps to as much as 80 kg of grain per capita per annum. But guess one must.

(3) Income from salt extraction. The earnings of salt producers, who accounted for very small shares of the total labor force and population, have not been reported systematically either. Besides publicizing the material gains of a few labor heroes, the SKN border region government did announce on one occasion the (gross?) receipts and tax burdens of all the salt producers in Kaochih, which was one of the four primary salt

Table 8.8.A
AVERAGE DAILY AND ANNUAL WAGES IN SELECTED OCCUPATIONS, 1931-1942

Unit: Yuan

Occupation by location	1931-1936	1937	1938	1939	1940	1941	1942
Average daily wages net of board							
Yang Chia K'ou [a]							
Carpenter	0.223	0.25	0.35	0.32	1.00	2.50	
Mason	0.235	0.30		0.40	1.00	4.25	
Blacksmith	1.000	1.00	1.00		8.00 ?		
Laborer, male	0.133	0.10	0.20	0.25	0.65	2.50	5.50
Laborer, female	0.034 [b]			0.044	0.08	0.12	
Yenan City [c]							
Bricklayer	0.225 [d]		0.45		1.10		
Yenan Hsien [e]							
Farm laborer				0.40	0.65		
Craftsman				0.50	1.00		

Table 8.8.A *(continued)*

Unit: Yuan

Occupation by location	1931-1936	1937	1938	1939	1940	1941	1942
Average annual wages net of board							
Yang Chia K'ou [a]							
Laborer, male	32.7	44	52	54	94	220	580
Laborer, female	11.0		9.6		9.6	12.25	12
Yenan Hsien [e]							
Farm laborer				62.5	112.5		
Shepherd				15	40		

a. Yenan nung-ts'un tiao-ch'a t'uan, *Mi-chih hsien*, pp. 128-129.
b. 1936 data.
c. *Shan Kan Ning 1939-1941*, p. 46.
d. 1932 data.
e. *Ibid.*, pp. 46-47.

Table 8.8.B

MILLET EQUIVALENT OF WAGES IN SELECTED OCCUPATIONS, 1931-1942 [a]

Unit: Kg

Occupation by location	1931-1936	1937	1938	1939	1940	1941	1942
Average daily wages net of board							
Yang Chia K'ou							
Carpenter	3.1	1.6	2.2	0.9	1.9	1.7	
Mason	3.3	1.9		1.1	1.9	2.8	
Blacksmith	13.9	6.3	6.3		15.1		
Laborer, male	1.9	0.6	1.3	0.7	1.2	1.7	1.2
Laborer, female	0.3			0.1	0.15	0.08	
Yenan City							
Bricklayer	(4.2)		2.1 [b]		2.0 [b]		
Yenan Hsien							
Farm laborer				1.1	1.2		
Craftsman				1.4	1.9		

Table 8.8.B *(continued)*

Unit: Kg

Occupation by location	1931-1936	1937	1938	1939	1940	1941	1942
Average annual wages net of board							
Yang Chia K'ou							
Laborer, male	454	275	325	154	177	147	124
Laborer, female	85		60		18	8	3
Yenan Hsien							
Farm laborer				179	212		
Shepherd				43	75		

a. Derived from tables 8.8.A, 2.11, and Yenan nung-ts'un tiao-ch'a t'uan, *Mi-chih hsien*, p. 149.
b. Derived from tables 8.8.A, 2.11, and 7.3.

producing areas.[51] The data appear in table 8.9. The source fails to provide estimates of the cost of production. At the June price, which probably understates the annual average price considerably, salt producers in Kaochih in 1943 had revenues after taxes of 2,256 kg of grain per capita. It may be assumed that similar revenues were common in other locations and during other years. In contrast, the living conditions of most salt producers prior to the soviet period were said to have been dismal.[52] A definite improvement is thus indicated, which also seems to reflect the priority assigned to salt production.[53]

(4) Income from other occupations. Information on the earnings of urban craftsmen, tradesmen, merchants, and other gainfully occupied persons, who together accounted for perhaps 10 percent of the private labor force, is most sketchy. Almost all of the available data concern the initial period. In 1939 the SKN border region government reported relative increases in wages net of payments in kind from unspecified prerevolutionary times to 1938 for selected occupations and locations. The former ranged from 15 to 30 percent, the latter from 50 to 100 percent.[54] In contrast, the price of wheat doubled during this interval, and the price of millet increased even more.[55] As a consequence, real wages declined, just as they did in the countryside. In the eight locations listed, daily wages averaged 0.184 yuan in prerevolutionary times and 0.322 yuan in 1938. Both averages are low in comparison with the data of tables 2.11 and 8.8.A,[56] which refer mostly to rural wages.

Another source, which reported daily wages of 0.30 to 0.40 and even 0.50 yuan for 1938, announced in addition the annual earnings presented in table 8.10. A comparison of these data with those of tables 2.11 and 8.8.A indicates that the cash earnings of most urban craftsmen and tradesmen exceeded those of the farm laborers by little if at all. Their per capita incomes probably differed similarly. Payments in kind on the pattern of table 2.11 may have added substantially to the earnings of all. In most instances, however, they apparently failed to raise them to the level of net value added during the early 1930s as estimated in table 2.12. The evident discrepancies between these two sets of data may be attributable to differences between the assumed numbers of workdays.

Table 8.9

RECEIPTS AND TAX PAYMENTS OF SALT PRODUCERS IN KAOCHIH, 1943

Receipts, tax payments	All households		Per household	Per capita
	SKN yuan [a]	kg of millet [b]	kg of millet [c]	kg of millet [d]
Subsidiary	8,000,000	267,380	1,385	457
Salt sales	33,000,000	1,102,941	5,715	1,885
Total receipts	41,000,000	1,370,321	7,100	2,342
Tax payments	1,500,000	50,134	260	86
Residual	39,500,000	1,320,187	6,840	2,256

a. *Salt Production*, p. 9.
b. Derived from table 7.3. Price: 29.92 yuan per kg.
c. Total divided by 193 households.
d. Total divided by 585 household members.

Table 8.10

ANNUAL CASH WAGES IN SELECTED OCCUPATIONS, APPARENTLY IN 1938.[a]

Occupations	Yuan	Kg of millet [b]
Blacksmiths, tailors, restaurant workers	100	500
Other craftsmen	50-60	250-300
Special store employees	130-140	650-700
Common store employees	40/50-70/80	225-375
Apprentices	8-12	40-60

a. Ch'i Li, *Shan Kan Ning pien ch'ü shih-lu,* p. 92.
b. Derived from table 7.3. Estimate: 0.20 yuan per kg.

Data for subsequent years are almost entirely lacking. Table 8.8.B contains a wage quotation for bricklayers in Yenan City in 1940 which points to constant real wages since 1938. Stein inquired into the fortunes of a few merchants in Yenan City and reported claims of great improvements from prerevolutionary times to 1944.[57] In the same year the SKN border region government asserted that urban craftsmen had experienced increases in *real* wages of 149.5 to 400 percent since the prewar period, without specifying either the initial or the eventual wages.[58] Information on the earnings of domestic servants in nonfarm households could not be found. It may be assumed, however, that they were similar to those of laborers in farm households as they appear in table 8.8.A and 8.8.B. The earnings of members of the professions, who constituted the largest segment of the employed nonfarm population in table 2.10, but who could not be accounted for in table 5.2, remain completely unknown.

In summary, the data simply do not suffice to reach firm conclusions about the income level in the private nonfarm sector and its development. It is therefore impossible to appraise claims of early hardships and subsequent improvements in response to the development of production, even though these claims may well be true.

Income Redistribution

Besides attempting to maintain and improve the levels of living in the public as well as in the private sector, the Chinese communists tried to change the structures of income in both sectors, for evident reasons. Limiting the members of the institutional households to small income differentials and to popular income levels served to keep them "close to the masses." But it also kept the cost of public service low, thereby presumably keeping the masses close to them. By taking a large share of the income (and initially the wealth) of the rich in the private sector, the Chinese communists could meet this cost as well as relieve the poor prior to the development of production. Moreover, in order to develop production sufficiently, they provided additional incentives to the producers in the forms of tax exemptions and rent reductions, which have been listed before. Unfortunately, it once again is problematic to specify the effects of such measures on the structure of incomes.

Public sector. The extraordinary reduction of income differentiation in the public sector has been discussed previously on two occasions. Chapter 4 dealt with the incentive problems which it posed,[59] and determining the level of living in the public sector involved comparisons of tables 2.12 and 8.2. Most revealing in the latter was the indication that the pay of common soldiers doubled while the average earnings of public officials halved during the change from prerevolutionary times to the period of the anti-Japanese war. The army's unusual degree of income equalization is also obvious from the following statement by Evans Carlson:

> Both of these armies [the Eighth Route Army and the New Fourth Army] were paid in accordance with the Central Government pay schedule (ranging from $7 a month for privates to several hundred dollars for the commander), but they disbursed the funds according to their own pay schedule ($1 per month for

fighters up to $6 per month for Commander-in-Chief Chu Teh). The difference went into a fund for the purchase of food, medical supplies and for the maintenance of Partisan troops, for which no provision was made by the Central Government.[60]

Since the cost of food appears to have been 4.5 yuan per month at that time,[61] the outlay per soldier of the Eighth Route Army tended to approach the national government norm, but the outlay per officer was at most twice the outlay per soldier, contrary to that norm. As a rule, the ratio appears to have been less than 2:1, and officers as well as men thus lived "close to the masses." Similar relations have been found for the employees of the newly formed public factories. Here the workers tended to receive as much in 1943, according to table 8.2, as craftsmen had earned in the early 1930s, according to table 2.12. Managers and technicians received more than that, according to table 8.3, but usually less than twice as much, again apparently in contrast with earnings relations outside the SKN border region. Forman's report of the ratios 4:3:2 between the wages of foremen or department chiefs, skilled workers, and apprentices may be indicative of the prevailing differences.[62] Table 8.2 indicates in addition that the differentiation of earnings within segments of the state administrative apparatus (communications workers) and in the school system was similarly limited, also doubtlessly in contrast with the practices elsewhere.[63]

Farm sector. Changes in the structure of income in the farm sector were attributable primarily to three causes: the land reform in the initial territory during the soviet period; the rent reduction in the territory incorporated during 1939-1940; and the institution of the unified agriculture tax in its successive versions. Temporary tax exemptions for cotton growers, immigrants, etc. were of secondary importance because they tended to affect relatively small numbers of people. The same was probably true of free land reclamation generally.

The redistributive effect of the initial land reform is hard to estimate in the absence of information on the scope of the reform. If the data of tables 2.5 and 2.8 are taken as indications, rental land accounted for 16.4 percent of the initial farm area.[64]

On the assumption that the landlords retained land in proportion to their rural population share of less than 1 percent,[65]
more than 15.4 percent of the entire farm area must have
changed owners during the reform. On the additional assumption that 50 percent of the product of the rental land used to be
collected as rent, at least 7.7 percent of the entire crop product
must have accrued to new owners after the reform. The pattern
of redistribution has not been discussed in detail, but it has
been mentioned that the primary beneficiaries were poor peasants and farm laborers, who apparently accounted for the majority of the rural population. As a result of such redistribution,
many of them in fact became middle peasants according to
several rural surveys.[66] The land reform thus changed the class
structure as well as the structure of income in the countryside.

The redistributive effect of rent reduction was evidently
much more limited. If after the territorial changes rental land
accounted for 8.3 percent of all the cultivated land and if rents
fell from 50 percent to 35 percent of the primary product of the
rental land,[67] then at least 1.24 percent of the total primary
crop was reallocated from landlords to tenants by means of
rent reduction. Table 2.5 suggests further that this redistribution may have benefitted more than just poor peasants.[68]

The redistributive effect of changes in the system of agricultural taxation cannot be calculated in the aggregate, for lack
of information on the actual distribution of income in the SKN
border region. However, the impositions on various peasant
classes have been reported for four locations in 1943, two of
which had not experienced land reform. By relating these peasant class rates to the tax rate schedules of table 7.4, it is possible
to reconstruct average class incomes before and after taxes for
three of these four locations.[69] The results, which appear in
table 8.11, are precarious in at least one respect. Landlords
were taxed more heavily, according to table 8.11, than the
schedules of table 7.4 permitted. As a consequence, landlord
incomes had to be estimated. They have been set at 1,500
catties of grain per capita per annum.

Peasant households were classified as either *rich* or *rich middle* or *middle* or *poor* in all locations, yet the standards of
wealth or poverty differed substantially from place to place.
Within each locality, of course, the income differences and

Table 8.11

THE EFFECT OF PROGRESSIVE TAXATION ON THE PER CAPITA INCOMES OF VARIOUS PEASANT CLASSES, 1943.

Location and peasant class	Income before taxes		Tax rate percent of income[c]	Income after taxes	
	index[a]	catties of grain[b]		catties of grain[d]	index[e]
Yenan Hsien, Yaotien Ch'ü[f]					
Rich peasants	2.300	605	22.17	471	1.938
Rich middle peasants	2.247	591	21.38	465	1.913
Middle peasants	1.711	450	16.01	378	1.555
Poor peasants	1.000	263	7.78	243	1.000
Chingyang Hsien[g]					
Landlords	4.983 ?	1,500 ?	41.50	877 ?	3.166 ?
Rich peasants	2.780	837	30.80	579	2.090
Rich middle peasants	2.322	699	25.30	522	1.884
Middle peasants	1.847	556	19.09	450	1.624
Poor peasants	1.000	301	8.05	277	1.000

Table 8.11 *(continued)*

Location and peasant class	Income before taxes		Tax rate percent of income[c]	Income after taxes	
	index[a]	catties of grain[b]		catties of grain[d]	index[e]
Suite Hsien, Tsutien Ch'ü[h]					
Landlords	7.281?	1,500?	36.50	952?	4.857?
Rich peasants	2.611	538	18.94	436	2.224
Rich middle peasants	1.980	408	13.59	353	1.801
Middle peasants	1.475	304	9.25	276	1.408
Poor peasants	1.000	206	4.85	196	1.000

a. Derived from catties of grain.
b. Derived from note c and *Ching-chi yen-chiu*, No. 2 (1956), p. 105.
c. See *ibid.*, p. 112.
d. Derived from incomes before taxes and tax rates.
e. Derived from catties of grain.
f. Tax rate schedule A of table 7.4.
g. Tax rate schedule B of table 7.4.
h. Tax rate schedule C of table 7.4.

differentials between the classes were also very great. The traditional system of agricultural taxation did not affect this pattern of differentiation significantly because it imposed the tax on land in accordance with its quality, i.e., its ability to produce income. The abolition of this system during the soviet period by itself did not change the structure either. But the introduction of the progressive income tax had a drastic effect, at least after 1941. A comparison of the indices of income before and after taxes in 1943, which appear in the first and final columns of table 8.11, demonstrates this point.

In the case of the landlords, the impact of the change to progressive income taxes was enormous. Moreover, it combined with the effect of simultaneous rent reductions. If the 1,500 catties in table 8.11 constitute 35 percent of the primary crop of rental land, the rent receipts prior to their reduction may be placed at 2,143 catties, on the basis of previous assumptions. Before their land became part of the border region, landlords may have had to pay 10 percent of this amount as land tax.[70] By 1943 they had to give up 56 or 59 percent of their original incomes to their tenants and to the government, depending on whether they lived in Suite or in Chingyang.

In summary, it appears that the income differentials between various rural classes narrowed substantially in response to the land reform, rent reduction, and progressive taxation. It also seems evident, however, that the farm sector did not achieve the extreme degree of income equalization which was characteristic of the public sector.

Nonfarm sector. The available information on income differentials in the nonfarm sector is inconclusive. Tables 8.8.A and 8.10 imply relations for selected occupations and skills which suggest that the differences between the wages in most crafts and trades were relatively small, especially when allowance is made for the fact that payments in kind have been omitted. Table 8.8.A intimates further that the differentials between common laborers and some craftsmen diminished during 1937-1941. Comparable information for subsequent years is lacking, and there is no information at all on the earnings of self-employed craftsmen and tradesmen, their relations to the wages of employees, changes in these relations, etc. The same is true of earnings in the professions.

Intersectoral relations. A comparison of the data for the public, private farm, and private nonfarm sectors suffers from the unevenness of the available information, but it points to several important changes in the structure of incomes in the SKN border region. As a result of the income equalization in the public sector, income differentials between the public officials and the mass of the people diminished greatly. Yet the incomes of common soldiers, which in presoviet times had been comparable to the incomes of common peasants, farm laborers, and domestic servants, apparently rose to twice that level during the good year 1938, remained above the original bench mark during the hard years 1940-1941, and regained the 1938 level by 1943. Peasant incomes in general, which probably fell less drastically than those of common soldiers during the hard years, by all indications did not improve to a similar degree.[71] It was only the earnings of special segments, such as the salt producers, that tended to become as large.

Correspondingly, the incomes of workers in the state-operated industrial enterprises, which were as high as the estimated earnings of craftsmen had been in presoviet times, seem to have been twice as high as the incomes of most craftsmen and common store employees in 1938. Only the incomes in a few crafts or trades and the wages of special employees appear to have come close to this level.[72] If the real wages of urban craftsmen increased as dramatically as has been claimed,[73] the worker-craftsman differential must have diminished greatly after 1938 and could have disappeared by 1944. However, for lack of evidence, it is impossible to demonstrate this development in absolute terms.

The evident changes in the structure of incomes add a new perspective to the equalitarianism in the public sector. By maintaining an unusually high level of living by local standards for all of its members, the SKN border region government in fact rewarded the majority of common soldiers, factory workers, and also students. It thus provided substantial material incentives in favor of three of the four priority sectors. The wage data for communications workers suggest in addition that the lower ranking employees in the fourth sector, public administration, may have been remunerated comparatively well, too. It was only the higher ranking cadres in all four sectors who were both absolutely and relatively less well provided for than the public officials had been during presoviet times. In their case, however, ideological incentives were probably fully effective. Such were the limits to the "mass line," according to the available evidence.

Accumulation of Surplus

The Chinese communists concerned themselves with the distribution of income not only for reasons relating to consumption but also and especially in the interest of producing and accumulating surplus. Indeed, the creation of surplus in various forms may be identified as their principal objective and the true measure of their success.[74] The development of production, which of course was essential for the maintenance or improvement of living standards, in view of the growing isolation of the SKN border region, required increases and improvements in the means and methods of production. Most of the additional tools and skills had to be produced internally, thus giving rise to the accumulation of surplus in relatively primitive forms. The consequent wellbeing of the people in turn promised to help create more output as well as more surplus in similar forms. Surplus thus governed the process of expansion which was to bring about the liberation of China.

Material accumulation. Changes in the capital stock of the SKN border region have been discussed in connection with the development of production in chapter 6. The incompleteness of the data renders any estimate of the overall rate of accumulation questionable. However, fairly firm impressions could be formed for some of the sectors.

(1) Agriculture. In the agricultural sector, which accounted for most of the population as well as for most of the output, capital formation in kind progressed fairly rapidly, more so in the case of crop growing than in the case of animal husbandry, as the following tabulation of average annual growth rates indicates:[75]

	1940-1945	1942-1945
Cultivated land	4.0%	5.3%
Oxen plus donkeys	4.2%	3.5%
Sheep	2.6%	2.8%

The construction of new irrigation facilities apparently added very little to the capital stock in agriculture.[76] Changes in the quantity and quality of tools, structures, etc. have not been reported in any detail. Moreover, the values of most increases cannot be determined directly. On the assumption that the incremental capital-output ratio in agriculture was near 2:1, one may infer from the grain production data that accumulation absorbed about 10 percent of the sector product during 1940-1944 and perhaps 15 percent of it during 1943-1944.[77]

(2) Salt extraction. The construction of salt fields and related facilities seems to have added greatly to the existing capacity. In contrast with the development in agriculture, however, the effort seems to have been concentrated on 1941, when the value added in capital construction may have been as great as the value added in salt production.[78] During 1939-1943 on the average accumulation accounted for close to 30 percent of the sector product, again on the premise that the incremental capital-output ratio was 2:1.[79] Moreover, its contribution to total accumulation was not so small either. At 1943 prices, the average annual addition to the capital stock during 1939-1943 was equivalent to 63,168 piculs of millet,[80] i.e., to perhaps 30 percent of the apparent capital formation in agriculture.

(3) Manufacturing and mining. The capital stock in manufacturing and mining grew with similar rapidity and also primarily prior to 1942. According to tables 6.8 and 6.9, state plus CIC enterprises together invested the equivalents of 41,868 piculs of millet in 1940 and of 14,044 piculs of millet in 1941. The additions in 1938 and in 1939 appear to have been equally large. Investment in industry thus accounted for 10 or more percent of the capital formation in agriculture during those years, but it seems to have diminished substantially thereafter to perhaps 5,000 piculs per annum, or less than 3 percent of the capital formation in agriculture.

(4) Road construction and transportation. The investment in roads and transport facilities, which occurred primarily during 1940-1942, cannot be approximated satisfactorily. The value of the outlay for construction materials is uncertain.[81] The maximum annual input of 4,500 man-years for road work was equivalent to 15,000-27,000 piculs of millet. The actual inputs of 1942

and 1943 were merely 2,040 piculs and 450 piculs, respectively.[82] Investment in roads thus appears to have been much less than investment in industry. The investment in pack animals has been counted already, and the value of other items cannot be ascertained.

A part of the capital stock in manufacturing and mining, transport, etc., which came from outside the SKN border region prior to the renewal of the blockade, was financed with central government and CIC grants. But the remainder and in particular all basic construction had to be accumulated internally in kind. The redistribution of income facilitated such spending in several ways. Rent and tax reductions or exemptions provided added incentives for peasants to engage in such construction; increasing tax revenues sustained the efforts of cadres, soldiers, students, and workers who undertook similar projects collectively; and high taxes plus low rents kept the landlords from disposing of their income as unproductively as in the past.[83] As a result of these changes, the overall rate of accumulation for the border region probably increased markedly over any prerevolutionary level. Moreover, growing inventory accumulation, the effort to save one year's crop in order to guard against famine and prepare for the counteroffensive, must have raised this rate still more.

Nonmaterial accumulation. By maintaining or improving most people's living standard in the SKN border region, material accumulation sustained the large variety of educational efforts which have been described in chapter 4. After the educational reform of 1942, most of these programs aimed particularly at expanding and improving production—by increasing the commitment as well as the technical know-how of all producers. In addition, however, during the years 1937-1945 the educational institutions of the border region trained more than 40,000 political and military cadres, plus thousands of cultural and technical cadres for the other liberated areas.[84] Such numbers may appear small in comparison with the more than 800,000 employed persons estimated to have lived in the SKN territory.[85] Nevertheless, their training may well have been Yenan's most important contribution to the conduct of the anti-Japanese war and more generally to the growth of the Chinese communist movement.

Summary

The strategy of the Chinese communists had significant distributive consequences according to all indications, but unfortunately, these indications are once again so few that many alleged changes in incomes and expenditures could not be reviewed in a meaningful way.

The levels of income and living in the public sector were comparable to presoviet times in 1938 and 1943, but they declined severely when the blockade was reimposed, then grew again on account of public production. The compensation for low-ranking members of the public sector rose while that for high-ranking members fell relative to prerevolutionary times, so that the degree of intrasectoral income differentiation diminished drastically.

The levels of income and living in the farm sector may have remained more stable during the years 1937-1945 as well as more comparable to the prerevolutionary period, but the inadequacy of the farm product data prevents a demonstration of this continuity in a conclusive form. Income from subsidiary work may have increased due to the development of home industry, but the balance of employment in subsidiary work is uncertain. Income differentials within the farm sector decreased substantially due to three important measures: the land reform in the original territory; the rent reduction in the newly incorporated areas; and the progressive taxation of incomes in all parts of the SKN border region.

The levels of income and living in the private nonfarm sector could not be determined with confidence. The few wages data suggest that persons on annual contracts may have experienced income losses due to progressing inflation while persons on daily contracts tended to keep their own. The annual number of workdays per craftsman may have increased as a result of the production campaign, and this increase may have been large enough to eliminate the apparent difference between annual net values added in presoviet times and wages earned in 1938. The information on intrasectoral income differentials is inconclusive, but it is probable that members of several traditional professions experienced setbacks comparable to those affecting the landlords.

All of these changes served to restructure incomes in favor of a few priority occupations, most of which were public, and in favor of the poor in all sectors. Improvements occurred especially in the living of soldiers relative to that of peasants and in the living of public manufacturing workers relative to that of private craftsmen, unless the latter gained greatly as a result of the production campaign. In contrast, the rewards for higher public office declined along with the returns to absentee ownership of land, money-lending, etc. Communist cadres could be expected to welcome this more equal distribution of income, and it was hoped that landlords would accept it, too.[86]

Finally, the restructuring of incomes affected not only the people's consumption but also the government's accumulation of surplus, which must be viewed as the critical variable. Most of the capital formation served to sustain the people of the SKN border region or to improve their sustenance, but part of the added output of consumer goods became a strategic reserve for offensive military operations. Another small part supported the training of experts for the anti-Japanese war, and this contribution to the growth of the Chinese communist movement appears to have been the SKN border region's most important accomplishment.

IX

Yenan
and the Yenan Period

Those cadres, experts, and troops who could be spared moved out to carry the struggle for liberation behind Japanese lines. In this endeavor they were to make use of what they had been taught: the lessons of Kiangsi, the Long March, and Yenan. The Chinese communists' strategy of military, political, economic, and cultural development, which had been formulated so laboriously and which was being implemented so comprehensively in the SKN border region, thus became a guide to action on a far grander scale. But did it serve this wider purpose well?

The reason for concern is readily apparent. The SKN border region was an extremely small part of China—an area of close to 100,000 square kilometers with about 1.5 million inhabitants, a garrison of at most 50,000 troops, and a peculiar resource base. Moreover, it was Free China's "little rear," which was well delineated and territorially stable at most times. It also had been under communist domination longest, even had experienced land reform, and had instituted elaborate formal organizational structures. In addition, it had benefited from free trade and outside aid during a brief but important interlude. Finally, as the central headquarters area and the model base of the Chinese communists, it both generated and received unusual publicity and attention. Characteristics such as these made the SKN border region an ideal object of strategy as well as of study.

In contrast, the base areas behind Japanese lines proliferated from very small beginnings to such an extent that early in 1945 they consisted of eighteen units with 95.5 million inhabitants,

910,000 regular troops, and two million local defense forces.[1] Much of this territory was being contested and fluctuated in size. Many parts had been liberated for brief periods of time, none had been exposed to land reform, and few had been penetrated organizationally to a comparable degree. The united-front windfalls did not reach that far, and the immigrating organizers had to spread themselves thin. However, practically all of the residents at one time or the other had been affected personally by the Japanese occupation. In many respects, the situation behind Japanese lines thus resembled that of the Kiangsi Soviet, which had inspired the strategy but had derived limited benefits from it, since it had to be abandoned as a base.

The different circumstances in the base areas behind Japanese lines could account for different experiences, but they also render inquiries highly problematic. The unspecified territorial fluctuations in particular preclude the calculation of bench-mark estimates on the pattern of chapter 2, and they also inhibited the systematic reporting of most social and economic indicators. It therefore appears impossible to match the presentations of chapters 4 to 8, even if no efforts are made to contrast the developments with norms for the prewar period.

Alternatively, it might be possible to study a cross-section of many small component areas of the eighteen bases, which found themselves in various stages of transition toward an ultimate state of complete consolidation. Such an approach should be expected to reveal that the core components of the bases, which were relatively secure for longer periods of time, tended to resemble the SKN border region during the final phase of the war. It should also be anticipated that the peripheral areas, which were insecure and which in many instances had come under communist influence more recently, would be more similar to the SKN border region during its formative phase—apart from differences due to active warfare. Unfortunately, it appears that most of the available information refers to the more consolidated core territory of the base areas, which were unlikely to exhibit substantial differences.

Short of such a cross-section study, which goes well beyond the scope of this inquiry, it is possible to deal with the problem of strategic continuity and effectiveness in a more impression-istic fashion. To this end, one may draw in particular on the accounts of Westerners who had occasion to pass through some of the base areas, notably through parts of the Shansi-Chahar-Hopei Border Region, the Shansi-Hopei-Honan Border Region, and the Shansi-Suiyuan Border Region. Reference may be made to Carlson's description of his tours as a military at-taché at the beginning of the war,[2] to the travelog of the Bands on their escape from Peking to Yenan after Pearl Harbor,[3] to Forman's report on his visit to the war zones in 1944,[4] and most of all to Lindsay's findings during his participant observation, which also began after Pearl Harbor.[5]

The composite picture which emerges from these accounts tends to support the conclusion of the US government,[6] as well as the implicit claim of the various border region governments,[7] that not only their strategy but also its effects were essentially the same as in the SKN border region. It does not seem neces-sary to reiterate the basic characteristics of this approach, but it should be noted that its principal unity did not preclude adaptations to different circumstances. For instance:

1. Territorial autarky was the goal, but for opposite reasons. The Japanese were to be isolated in the cities, deprived of the foodstuffs and raw materials which the surrounding country-side produced. To this end, trade was to be prevented rather than promoted. In the extreme, the base areas had to revert to subsistence economy to the greatest possible degree, against the will and the active intervention of the enemy.[8]

2. Since most of the territory of the base areas was poten-tially subject to Japanese invasion, import-substituting indus-tries—whenever possible—had to be built and operated in a form which made them easily removable. The primitive tech-nology and especially the lack of mechanical power, which was characteristic of all the base areas, facilitated such an adjustment to war conditions.[9]

3. Since they had to engage in fighting, army units behind Japanese lines usually could not participate as much in produc-tion as those in the SKN border region did. The base areas therefore continued to depend more heavily on taxation. Nev-ertheless, the consequent burden on the private population

tended to remain bearable because the public sector accounted for a much smaller share of the total population.[10]

4. In taxation, a distinction had to be made between the more and the less secure regions within each base. Because the Japanese imposed more heavily on the latter, the base-area government could not collect as much there as in the core regions, where the benefits of the development strategy could materialize with fewer inhibitions.[11]

5. Because of the continuing warfare, much of the development effort in the base areas behind Japanese lines aimed at the rehabilitation of the economy rather than at its improvement over some prewar state. For this reason, Mao Tse-tung noted in his endorsement of production campaigns of 1 October 1943 that "... the slogan of 'ample food and clothing' should not be raised for the time being except in the Shensi-Kansu-Ninghsia Border Region...."[12]

In short, these and other adaptations to different circumstances appear to have been comparable to the changes from Kiangsi to Yenan. They evidently served to implement the strategy of development more effectively, and they certainly did not challenge its principal concept, which Mao Tse-tung stated succinctly once again toward the end of the period, in his report "On Coalition Government" of 24 April 1945:

> "Faced with a formidable enemy, it is impossible for us to build up bases against the Japanese and resist their attacks unless we settle the question of democracy and the people's livelihood"—this is what the Chinese Communist Party has been advocating and, moreover, has already put into practice with excellent results.[13]

Appendix

Results of the Investigation of Suite Hsien

The Rural Reconstruction Commission of the Executive Yuan studied four villages of Suite Hsien in Shensi Province as part of its inquiry into *land relations* during the late 1920s and early 1930s in that province (cf. Nung-ts'un fu-hsing wei-yuan hui, *Shan-hsi sheng nung-ts'un tiao-ch'a,* pp. 79 ff.) Most of the basic findings of this study are reproduced in this appendix.

The source defines five classes of rural households in the following terms: a household which engages in agriculture and which experiences average living conditions is a *middle peasant* household. A household which is short of land or which rents land or which supplies hired labor is a *poor peasant* household. A household which experiences living conditions better than those of the middle peasant or which hires labor for field work or which owns relatively many draught animals is a *rich peasant* household. A household which amasses relatively much land yet does not engage in the field work is a *landlord* household. Those who manage the cultivation of the greater portion of their land are *landlord-managers.* Those who lease the greater portion of their land are *landlord-letters.* A household which is not engaged in agriculture or which does not use agriculture as its primary occupation belongs to the *other* village households (cf. *ibid., instructions to the reader,* p. 1).

The definitions appear to be in most respects the same as those used by the Chinese communists. But they are or may be in conflict with the terms and findings of Buck. Buck limits the term *landlord* to a person who leases land, and he classifies *landlord-managers* as owners of farms, presumably of large ones. In addition, Buck does not presume nor find that tenant farmers are necessarily poor peasants. (Cf. Buck, *Land Utilization in China,* pp. 194 ff.) However, the evidence for the four villages in Suite Hsien suggests that a definition which is at least problematic for most parts of China, is meaningful in a specific situation. It thus serves to point to the unusual conditions in North Shensi. The findings of the Rural Reconstruction Commission in Weinan Hsien in the eastern part and in Fenghsiang Hsien in the western part of the Kuanchung region in Central Shensi reenforce this point.

Table A.1 depicts a rather unusual social structure. Local landlords and rich peasants are relatively small in numbers, but their numbers do not change significantly from 1928 to 1933. The number of middle peasants is relatively small, too, and it decreases drastically from 1928 to 1933. The number of poor peasants accounts for three-fourths of all households in 1928, and it grows to four-fifths of all households by 1933. Among them, tenants constitute the largest share which grows drastically, and farm laborers constitute the second largest share which declines strongly. From 1928 to 1933 many middle peasants descend to the status of poor peasant-owners, and fewer become tenants or laborers. Many poor peasant-owners become tenants, and many farm laborers become tenants as well. Even several *other* village households become tenant households. In comparison, very few households ascend socially to original or higher proprietary status.

Table A.2 demonstrates that the trend toward tenancy is associated with an increase in the share of rental land in general and in the share of land owned by distant landlords in particular. The latter increases from about 30 percent of the cultivated land in 1928 to about 45 percent of the cultivated land in 1933. The most important distant landlord is the *Ma* clan of Yang Chia K'ou in Michih Hsien next to Suite Hsien (cf. Nung-ts'un fu-hsing wei-yuan hui, *Shan-hsi sheng,* p. 84). This clan, which also engages in usurious money-lending, in mortgaging of land, etc., appears again as an object of study during the rural investigation in the SKN border region (cf. Yen-an nung-ts'un tiao-ch'a t'uan, *Mi-chih hsien Yang Chia K'ou tiao-ch'a*). Local landlords are comparatively unimportant in 1928 and become even more unimportant by 1933. Curiously, the share of land cultivated by hired labor increases notably, too, due to the hiring of labor by middle peasants.

Table A.3 yields information on the structure of the population. To be noted are the following developments. The population of the four villages increases 1.5 percent per annum from 1928 to 1933. The average household size grows 1 percent per annum from 5.44 in 1928 to 5.71 in 1933. The share of employable persons in the population of rich, middle, and poor peasant households falls for obscure reasons from 51 percent in 1928 to 42.5 percent in 1933. The share of persons cultivating their own or rented land does not vary greatly, from 22.8 percent in 1928 to 22.3 percent in 1933. But the share of persons working elsewhere declines drastically, from 5.3 percent in 1928 to 1.7 percent in 1933.

Table A.3 reveals in addition some unusual changes in average household sizes which modify the effects of changes in the structure of households. Tables A.2 and A.3 yield the following land-population ratios (*hsiang* @ three *mou* per capita):

Class of household	Land owned		Land cultivated	
	1928	1933	1928	1933
Local landlords	8.9	9.8	4.7	4.4
Rich peasants	7.0	5.4	7.0	4.8
Middle peasants	2.7	2.3	2.7	2.9
Poor peasants	0.6	0.4	1.7	1.6
Total	1.4	1.0	2.1	2.0

The average per capita data suggest a deterioration of the living conditions of most classes in addition to the increasing preponderance of the lower classes. The data also point to an increasing inequality in the distribution of land and presumably of income.

Table A.4 finally substantiates the initial statement that the designation of tenants as poor peasants is appropriate in the case of the four villages in Suite Hsien. More than 50 percent of all poor peasant households are totally landless in 1928 and in 1933. An additional 25 or more percent own very little land in both years. About 20 percent do not cultivate land on their own account. The remaining households are not as heavily concentrated on the smallest land classes. However, in view of the fact that they have to pay a large portion of the product of rental land as land rent, the greater dispersion is not indicative of better living conditions. Only a few extreme cases may be called inadequately classified.

Table A.1

CHANGES IN THE CLASS STRUCTURE OF HOUSEHOLDS IN FOUR VILLAGES OF SUITE HSIEN, SHENSI PROVINCE, FROM 1928 TO 1933. [a]

Class of household	1928	1933									Total
		(1)	(2)	(3)	(4)	(5)	(6)	(7)	(8)	(9)	
(1) Landlord-manager	2	1			1						2
(2) Landlord-letter	3	1	2								3
(3) Rich peasant	9			8			1				9
(4) Middle peasant	41			1	29	7	3	2			43
(5) Poor peasant-owner	47				1	34	10		2	1	47
(6) Poor peasant-tenant	89					2	85	2	2		91
(7) Poor peasant-laborer, purely	42					2	4	32	2	2	42
(8) Poor peasant-laborer, partly	19					3	15		3	1	22
(9) Other [b]	13						4	1	1	7	13
Total	265	2	2	9	31	48	122	37	10	11	272

a. Nung-ts'un fu-hsing wei-yuan hui, *Shan-hsi sheng*, p. 81.
b. Including shepherds, stone masons, blacksmiths, salt traders, and beggars.

Table A.2

OWNERSHIP AND CULTIVATION OF LAND IN FOUR VILLAGES OF SUITE HSIEN, SHENSI PROVINCE, IN 1928 AND 1933. [a]

Unit of land: *hsiang* @ three *mou*. [b]

Year	Class of household	Land owned locally	Land rented in	Land rented out	Land cultivated total	by own labor	by hired labor
1928	Local landlords	436.4	0.0	204.4	232.0	91.0	141.0
	Rich peasants	341.5	40.0	38.0	343.5	152.5	191.0
	Middle peasants	696.5	5.5	0.0	702.0	702.0	0.0
	Poor peasants	604.6	1,163.6	5.0	1,763.2	1,755.2	8.0
	All classes	2,079.0	1,209.1	247.4	3,040.7	2,700.7	340.0
1933	Local landlords	273.4	0.0	150.4	123.0	25.0	98.0
	Rich peasants	369.5	4.0	42.0	331.5	115.5	216.0
	Middle peasants	459.0	124.3	0.0	583.3	487.3	96.0
	Poor peasants	514.5	1,488.2	11.0	1,991.7	1,991.7	0.0
	All classes	1,616.4	1,616.5	203.4	3,029.5	2,619.5	410.0

Table A.2 *(continued)*

Unit of land: *hsiang* @ three *mou*.[b]

Year	Class of household	Land owned locally	Land rented in	Land rented out	Land cultivated total	by own labor	by hired labor
Change	Local landlords	− 163.0	0.0	− 54.0	−109.0	− 66.0	− 43.0
	Rich peasants	+ 28.0	− 36.0	+ 4.0	− 12.0	− 37.0	+ 25.0
	Middle peasants	− 237.5	+118.8	0.0	−118.7	−214.7	+ 96.0
	Poor peasants	− 90.1	+324.6	+ 6.0	+ 228.5	+ 236.5	− 8.0
	All classes	− 462.6	+407.4	− 44.0	− 11.2	− 81.2	+ 70.0

a. Nung-ts'un fu-hsing wei-yuan hui, *Shan-hsi sheng,* pp. 99-100, 109.
b. Cf. *ibid.,* directions to the reader, pp. 1-2.

Table A.3

STRUCTURE OF POPULATION IN FOUR VILLAGES OF SUITE HSIEN, SHENSI PROVINCE, 1928 AND 1933.

Year	Class of household	House-holds	House-hold members	Employ-able persons	Persons working elsewhere	Culti-vators	Draught animals
1928	Local landlords	5	49				11
	Rich peasants	9	49	12	1	11	14
	Middle peasants	41	259	131	2	68	23
	Poor peasants	197	1,038	544	68	228	24
	Others	13	46				
	All classes	265	1,441				72
1933	Local landlords	4	28				4
	Rich peasants	9	69	34	1	17	8
	Middle peasants	31	200	74	1	51	14
	Poor peasants	217	1,222	526	24	265	36
	Others	11	33				
	All classes	272	1,552				62

Table A.3 *(continued)*

Year / Class of household	House-holds	House-hold members	Employ-able persons	Persons working elsewhere	Culti-vators	Draught animals
Change						
Local landlords	− 1	− 21				− 7
Rich peasants	0	+ 20	+ 22	0	+ 6	− 6
Middle peasants	− 10	− 59	− 57	− 1	− 17	− 9
Poor peasants	+ 20	+ 184	− 18	− 44	+ 37	+ 12
Others	− 2	− 13				
All classes	+ 7	+ 111				− 10

a. Nung-ts'un fu-hsing wei-yuan hui, *Shan-hsi sheng*, pp. 92-93, 105-107, 111-112.

Table A.4

DISTRIBUTION OF POOR PEASANT HOUSEHOLDS IN FOUR VILLAGES OF SUITE HSIEN, SHENSI PROVINCE, 1928-1933, ACCORDING TO LAND OWNED AND LAND CULTIVATED. [a]

Land hsiang @ three *mou*	Distribution of households according to					
	Land owned			Land cultivated		
	1928	1933	Change	1928	1933	Change
0	106	124	+18	43	39	− 4
1-5	51	61	+10	50	58	8
6-10	26	21	− 5	36	47	11
11-15	7	7	0	34	33	1
16-20	4	2	− 2	14	20	+ 6
21-25	2	2	0	11	8	− 3
26-30	0	0	0	3	2	− 1
31-35	0	0	0	2	4	+ 2
36-40	0	0	0	0	3	+ 3
41-45	0	0	0	1	1	0
46-50	0	0	0	0	1	+ 1
51-55	0	0	0	0	0	0
56-60	1	0	1	1	0	− 1
61-65	0	0	0	0	0	0
66-70	0	0	0	1	0	− 1
71-75	0	0	0	1	1	0
Total	197	217	+20	197	217	+20

a. Nung-ts'un fu-hsing wei-yuan hui, *Shan-hsi sheng,* pp. 91, 102.

Notes to Chapter 1

1. Mao Tse-tung, *Selected Works* (Peking: Foreign Languages Press, 1965), Vol. I, pp. 23-24 (Hereinafter cited as *Mao I* to *Mao IV*).
2. Edgar Snow, *Red Star Over China* (New York: Grove Press, 1938), p. 73.
3. Victor A. Yakhontoff, *The Chinese Soviets* (New York: Coward-McCann, 1934), p. 12.
4. See in particular Benjamin Schwartz, *Chinese Communism and the Rise of Mao* (Cambridge: Harvard University Press, 1958); Karl August Wittfogel, "The Legend of 'Maoism'," *The China Quarterly*, No. 1 (1960): 72-86, and No. 2 (1960): 16-34, plus Schwartz's rejoinder *ibid.*, pp. 35-42; Tso-liang Hsiao, *Power Relations within the Chinese Communist Movement, 1930-1934* (Seattle: University of Washington Press, 1961); John Rue, *Mao Tse-tung in Opposition, 1927-1935* (Stanford: Stanford University Press, 1966); and Richard C. Thornton, *The Comintern and the Chinese Communists, 1928-1931* (Seattle: University of Washington Press, 1969).
5. On the origins of the Northwest Soviet, see Mark Selden, "The Guerrilla Movement in Northwest China: The Origins of the Shensi-Kansu-Ninghsia Border Region," *The China Quarterly*, No. 28 (1966): 63-81, and No. 29 (1967): 61-81.
6. T. A. Bisson, *Yenan in June 1937; Talks with the Communist Leaders* (Berkeley: Center for Chinese Studies, University of California, 1973), p. 30.
7. Edgar Snow, *Random Notes on Red China 1936-1945* (Cambridge: East Asian Research Center, Harvard University, 1957), pp. 100-102.
8. *Mao III*, pp. 167-168. Included in the population estimate are the people of contested areas who paid taxes to both the Japanese and the Chinese communist base-area governments.
9. *Ibid.*
10. The documents of the campaign appear in Boyd Compton, *Mao's China. Party Reform Documents, 1942-1944* (Seattle: University of Washington Press, 1952). A more comprehensive analysis is provided by Mark Selden, *The Yenan Way in Revolutionary China* (Cambridge: Harvard University Press, 1971).
11. Selden, *Yenan Way*.
12. Guenther Stein, *The Challenge of Red China* (New York: McGraw-Hill, 1945), p. 97.
13. *Ibid.*, pp. 99, 102, 328.

Notes to Chapter 2

1. See Shan Kan Ning pien ch'ü cheng-fu wei-yuan hui, *Shan Kan Ning pien ch'ü cheng-fu kung-tso pao-kao (28 nien-30 nien)* (Border Region Government Secretariat, July 1941), p. 8 (Hereinafter cited as *Shan Kan Ning 1939-1941*).

2. See Mark Selden, "The Guerrilla Movement in Northwest China: The Origins of the Shensi-Kansu-Ninghsia Border Region (Part I)," *The China Quarterly*, No. 28 (October-December 1966): esp. 74-78.

3. See John Lossing Buck, *Land Utilization in China. Atlas* (Nanking: The University of Nanking Press, 1937), maps 3 and 6, pp. 3 and 8. Note that Hsunyi Hsien was lost during 1939/40. Note also that Buck investigated to a more limited extent Yenan, Yenchang, and Fu Hsien. Cf. *ibid.*, p. 4.

4. Nung-ts'un fu-hsing wei-yuan hui, *Shan-hsi sheng nung-ts'un tiao-ch'a* (Shanghai, 1934), pp. 79 ff. In addition, the investigation dealt with Weinan Hsien in the eastern part and with Feng hsiang Hsien in the western part of the Kuangchung region of Shensi.

5. Yen-an nung-ts'un tiao-ch'a t'uan, *Mi-chih hsien yang chia k'ou tiao-ch'a* (Peking: San Lien Bookstore, 1957). A more comprehensive and potentially more useful study is *T'ai Hang Ch'ü 1944 nien kuo-min ching-chi tiao-ch'a ch'u-pu yen-chiu* which, however, depicts the state of affairs in part of the Shansi-Hopei-Shantung-Honan Border Region.

6. The twenty-six hsien were: Yenan (Fushih) (S), Yenchuan (S), Yenchang (S), Chingchien (S), Suite (S), Michih (S), Chia (S), Wupao (S), Shenfu (i.e., the greater part of Shenmu and Fuku) (S), Anting (S), Ansai (S), Chingpien (S), Tingpien (S), Chihtan (Paoan) (S), Kanchuan (S), Ning (K), Chingyang (K), Hoshui (K), Chenyuan (D), Huan (K), Yuwang (N), Yenchih (N), Fu (S), Chunhua (S), Hsunyi (S), and Chengning (K). See *Shan Kan Ning 1939-1941*, pp. 7-8 (Yuwang omitted) and *Brief Account of the Reconstruction in the Shensi-Kansu-Ninghsia Border Region*, (unpublished translation of a SKN border region government report, no author, no date) (Hereinafter cited as *Brief Account*). The text implies that the report was made in 1944.

7. See *Shan Kan Ning 1939-1941*, pp. 12-13, for such a dating in the cases of Suite, Chingchien, and Wupao. The source does not state when Michih and Chia Hsien came under SKN control.

8. See *Mao II*, p. 394, reference 7, and *Brief Account*, p. 2: "The whole district of Yuwang, five district towns: Chenyuan, Ninghsien, Chengning, Hsunyi, Chunhua, and several thousand small and big villages in the North, South-East, and West of our border were occupied in succession, . . ." For a more detailed review of the territorial changes see Yung Ying Hsü, *A Survey of Shensi-Kansu-Ninghsia Border Region* (New York: Institute of Pacific Relations, 1945), part 1, pp. 5-8 (hereinafter cited as Hsü, *A Survey*).

9. See Hsü, *A Survey*, pp. 10 ff., for evidence in support of this position.

10. See Snow, *Red Star*, p. 472. Note, however, that Snow's area estimate of "some fifty counties—an area between sixty and seventy thousand square miles" (i.e., 155 to 180 thousand km²) appears to exaggerate the size of the territory. Note also that Snow obtained a reference to 600,000 persons from Chou En-lai in an interview on 9 July 1936. See Snow, *Random Notes*, p. 61. This estimate clearly pertains to part of the eventual SKN border region.

11. See Ta-chung Liu and Kung-chia Yeh, *The Economy of the Chinese Mainland, 1933-1959* (Princeton, N. J.: Princeton University Press, 1965), pp. 178-179.

12. See *ibid.*
13. See Buck, *Land Utilization in China. Statistics* (Nanking: The University of Nanking Press, 1937), p. 426. (Hereinafter cited as Buck, *Statistics*).
14. According to Buck, *Statistics,* pp. 21 ff., 416 ff., the SKN border region was located as follows:

	Spring wheat area %			Winter wheat-millet area %		
	gross area	house-holds	farm house-holds	gross area	house-holds	farm house-holds
Designated area	36.9	29.3	28.5	63.1	70.7	71.5
Area until 1939/40	39.3	35.5	35.4	60.7	64.5	64.6
Area after 1939/40	34.3	31.8	31.5	65.7	68.2	68.5

15. See *ibid.,* p. 426.
16. See *Shan Kan Ning (1958),* p. 379. Note that these rates have been reprinted repeatedly. It is therefore unlikely that they embody printing mistakes.
17. See Buck, *Land Utilization,* pp. 388-390.
18. See *ibid.,* pp. 377, 383.
19. The population of the four villages of Suite Hsien grew from 1928 to 1933 at an average annual rate of 1.5 percent. The average household size increased during the same period at an average annual rate of 1 percent. See table A.3. The cause of this growth cannot be ascertained.
20. Government reports state a total immigration of about 100,000 persons during 1937-1940 (see *Shan Kan Ning 1939-1941,* p. 44) and of 85,800 persons during 1941-1944 (see *Shan Kan Ning (1958),* pp. 284-285). Data on emigration are lacking, but the population loss due to it seems to have been negligibly small.
21. The SKN border region government has published data on the numbers of reorganized administrative subdivisions within the region which imply the following averages for the end of 1944:

Name of unit	Number of units	Average per unit, end of 1944			
		area in km²	radius in km	house-holds	popu-lation
Hsien (district), Shih (city)	33	3,000	30.9	9,484	48,335
Ch'ü (region)	216	458	12.1	1,449	7,385
Hsiang (township)	1,254	79	5.0	250	1,272
Administrative village	4,852	20.4	2.6	65	329
Natural village	18,730	5.3	1.5	17	85

See *Shan Kan Ning (1958)*, pp. 378-379, and *Brief Account*, p. 2. An incomplete account for 1941 yields similar averages at the hsien, ch'ü, and hsiang levels. The number of administrative villages was considerably larger. See *Shan Kan Ning 1939-1941*, pp. 11-15.

22. Estimate: .355 times share in *spring wheat area* plus .645 times share in *winter wheat-millet area*. See note 14 (share of households) and Buck, *Statistics*, p. 420. Note that in the case of the *spring wheat area*, we correct an apparent printing mistake by changing the share of families in farm villages and hamlets from 75.3 to 73.5 percent.

23. Estimate: .318 times share in *spring wheat area* plus .682 times share in *winter wheat-millet area*. See note 22.

24. In comparison, a hsien on the average incorporated 40,600 households in the *wheat region* and 46,800 households in Buck's eight agricultural areas according to the data of the national government. See Buck, *Statistics*, pp. 21, 416.

25. See Buck, *Land Utilization*, p. 372.

26. See table 2.3 for evidence in support of this hypothesis.

27. See table 2.3 for unusually large numbers of merchants and of home-industry workers.

28. See Buck, *Land Utilization*, p. 372.

29. See *Brief Account*, p. 16.

30. See *Shan Kan Ning (1958)*, p. 90.

31. Derived from Buck, *Land Utilization*, p. 373. The average length of schooling was 4.1 years for men and 2.7 years for women. See *ibid.*, p. 374.

32. See *Shan Kan Ning (1958)*, p. 86.

33. See the discussion of urban-rural structure.

34. 76.5 percent times *spring wheat area* weight plus 87.5 percent times *winter wheat-millet area* weight. See Buck, *Statistics*, p. 420, and notes 22, 23.

35. 72.3 percent times *spring wheat area* weight plus 79.4 percent times *winter wheat-millet area* weight. See Buck, *Statistics*, p. 420, and notes 22, 23.

36. Derived from Buck, *Statistics*, p. 416.

37. I.e., 74.6 times 83.6/76.9 and 76.8 times 84.0/77.1. See notes 34, 36.

38. Derived from Buck, *Land Utilization*, p. 368 and note 37. Buck's data imply the following relative shares:

Tenure of farm in North China	% families	population
Owners, part-owners, plus tenants	83.5	85.3
Landlords, tenure unknown, plus nonfarm	16.5	14.7

We multiply the family shares of reference 37 by 85.3/83.5 in order to arrive at estimates of the shares of the farm population.

39. Derived from table A.1.

40. See Nung-ts'un fu-hsing wei-yuan hui, *Shan-hsi sheng*, pp. 6 and 46.

41. See Yen-an nung-ts'un tiao-ch'a t'uan, *Mi-chih hsien*, pp. 1, 15-21. Note that the village as well as the methods of its study were unusual.

42. See table A.3. The source refers to *yu kung-tso neng-li jen* (persons able to work).

43. Derived from Buck, *Statistics,* pp. 305, 309, and Buck, *Land Utilization,* p. 475.

44. Derived from Buck, *Land Utilization,* as well as Buck, *Statistics,* p. 303, and note 14.

45. See note 47.

46. In Hsunyi, 71.7 percent of all employed persons engaged in farm work only and 10.6 percent of them engaged in both farm and subsidiary work. In Tingpien, the corresponding shares were 51.4 percent and 35.1 percent. See Buck, *Statistics,* p. 303.

47. The estimates of tables 2.2 and 2.3 suggest such an inference, as the following contrast shows:

Kind of occupation	Table 2.2 1936	1940	Table 2.3 1936	1940	Kind of employment
Agriculture only	322.0	345.0	338.4	379.6	Farm work only
Agriculture plus other	91.0	97.5	97.4	103.9	Farm work plus subsidiary work
Subtotal	413.0	442.5	435.8	483.5	Total
Agriculture plus domestic service	196.0	210.0			
Total	609.0	652.5			

48. See Appendix A for much smaller shares of cultivators in four villages in Suite.

49. See *Shan Kan Ning pien ch'ü cheng-ts'e t'iao-li hui-pien* (Shan Kan Ning pien ch'ü cheng-fu pan kung t'ing pien, May 1944), p. 30. Note that the source does not define the term.

50. The shares of persons employed in subsidiary work only were small in both Hsunyi and Tingpien and smaller in the latter. But the very large share of part-time subsidiary work there resulted in a 36.2 percent share of subsidiary effort in total effort, in comparison with a 17.7 percent share in Hsunyi. See Buck, *Statistics,* p. 305.

51. The dominant subsidiary occupations were merchant and agricultural laborer in Tingpien but home-industry worker and merchant in Hsunyi. Correspondingly, there was emphasis on male subsidiary work in Tingpien but on female subsidiary work in Hsunyi. See *ibid.,* pp. 303, 309.

52. To demonstrate these relations, we proceed as in reference 47:

Kind of occupation	Table 2.2 1936	1940	Table 2.3 1936	1940	Kind of employment
Home industry	21.0	22.5	53.3	62.8	Home industry
Trade	68.6	73.5	70.7	74.4	Merchant

Transport	12.6	13.5		
Manufacturing	22.4	24.0	18.5	19.2 Laborer, nonagricultural
Professions	70.0	75.0	5.8	6.4 Professional, scholar
Public Service	8.4	9.0	2.4	2.6 Official, soldier

Note that the data from Table 2.2 add part-time and full-time occupation in nonagricultural activities.

53. For a discussion of marketing, see Buck, *Statistics*, p. 343. The marketing of the farm's products required 6.8 man-work days per farm in Tingpien and 40.0 man-work days per farm in Hsunyi. The greater employment in merchant activities in Tingpien (see notes 50, 51) may be a form of disguised unemployment which was attributable in part to the disasters of the late 1920s.

54. Derived from John Lossing Buck, *Chinese Farm Economy* (Chicago: University of Chicago Press, 1930), pp. 49, 52. In his *Land Utilization in China*, Buck measured merely the utilization of adult males in terms of months of work. We estimate for the border region that close to 20 percent of them had full-time work, about three-quarters had part-time work, and less than 1 percent had no work at all. The number of idle months per able-bodied male was 1.7 per annum. Derived from Buck, *Statistics*, p. 306, and note 14.

55. See note 50 for an implicit share of such a magnitude.

56. See Peter Schran, *The Development of Chinese Agriculture, 1950-1959* (Urbana: University of Illinois Press, 1969), table 3.10, for estimates of the average numbers of workdays of men, women, and children in Buck's eight agricultural areas.

57. See *Shan Kan Ning (1958)*, p. 4.

58. In Tingpien, forty *times* the cultivated area was said to be arable. In Fu, Yenan, and Yenchang, the cultivated area could be increased on the average by 40 percent. Hsunyi contained relatively little uncultivated land which was arable. See Buck, *Statistics*, pp. 21-31, 38.

59. For a detailed discussion of these physiographic features, see Hsü, *A Survey*, part 1, pp. 27-42.

60. Derived from Buck, *Statistics*, pp. 21-22 and 416 on the assumption of an average household size of 5.2 persons. Note that the average of 6.0 *mou* per capita is comparable to the averages in four villages in Suite (average area utilized per capita: 6.26 *mou* in 1928 and 5.85 *mou* in 1933). Derived from tables A.2 and A.3.

61. Derived from Buck, *Statistics*, pp. 286, 420, and note 14.

62. Estimate: 8,431,000/1,159,200. See tables 2.3, 2.4.

63. See Snow, *Random Notes*, pp. 36-37. Selden presents even more extreme data of the same kind for one hsiang (township) in Yenchuan Hsien in January 1935. See Selden, *The Yenan Way*, p. 81. Note in addition that most hsien in the border region territory had instituted land reform measures

during the soviet period, at a time when the government published practically no aggregate information. For the effects of land redistribution on social structure in the instance of the one hsiang in Yenchuan Hsien, see Selden, *The Yenan Way.*

64. See Appendix A and Peter Schran, *The Development of Chinese Agriculture,* chapter 2, for information which suggests such a correspondence.

65. See table A.2 and Buck, *Statistics,* p. 55.

66. See Buck, *Statistics,* p. 57, and table A.4.

67. See Yen-an nung-ts'un tiao-ch'a t'uan, *Mi-chih hsien,* and note that the data in this source cannot be made comparable to those of Buck and of the Rural Reconstruction Commission.

68. See Buck, *Land Utilization,* p. 194.

69. See *ibid.,* p. 288.

70. See Buck, *Statistics,* p. 40.

71. Derived from *ibid.,* pp. 43, 286, and reference 14.

72. See *ibid.,* pp. 53, 215.

73. See *Shan Kan Ning (1958),* p. 285.

74. See Buck, *Statistics,* p. 50.

75. Derived from *ibid.,* pp. 172, 286, and reference 14. According to Hsü, *A Survey,* Part 2, p. 69, eight other hsien within the SKN border region reported a total of 25,700 *mou* of cotton land for 1931.

76. See *Brief Account,* p. 11.

77. Derived from Buck, *Statistics,* pp. 172, 174, 209, 286.

78. See *ibid.,* p. 208.

79. Derived from notes 14, 77, and 78.

80. Derived from *Shan Kan Ning 1939-1941,* pp. 41-42, and *Ching-chi yen-chiu,* No. 2 (1956): 108. Note that the SKN border region government operated originally with piculs of 400 catties @ 500 grams (see *Shan Kan Ning (1958),* p. 21) and—seemingly—since 1939 with piculs of 300 catties @ 500 grams (see table 7.3). The standard weights appear to have differed from the actual weights used in various localities. Buck lists the weight of a catty in Tingpien in 1930 as 457.14 grams and that of a catty in Hsunyi as 596.82 grams. See Buck, *Statistics,* p. 473.

81. Changes in the quality of the agricultural year have been recorded for Yang Chia K'ou of Michih Hsien, but the entry for 1937 is missing. Other data suggest that it was probably poor. See Yen-an nung-ts'un tiao-ch'a t'uan, *Mi-chih hsien,* pp. 140-142, 146, 148-149.

82. See *Shan Kan Ning (1958),* p. 283.

83. See *Brief Account,* p. 11, for the statement that the mortality rates of cattle and of sheep were high in the SKN border region.

84. See *Shan Kan Ning 1939-1941,* pp. 43, 51.

85. Buck himself concluded that the number of sheep per farm in Tingpien was unusually large. He therefore excluded Tingpien from his area, regional, and national averages. The numbers of oxen and donkeys were relatively large, too, but they did not exceed the aggregate averages as drastically. See Buck, *Statistics,* pp. 122-123.

86. Derived from *ibid.*, and note 14.

87. See Buck, *Statistics*, p. 122.

88. See Liu and Yeh, *Economy of the Chinese Mainland*, pp. 310-311.

89. For a discussion of these possibilities, see, e.g., Ralph W. Phillips, Ray G. Johnson, and Raymond T. Moyer, *The Livestock of China* (Washington: United States Government Printing Office, 1945). Note that maturation periods of less than one year were of limited significance due to the fact that births tended to cumulate in the spring.

90. Note in particular that meat consumption data are of limited importance in this connection. The reproduction of hogs appears to offset the consumption of pork. But the consumption of mutton accounts for a small fraction of the reproduction of sheep.

91. See Buck, *Statistics*, pp. 305, 309.

92. Derived from *ibid.* and note 14.

93. See Buck, *Statistics*, p. 309.

94. See *ibid.*, p. 328.

95. See *Shan Kan Ning (1958)*, pp. 23-24.

96. See Buck, *Land Utilization*, p. 306, and note 14.

97. Note that the deflation of the money earnings in Tingpien and Hsunyi by the average wheat prices in the reference areas would yield much higher earnings in Tingpien than in Hsunyi and lower SKN averages.

98. Derived from Buck, *Statistics*, p. 309, and note 96.

99. On a nationwide scale, the farm prices of most coarse grains appear to have been much lower than the farm price of wheat. See Liu and Yeh, *Economy of the Chinese Mainland*, pp. 325 ff. However, data for Yang Chia K'ou indicate that yellow millet was more expensive than wheat. See Yen-an nung-ts'un tiao-ch'a t'uan, *Mi-chih hsien*, p. 149.

100. In the case of Hsunyi, we use the ratio of man-equivalents in subsidiary work to total man-equivalents as an approximate measure of the share of subsidiary income in total income. See table 2.8, note i.

101. Note that we may overestimate the cost of crop production due to the fact that farmers in Tingpien apparently used fertilizers to a very limited extent. See Buck, *Statistics*, pp. 138, 140. Fertilizers accounted for about half of the cost of crop production. See Liu and Yeh, *Economy of the Chinese Mainland*, p. 414.

102. Note that grain consumption according to table 2.9 accounted for 75.4 percent of the grain-equivalent of net income in Tingpien and for 76.0 percent of the grain-equivalent of net income in Hsunyi according to table 2.8.

103. Derived from Buck, *Statistics*, pp. 289, 297, 300, 302, and note 14, 77, 78.

104. See *Brief Account*, p. 13.

105. See note 103 and Buck, *Statistics*, p. 311.

106. Note that the data are not very conclusive. Information on the distribution of animal husbandry by farm size is lacking in general and estimates of the share of subsidiary income by farm size are lacking for Hsunyi.

107. See Nung-ts'un fu-hsing wei-yuan hui, *Shan-hsi sheng*, p. 152, for

the information that the land taxes in Suite in 1933 amounted to one *tou* (at the standard rate four kg of wheat) per *hsiang* of hill land and to 2.8 *tou* (i.e., 11.2 kg of wheat) per *hsiang* of river land. Since the average area of cultivated land was about two hsiang per capita of the peasant population (see Appendix A), average per capita taxes ranged in between 8 and 22.4 kg of wheat per annum.

108. See *ibid.,* pp. 151-152, for comparisons of the situation in Weinan, Fenghsiang, and Suite. See also Buck, *Land Utilization,* pp. 327-328, for a reference to "comparatively oppressive" taxation in the *winter wheat-millet area.*

109. Derived from tables 2.3 and 2.8.

110. Derived from table 2.3 and note 107 (estimate: total farm population times 15 kg, divided by 1,000).

111. Note that the share of land rent presumably varied closely with the share of rental land in total farm land. For variations see Buck, *Land Utilization,* p. 194.

112. Derived from tables 2.3 and 2.8.

113. See Buck, *Statistics,* pp. 403-406.

114. See *ibid.,* pp. 87, 93.

115. See *ibid.,* p. 73, and Buck, *Land Utilization,* p. 406.

116. Derived from tables 2.2, 2.3 and 2.9.

117. See Liu and Yeh, *Economy of the Chinese Mainland,* p. 414, for the information that seeds accounted for about 4 percent of the gross value of output. T. H. Shen, *Agricultural Resources of China* (Ithaca, N.Y.: Cornell University Press, 1951), p. 378, implies that seeds accounted for 5.1 percent and feed for 5.9 percent of the total output of grains in the twenty-two provinces of China during 1931-1937.

118. For crop product, see Buck, *Land Utilization,* p. 286. Farm wages derived from *ibid.,* pp. 278, 297, 306. Total net income derived from farm wages and share of subsidiary income in net income, see *ibid.,* p. 297. Grain consumption derived from Buck, *Statistics,* pp. 66, 67, 73 (share of grain in total caloric intake times caloric intake per adult male unit times share of adult male units in population, divided by calories per kg of grains).

119. Derived from tables 2.8 and 2.9 (average of territory before and after 1939/40).

120. See Buck, *Statistics,* p. 73.

121. See note 38.

122. Derived from tables 2.2 and 2.3.

123. Note in particular that the contrast concerns the occupational structure of the total population in North China and the employment structure of the farm population in SKN as inferred from the Hsunyi and Tingpien data. However, the use of wheat region averages for the farm population would not change the results of table 2.10 greatly. The numbers of nonfarm population occupied in the professions and in public service would be somewhat smaller. The number of nonfarm population in trade would be positive, but that of nonfarm population in manufacturing would be negative. The

negative residual in home industry would be smaller.

124. See Nung-ts'un fu-hsing wei-yuan hui, *Shan-hsi sheng,* pp. 6, 46, 80, for the absence of any reference to the professions in the enumeration of the occupations of "other" households.

125. See *ibid.* for references to a variety of crafts and trades, including begging.

126. See notes 26, 27, 52, 53.

127. See notes 22, 23, and 39-41 for this implication.

128. See tables 5.2 and 5.4 for evidence on this point.

129. Note that some of the "factories" which Snow encountered in 1936 appear to have been owned privately. See Edgar Snow, *Red Star,* p. 268.

130. See *Brief Account,* pp. 2-3, for a description of the products of the SKN border region. See also Hsü, *A Survey,* part 1, pp. 35-38, for a discussion of its mineral endowment.

131. See *Salt Production* (unpublished translation of a SKN border region government report, no author, no date) (hereinafter cited as *Salt Production*), p. 1.

132. See *ibid.,* p. 8. The source refers to Yenchih, which produced most of the salt of the border region.

133. See Edgar Snow, *Red Star,* p. 269, and note that the total output of oil was quite small.

134. To this end, net value added (see Liu and Yeh, *Economy of the Chinese Mainland,* pp. 154, 161, 164-166, 600, 608) is divided by 0.09 yuan per kg of wheat (see *ibid.,* p. 332).

135. A ratio of $630/850 = 0.74118$ is used. See note 96 and table 2.11.

136. Note the omission of trade and home industry, on the assumption that the two offset each other. The estimates are as follows:

Occupation	Persons	Average wages	Total wages
Professions	64,200	1,501	96,364,200
Domestic service	36,400	535	19,474,000
Public service	6,000	1,153	6,918,000
Transport	12,600	906	11,415,600
Handicrafts	3,900	1,070	4,173,000
Total	123,100	*1,124*	138,344,800

137. I.e., $138,344,800/240,800 = 574.5$ kg of wheat. See notes 122 and 136.

138. Derived from *ibid.,* and table 2.8.

139. See *T'ung-chi yen-chiu,* No. 1 (1958): 13, for similar ratios of average per capita commodity expenditures of nonagricultural labor force and peasantry.

140. See note 118 and note the failure to account for urban-rural cost-of-living differentials which may account for much of the difference between 490 kg and 575 kg. See note 139 for an implicit cost-of-living differential of about 15 percent.

141. See Buck. *Statistics,* p. 413. Note that the reference is to the larger agricultural areas. The sample included from the SKN territory respondents in Yenan, Yenchang, and Hsunyi. There were no complaints from Yenan, reference to heavy taxes from Yenchang, and reference to banditry from Hsunyi.

142. Note that Buck's agricultural survey schedules contained a question concerning acute farm tenancy problems in the region. See *ibid.,* p. 441. Responses to this question have not been published.

143. See, for example, Edgar Snow, *Red Star,* pp. 228-232, for a summary of the views of Dr. A. Stampar of the League of Nations and for references to various missionaries in the area.

144. Note that although Buck excluded explicit disaster areas as well as much of the SKN territory (see note 3), he studied the Northwest rather comprehensively (twenty-nine locations in Shensi, eight locations in Kansu). Stampar's statements are more impressionistic and also not SKN specific. Snow's summary seems to refer especially to disaster areas.

Notes to Chapter 3

1. Snow, *Red Star Over China,* p. 243.

2. *Mao I,* pp. 69-70.

3. For a summary of the contents of the resolution see Richard C. Thornton, *The Comintern and the Chinese Communists 1928-1931,* pp. 56-57.

4. *Ibid.,* p. 57.

5. See his report on "The Struggle in the Chingkang Mountains," *Mao I,* pp. 73 ff., esp. pp. 89-90, 95, 98.

6. See *ibid.,* pp. 103-104, for editorial comment to this effect.

7. Yakhontoff, *The Chinese Soviets,* p. 270, notes that according to Mao's report to the second soviet congress, which was held in January 1934, confiscation and requisitioning in both Kuomintang and soviet territory constituted the largest item in the revenue of the soviet government.

8. Snow, *Red Star Over China,* p. 249, reports that according to Lin Pai-ch'ü, then commissioner of finance, the most important source of revenue in 1936 was confiscation.

9. See Ilpyong J. Kim, *The Politics of Chinese Communism* (Berkeley: University of California Press, 1973), pp. 32 ff., esp. p. 38, for evidence to this effect.

10. See Hsiao, *Power Relations,* pp. 176 ff., for repeated references to the close correspondence between COMINTERN directives and specific enactments of the first soviet congress.

11. *Fundamental Laws of the Chinese Soviet Republic* (New York: International Publishers, 1934), pp. 19-20. Article 8, which concerned the privileges of foreigners in China, was irrelevant for the base areas of 1931. Note that all of these articles amplified demands of the ten-point program which the sixth party congress had adopted in July 1928. See *Mao III,* p. 175, note 5.

12. See *Fundamental* Laws, pp. 52-68. Note that the number of ". . . persons working for wages in industrial enterprises, workshops, or in any other productive undertaking, or in any institution (including government, cooperative, and private institutions) . . ." was relatively small.

13. See Tso-liang Hsiao, *The Land Revolution in China 1930-1934* (Seattle: University of Washington Press, 1969), for the development of this point and the full text of the law. Other translations usually contain merely its first seven articles. See *Fundamental Laws*, pp. 24-27.

14. See *Fundamental Laws*, pp. 39-43.

15. *Ibid.*, pp. 69-77.

16. *Ibid.*, p. 38.

17. See Buck, *Land Utilization*, p. 462.

18. For Mao's *ex post facto* interpretation of the disagreement, see the "Resolution on Certain Questions in the History of Our Party" of 20 April 1945, *Mao III*, esp. pp. 165, 196.

19. Kim, *The Politics of Chinese Communism*, pp. 49 ff., esp. p. 51.

20. *Ibid.*, p. 94.

21. *Mao I*, pp. 147-148.

22. See *ibid.*, pp. 129-136, for the text of a speech delivered at the economic construction conference of seventeen hsien in southern Kiangsi in August 1933.

23. The resolution is reproduced in Hsiao, *Power Relations*, Vol. 2, pp. 741-744.

24. See Hsiao, *Land Revolution*, pp. 198 ff., esp. p. 204, and Kim, *The Politics of Chinese Communism*, pp. 9-11.

25. *Mao I*, pp. 197-254.

26. *Ibid.*, p. 240.

27. Note that Mao stressed this implication *ibid.*, p. 249, in the following form:

> In establishing our own war industry we must not allow ourselves to become dependent on it. Our basic policy is to rely on the war industries of the imperialist countries and of our domestic enemy. We have a claim on the output of the arsenals of London as well as Hangyang, and, what is more, it is delivered to us by the enemy's transport corps. This is the sober truth, it is not a jest.

28. Edgar Snow in his *Red Star Over China*, p. 217, describes the Long March in this perspective as follows:

> In one sense this mass migration was the biggest armed propaganda tour in history. The Reds passed through provinces populated by more than 200,000,000 people. Between battles and skirmishes, in every town occupied, they called great mass meetings, gave theatrical performances, heavily "taxed" the rich, freed many slaves (some of whom joined the Red Army), preached "liberty, equality, democracy," confiscated the property of the "traitors" (officials, big landlords, and tax collectors) and distributed their goods among the poor. . . .

29. See Donald G. Gillin, " 'Peasant Nationalism' in the History of Chinese Communism," *Journal of Asian Studies* 23, 2 (February 1964): 269-289, for a discussion of this event.

30. See Snow, *Red Star Over China*, pp. 232-251, for a vivid description of the considerations and activities at that time.

31. See *ibid.* and Mark Selden, *The Yenan Way in Revolutionary China* (Cambridge: Harvard University Press, 1971), pp. 109-111, 124, for a summary of the accomplishments.

32. See *Mao I*, p. 269, for a paraphrased version of the actual pledges. The original communication is reproduced *ibid.* on page 281.

33. See Selden, *The Yenan Way*, pp. 100, 102, for data on the extent to which land redistribution had been carried out.

34. See Maxwell S. Stewart, *Wartime China* (I.P.R. Pamphlets No. 10; New York: American Council, Institute of Pacific Relations, 1944), p. 47, for the following statement: "According to the agreement entered into between the Communists and the National Government in 1937, the Red armies were to receive about $700,000 in Chinese currency monthly to meet their payrolls, and they were also to be armed and equipped like any other branch of the Chinese Army. . . ." Nym Wales noted on 29 August 1937 that "the whole Chinese Red Army is now clothed in regulation Kuomintang uniforms supplied by Nanking. . . ." See Nym Wales, *Inside Red China*, p. 211.

35. For a description of such policies see *Shan Kan Ning (1958)*, pp. 14-16. Note in this connection that the land reform, which had been carried out in most of the hsien within the base area, was not to be undone. Efforts at reestablishing the status which had prevailed before were made privately and resisted publicly. See *Mao II*, p. 76, for the following statement which was made on 15 May 1938:

> However, recent investigations in the Border Region have disclosed that, disregarding the public interest, some persons are using various means to force the peasants to return land and houses that have been distributed to them, to compel debtors to pay back old cancelled loans, . . ." etc.

36. Rue, *Mao Tse-tung in Opposition, 1927-1935*, p. 279.

37. Selden, *The Yenan Way*, pp. 173-175. Note that the issue came to the fore most clearly in education.

38. See *Shan Kan Ning (1958)*, pp. 20-21.

39. See *ibid.*, pp. 32-33.

40. See *ibid.*, p. 37.

41. See *ibid.*, p. 38.

42. See *Mao III*, pp. 99-102 ("A Most Important Policy," 7 September 1942).

43. See *ibid.*, p. 205 (Resolution on Certain Questions in the History of Our Party, 20 April 1945), for the following restatement of the tactical argument: "The Red Army must simultaneously shoulder the threefold task of fighting, doing mass work and raising funds (which at present means production); . . ."

44. See *ibid.,* pp. 243-244 ("We Must Learn To Do Economic Work," 10 January 1945). See also *ibid.,* p. 326 (27 April 1945), for the following statement: "In our circumstances, production by the army for its own support, though backward or retrogressive in form, is progressive in substance and of great historic significance. Formally speaking, we are violating the principle of division of labor. However, in our circumstances—the poverty and disunity of the country (resulting from the crimes of the chief ruling clique of the Kuomintang), and the protracted and dispersed people's guerrilla war—what we are doing is progressive. . . ."

45. Most important as a bench mark is Mao Tse-tung's report to the meeting of higher cadres of the SKN border region in December 1942. This report appears in full under the title "Ching-chi wen-t'i yü ts'ai-cheng wen-t'i" in *Mao Tse-tung hsüan-chi,* 1947 ed., Vol. 5, pp. 1-179.

Notes to Chapter 4

1. For a description of the structure of government in the base area and its transformation from soviet to united-front times, see Hsü, *A Survey,* Part 1, pp. 43-62.

2. See Ch'i Li, *Shan Kan Ning pien ch'ü shih-lu* (Yenan?: Chieh-fang she, 1939; reproduced by Center for Chinese Research Materials, Association of Research Libraries, Washington, D. C., 1969), pp. 79-80. Note that union membership rose to about 60,000 by 1945. See Gunther Stein, *The Challenge of Red China* (New York: McGraw-Hill, 1945), p. 180. Note also that according to Nym Wales, *Inside Red China,* p. 192, about 130,000 women participated in mass movements in the summer of 1937, and about 80,000 of them dependably.

3. For instance, the general union, which was composed of a (nonagricultural) production workers' union, an agricultural workers' union, a store employees' and handicraft workers' union, and a communication and transportation workers' union, organized its members along regional, hsien, ch'ü, hsiang, and small group lines (Ch'i Li, *Shan Kan Ning,* pp. 84-86). The women's federation, which also instituted such territorial divisions, in addition created a variety of functional units such as the women's self-defense corps, the women's vanguards, the girls' guards, and brigades for nursing, consoling, garment-making, laundering, air-raid warning, sanitation, and several other tasks (*ibid.,* p. 105).

4. See *ibid.,* p. 87, for the variety of union tasks, p. 100 for the functions of the youth corps, and pp. 108-118 for the functions of various other organizations, most of which were concerned primarily with education.

5. See Selden, *The Yenan Way,* pp. 142-143, for this view.

6. *Ibid.,* 212-216, and *Shan Kan Ning (1958),* p. 315. Note that there are no differences of classification indicated, so that the apparent increase from 1943 to 1945 may have been real.

7. Stein, *The Challenge,* pp. 137-138. Stein also lists their distribution on administrative levels as follows: hsiang level—2,000 officials; ch'ü

level—1,000 functionaries; hsien plus subregional level—1,200 officials; border region government—300 persons.

8. See *Shan Kan Ning (1958)*, pp. 7-8, and *Brief Account*, pp. 6-7.

9. See Ch'i Li, *Shan Kan Ning*, pp. 67, 100, 105. The difference is implied by conflicting references to the women's self-defense corps which is listed as 10,200 strong on p. 67 and as 40,212 strong on p. 105. The number on p. 67 is explained as unusually small due to the fact that most women in the area had bound feet.

10. See note 8.

11. See *Brief Account*, p. 7, for the statement that a total of 7,000 persons were thus mobilized.

12. See Snow, *Red Star*, p. 284. See also Snow, *Random Notes*, pp. 100-102, for an accounting of the strength of the Red Army and for Snow's lower ,personal estimate of 30,000 to 50,000 troops.

13. See Stein, *The Challenge*, p. 166, and Harrison Forman, *Report from Red China* (New York: Henry Holt, 1945), p. 73. An estimate of 46,000 troops in 1944 can be derived from the claims that the army cultivated 830,000 *mou* of land in *toto* (*Shan Kan Ning (1958)*, p. 282) and that each soldier on the average cultivated 18 *mou* of land (*Mao III*, p. 154).

14. The estimate of 45,000 men in 1941 assumes that the garrison reached its subsequent strength as a result of the conflicts culminating in the New Fourth Army incident. The estimate of 40,000 to 41,500 men in 1940 is based on the statement that in spring 1940, when the troop strength of the garrison was to be increased by 3,500 men, 5,000 men volunteered for service. The actual number of enlistments has not been made public. See *Shan Kan Ning (1958)*, p. 85. The estimate of 33,000 men in 1938 is derived from the estimate for 1941 and the claim that the troop strength increased 36 percent during those three years. See *Shan Kan Ning 1939-1941*, p. 30.

15. See *Shan Kan Ning (1958)*, p. 315, and note that by the end of 1945, many troops had been shifted to the Northeast.

16. See *ibid.*, p. 8, and note that the "original" strength of the garrison (pao-an tui) was said to have been more than 20,000 men. See *Shan Kan Ning 1939-1941*, pp. 26, 34.

17. See *Shan Kan Ning (1958)*, p. 8, for the statement that total enlistments until 1939 reached 30,000 men.

18. See Nym Wales, *Inside Red China*, p. 197, for a description of the army garment shops.

19. See Selden, *The Yenan Way*, p. 248, and Shih Ching-t'ang et al., ed., *Chung-kuo nung-yeh ho-tso-hua yün-tung shih-liao* (Peking: San Lien Bookstore, 1962), Vol. 1, pp. 211, 258.

20. Precise information on the number of cooperators in spinning and weaving is lacking. However, *Shan Kan Ning pien ch'ü cheng-ts'e t'iao-li hui-pien*, p. 27, states that most of the 137,600 spinning women in 1943 were affiliated with cooperatives.

21. Such a conclusion follows from the statement that most spinning women were organized. The implication can be made explicit for 1939 when 137

cooperatives with 28,326 members engaged in cotton textile production while ten cooperatives with 205 members undertook other types of production (porcelain-making, oil-pressing, flour-milling, bean-curd-making, brick-making, etc.) See Nym Wales, *Notes*, p. 59. Note, however, that cooperatives may have been strategically important also in activities such as salt extraction which employed relatively few persons yet contributed decisively to the development of the SKN border region. See *Salt Production*, pp. 3-4, for the organizational techniques, esp. the formation of salt production management committees and labor-exchange brigades.

22. For a detailed description of the South Ch'ü cooperative and for Mao's endorsement see *Chieh-shao nan ch'ü ho-tso she* (Hong Kong: Hsin Min Chu Press, 1949). See also Mao Tse-tung, "Ching-chi wen-t'i," pp. 54 ff. and Selden, *The Yenan Way*, pp. 239-241.

23. See *Shan Kan Ning pien ch'ü cheng-ts'e t'iao-li hui-pien*, pp. 26-27, as well as *Brief Account*, p. 12.

24. Derived from table 4.1 and chapter 2, reference 21.

25. See Nym Wales, *Notes*, pp. 59-63, for a reference to this organization which operated thirteen units with 120 members.

26. See *Mao III*, pp. 155-156 ("Get Organized," 29 November 1943), for the following statement: "The cooperatives are now the most important form of mass organization in the economic field. Although it is unnecessary to insist on attaching the label cooperative to the production activities of the masses in our army, our government and other organizations and our schools, these activities are of a cooperative nature, being carried on under centralized leadership to meet the material needs of various departments, units and individuals through mutual help and joint labor. They are cooperatives of a sort." Note in this connection the description of the Nanniwan project, for example in Gunther Stein, *The Challenge*, pp. 66-74, and in Harrison Forman, *Report*, pp. 38-45.

27. For a description of the origin of this movement, which was meant to provide a substitute for the industries that the interior of China lacked, see Nym Wales, *Notes*. The extension of the movement into SKN is dealt with *ibidem* on pp. 56 ff.

28. See Snow, *Random Notes*, p. 71.

29. See Nym Wales, *Notes*, p. 56.

30. During the years 1939-1943, outside contributions accounted for about 12 percent of the receipts of the CIC branch in the SKN border region. The remaining 88 percent were given by the border region government. See *ibid.*, pp. 63-64. Note that these proportions may not be indicative of the real contributory shares, due to the inflationary spiral.

31. The initial set of ten societies with 215 members produced colored cotton stockings, military uniforms, tin-plate articles, oil lamps, shoes, soap, tooth powder, and hemp-seed oil. See *ibid.*, p. 59.

32. In 1942, CIC textile producers numbered thirty societies with 385 members. See Mao and others, *New Life*, pp. 48-50. Total CIC membership reached 563 members in that year. See table 4.1.

33. Note that in addition, the government of course operated the SKN border region bank, which began to issue notes in substantial amounts in 1941, and it also engaged in regulatory activities through agencies such as the salt bureau, the materials bureau, etc.

34. See note 18 for the early examples. See also Mao, "Ching-chi wen-t'i," pp. 81 ff., 98 ff., for later examples.

35. See Mao "Ching-chi wen-t'i,", pp. 138 ff., esp. pp. 153-154, and note the emphasis on commercial profit. The overall estimate for 1942 was that of the product of central administration enterprises and after-hours enterprises, 57.5 percent were for own consumption and 42.5 percent for the market.

36. See Stein, *The Challenge*, p. 180, and note that his references to factories rather than employed persons appear to be mistaken. See table 4.1 for appropriate proportions between persons employed in state enterprises and CIC enterprises.

37. Data on the average sizes of establishments in various sectors and branches present a confusing picture. E.g., table 5.4 implies an average size of about three persons per shop for selected handicrafts in thirteen hsien cities in 1942/1943. This average probably exaggerates that of all handicraft establishments in the entire border region. CIC units on the average counted about ten members per establishment in 1939 but less than four members per establishment in 1944 (see Nym Wales, *Notes,* pp. 59-63). CIC weaving units in 1943 had twelve persons per cooperative while private weaving mills employed six persons per establishment (see *Wei kung-yeh p'in;* p. 59). The average size of state enterprises fluctuated wildly over time but remained above thirty persons. In addition, the size of state enterprises varied substantially by branch of industry (see tables 4.4, 5.3).

38. See *Shan Kan Ning (1958),* p. 86, for a reference to 90 percent illiteracy among soldiers during the late 1930s.

39. For an early example of the training of women in farm work, see Nym Wales, *Inside Red China,* p. 195. Note also that the effectiveness of "how to do it" literature in all lines of production and notably in farming depended in part on an adequate degree of literacy.

40. Note that students in the fourth and fifth grades numbered merely 222 in 1938, 1,586 in 1940, and 1,250 in 1944. See *Shan Kan Ning 1939-1941,* p. 61, and *General Survey of National Education,* pp. 1-2.

41. Note that whereas originally at least two-thirds of the middle plus normal school students had immigrated into the SKN border region, by 1940 more than two-thirds of them were of local origin. See *Shan Kan Ning 1939-1941,* pp. 67-68.

42. For a detailed description of the student body of the Anti-Japanese Military Academy during the late 1930s see Ch'i Li, *Shan Kan Ning,* pp. 121 ff.

43. Note also the 1945 statement that during the entire period 1937-1945, the school system produced 40,000 political and military cadres plus thousands of educational and technical cadres for the liberation of other areas. See *Shan Kan Ning (1958),* p. 287.

44. For an illuminating discussion of the educational system in the SKN border region and the conflict over educational policies between the educational reformers and the Maoists during the years 1942-1944, see Peter J. Seybolt, "The Yenan Revolution in Mass Education," *The China Quarterly,* No. 48 (October/December 1971): 641-664.

45. See chapter 2, notes 29 to 32. Note also the absence of information on old-style learning, which probably predominated in the area.

46. See *Brief Account,* p. 16, and *General Survey of National Education,* pp. 1-2, for references to a variety of measures which involved a (temporary) contraction of enrollment. Noteworthy are the consolidation of schools, elimination of inferior teachers, diminution of compulsion in inducing school attendance, accommodation to the labor requirements of the farms, etc.

47. The results of the 1953 census suggest that children of ages seven to ten constituted 5 to 6 percent of the entire population (see John S. Aird, "Present and Prospective Population of Mainland China," Milbank Memorial Fund, *Population Trends in Eastern Europe, the USSR and Mainland China* [New York: Milbank Memorial Fund, 1960], p. 105). The corresponding absolute numbers for the SKN border region would be 75,000 to 90,000 children (derived from *ibid.* and table 2.1). The number of primary school students in the first three grades was 30,540 in 1944 (see table 4.5 and note 40). Note also a statement in *Shan Kan Ning (1958),* p. 90, that merely one in four children of school age attended school in 1940.

48. See Stein, *The Challenge,* p. 263, for an observation of this fact in one specific instance.

49. Note that the student bodies of the major educational institutions grew very rapidly from 1936 to 1938. For instance, the Anti-Japanese Military Academy started with 300 students in June 1936; the second class in 1937 had 800 students; the third and fourth classes in 1938 each had 5,000 to 6,000 students; and the fifth class at the end of 1938 numbered 10,000 students. See Ch'i Li, *Shan Kan Ning,* pp. 118-121. Correspondingly, the North Shensi Public School began with 500 students in September 1937, reached 1,400 students in March 1938, and grew to more than 3,000 students soon thereafter. See *ibid.,* pp. 139-140.

50. For a comprehensive discussion of the efforts of 1943, see Mark Selden, *The Yenan Way,* pp. 208 ff.

51. For early examples of Mao's concern, see the section on Questions of Party Organization in "The Struggle in the Chingkang Mountains" (25 November 1928), *Mao I,* pp. 92 ff., as well as the sections On Ultra-Democracy and On the Disregard of Organizational Discipline in his article "On Correcting Mistaken Ideas in the Party" (December 1929), *Mao I,* pp. 108-110.

52. *Mao I,* p. 291.

53. *Mao II,* pp. 195-211.

54. See *ibid.,* p. 198.

55. See *ibid.,* p. 203, for the following list:

First, give them guidance. This means allowing them a free hand in their work so that they have the courage to assume responsibility and, at the same time, giving them instructions so that, guided by the Party's political line, they are able to make full use of their initiative.

Second, raise their level. This means educating them by giving them the opportunity to study so that they can enhance their theoretical understanding and their working ability.

Third, check up on their work and help them sum up their experience, carry forward their achievements, and correct their mistakes. To assign work without checking up and to take notice only when serious mistakes are made—that is not the way to take care of cadres.

Fourth, in general, use the method of persuasion with cadres who have made mistakes and help them correct their mistakes. The method of struggle should be confined to those who make serious mistakes and nevertheless refuse to accept guidance. Here patience is essential. It is wrong lightly to lable people "opportunists" or lightly to begin "waging struggles" against them.

Fifth, help them with their difficulties. When cadres are in difficulty as a result of illness, straitened means, or domestic or other troubles, we must be sure to give them as much care as possible.

56. For a comprehensive study of the rectification campaign and Mao's contribution to it, see Boyd Compton, *Mao's China: Party Reform Documents, 1942-1944* (Seattle: University of Washington Press, 1952).

57. *Mao III*, p. 18, note.

58. *Ibid.*, pp. 117-122: "Some Questions Concerning Methods of Leadership" (1 June 1943).

59. *Ibid.*, pp. 69-98.

60. See *General Survey of National Education in the Shensi-Kansu-Ninghsia Border Region,* pp. 8-15, and note the emphasis on work-study programs as well as on the formation of yangko (song and play) brigades for the propagation of the development program in the countryside.

61. See *ibid.,* pp. 15 ff., esp. p. 16: ". . ., since 1942, the Border Region Education Bureau enlarged and transformed the various forms of character learning movement to carry out general social education. Moreover, in the winter of 1943, there were clear and definite instructions that social education should be closely coordinated with the other tasks in every Hsien such as production movement, guard against traitors and self-defense, support the army and government and love the people movement, reducing rent and interest, etc. During the realization of the above-mentioned work, social activities were organized according to plan and education was carried out amongst the people."

62. Note that not only the normal schools but also the middle schools, arts academy, and university served primarily the purpose of training teachers for the lower educational institutions.

63. For a description of the educational objectives and techniques of the Anti-Japanese Military Academy (K'ang Ta) see Ch'i Li, *Shan Kan Ning,* pp. 121-126.

64. See Stein, *The Challenge*, pp. 260-267, and Forman, *Report*, pp. 86-97, for summaries of their impressions of the educational system in the border region. See also Stein, *The Challenge*, pp. 150-153, for a description of the working of the CCP party school and Forman, *Report*, pp. 44-45, for a description of the education of troops in Nanniwan.

65. See *Mao III*, pp. 99-101.

66. See *ibid.*, pp. 111-116.

67. See *ibid.*, p. 101.

68. See *ibid.*, p. 133.

69. See *ibid.*, pp. 133-134.

70. See Mao Tse-tung, "Get Organized," speech made at a reception in honor of the labor heroes of the Shensi-Kansu-Ninghsia Border Region on 29 November 1943, *Mao III*, p. 153.

71. Both books are filled with references to the involvement of almost everyone in production. Note in this connection that Forman questioned the wisdom of having medical students spend three hours daily at spinning. His criticism of the practice apparently led to the abolition of the requirement. See Forman, *Report.*, pp. 51-52.

72. See *ibid.*, p. 74, and note that the most significant change took place in 1944.

73. See Maos speech on "We must learn to do economic work" (10 January 1945), *Mao III*, pp. 239-245, and his editorial on "Production is also possible in the guerrilla zones" (31 January 1945), *ibid.*, pp. 247-250.

74. See *Shan Kan Ning pien ch'ü cheng-ts'e t'iao-li hui-pien*, p. 58, for an appraisal of the progress of the campaign by Li Ting-ming, Vice-Chairman of the SKN border region government.

75. See *ibid.*, Appendix, pp. 82 ff., for the texts of various regulations, most of which dated from February 1943.

76. See *ibid.*, pp. 59-71, for a description of these changes. Note that the production campaign was referred to in the context of economizing.

77. See *ibid.*, p. 59.

78. See especially Stein, *The Challenge*, pp. 136, 141.

79. See chapter 5, notes 16 to 19. Note further that the interpretation of the evidence is ambiguous because administrative personnel assigned to (part-time or full-time) material production may have been counted twice, i.e., in administration as well as elsewhere such as in industry.

80. See *Wei kung-yeh p'in*, pp. 14-15, 63.

81. See *ibid.*, p. 17.

82. See *ibid.*, p. 63.

83. See *ibid.*, p. 64. Note that the source refers especially to the training of apprentices.

84. See *ibid.*, pp. 20 and 51-52. Note that the cited examples, which concern changes during 1943-1944, appear to be extreme and therefore unrepresentative.

85. See *ibid.*, pp. 17 and 74, as well as Mao, "Ching-chi wen-t'i," p. 96.

86. See *Mao I*, pp. 81-83.

87. See *Mao II*, p. 198.

88. See *Mao I*, pp. 110-111.

89. See note 55, point 5.

90. See *Mao III*, p. 133.

91. See *ibid.*, p. 132.

92. See Ch'i Li, *Shan Kan Ning*, pp. 126-127, 169.

93. See *ibid.* and *Ching-chi yen-chiu*, No. 2 (1956), p. 101.

94. Derived from Yen-an nung-ts'un tiao-ch'a t'uan, *Mi-chih hsien*, p. 149.

95. See *Shan Kan Ning (1958)*, p. 19, and Ch'i Li, *Shan Kan Ning*, p. 169, for references to this limit. See also Edgar Snow, *Red Star*, p. 477, for the note that the commissioner of finance in 1936 received an allowance of five yuan.

96. See *Ching-chi yen-chiu*, No. 2 (1956), p. 101, for the estimate that the cost per soldier amounted to six to eight piculs (0.9 to 1.2 tons) of millet per annum. See also Ch'i Li, *Shan Kan Ning*, p. 169, for estimates of 4.5 yuan food expenditure and 1 yuan pocket money per month. The cost of clothing cannot have exceeded 1.5 yuan per month.

97. See *Shan Kan Ning (1958)*, p. 19, for a reference to 2.5 yuan allowance for hsien chiefs. See Ch'i Li, *Shan Kan Ning*, pp. 155 and 158, for the allowances of teachers in the Lu Hsun Art Academy (2.0-3.0 yuan per month) and in the border region middle school (3.0-5.0 yuan per month).

98. Note that information on cadre allowances during later years could not be found.

99. The most likely exception to the rule appeared during the mass production campaign in the form of the labor hero who in many instances could achieve high status as well as individual wealth.

100. See *General Survey of National Education*, p. 7, for indications of extraordinarily equalitarian conditions for teachers and principals of various grade schools.

101. See Forman, *Report*, p. 76.

102. See Stein, *The Challenge*, p. 179.

103. See *ibid.*, p. 178, and table 8.3.

104. See *Wei kung-yeh p'in*, p. 77.

105. See *ibid.*, p. 76. The source mentions several extreme changes in the wages system but does not specify other earlier forms of wage payment.

106. See *ibid.*, p. 46.

107. See *ibid.*, p. 22. Note also the identification of petty bourgeois values in this conclusion.

108. See *ibid.*, p. 108, for the points that the mixed system failed to encourage individual study of technology as well as individual economizing of rationed supplies, e.g. of clothing.

109. See *ibid.*, p. 79, and note that the source does not specify inter-industry differentials. For a discussion of Chinese practices during the 1950s and their relation to Soviet practices, see Peter Schran, "Unity and Diversity of Russian and Chinese Industrial Wage Policies," *Journal of Asian Studies*, 23, 2 (February 1964): 245-251.

110. See *Wei kung-yeh p'in,* p. 79, and note that the Kuang Hua printing plant, which was being criticized for this reason, had narrowed wage differentials while adopting an all-wages system!

111. See *ibid.* The details of such a wage grade system have not been specified. For a description of later practices, which usually abstracted from seniority as a criterion, see Peter Schran, "Unity and Diversity."

112. See *Wei kung-yeh p'in,* p. 79.

113. See Mao, "Ching-chi wen-t'i," p. 96.

114. See *Wei kung-yeh p'in,* p. 77, for this observation.

115. See note 110.

116. See *Shan Kan Ning pien ch'ü cheng-ts'e t'iao-li hui-pien,* p. 175. Communications workers were stationed in Yenan as well as along the major roads in the SKN border region.

117. See *ibid.*

118. See *Shan Kan Ning 1939-1941,* p. 44, and *Shan Kan Ning (1958),* pp. 284-285.

119. See *Shan Kan Ning (1958),* pp. 32-33.

120. See *Wei kung-yeh p'in,* p. 42.

121. See *Salt Production,* p. 3, for the following rewards for recruiters of salt farmers: one family—one sheep; two families—two sheep; five families—half an oxen; ten families—one oxen. To encourage the transportation of salt, the government exempted income earned in this line of business from taxation (see *ibid.,* p. 7). It also exempted animals used full time in salt transportation from corvée. See *Shan Kan Ning (1958),* p. 126.

122. See *Brief Account,* p. 11.

123. See *Wei kung-yeh p'in,* p. 45. Note also that the constraints to external trade and the resulting price structure appear to have been such that the tariff reductions did not impede cotton-growing and cotton-spinning. Note further that the government organized and financed the Yung Ch'ang local cloth production and marketing company of Suite which in turn organized putting-out systems in spinning and weaving.

124. See *ibid.* Note that the source asserts positive responses to the policy by two private firms.

125. See Mao III, pp. 131-132 ("Spread the Campaigns to Reduce Rent, Increase Production and 'Support the Government and Cherish the People' in the Base Areas," 1 October 1943). Note that the rent-reduction campaign basically aimed at securing mass support. However, such support was to result in increased productive efforts. "If during this autumn we check on how far the policy has been carried out and perform the task of rent reduction thoroughly, we shall be able to arouse the initiative of the peasant masses and, in the coming year, intensify our struggle against the enemy *and give impetus to the production campaign.*" (Italics added).

126. See *ibid.,* p. 132.

127. See note 109. Note also, however, that subsidies and protection were to be reduced during the course of increasing self-sufficiency, e.g. in match-manufacturing. See *Wei kung-yeh p'in,* p. 60.

128. See *Shan Kan Ning (1958)*, p. 285.

129. As part of this program, external trade in 1943 was unified under the government's materials bureau. In addition, efforts were made to separate salt transport and salt production organizationally. See Mao, "Ching-chi wen-t'i," p. 147.

130. See *Shan Kan Ning pien ch'ü cheng-ts'e t'iao-li hui-pien*, pp. 45-46, for the plans to integrate state and cooperative organizations in commerce during 1944. See *Wei kung-yeh p'in*, esp. p. 90, for the call to adopt the planning of production at the same time.

Notes to Chapter 5

1. See chapter 2, note 13, and Snow, *Red Star*, pp. 228-232, for an abstract of the findings of A. Stampar. Stampar's report on *The Northwestern Provinces and their Possibilities of Development* could not be located.

2. See chapter 4, notes 118-121.

3. See Stein, *The Challenge*, p. 163, and *Brief Account*, p. 7.

4. Note that the official population estimates of 1941 and 1944 exclude these groups explicitly.

5. See chapter 2, note 20.

6. Note that the one reference in table 5.1 to 8,800 labor-force members in 1943, a number which barely exceeds that of the immigrant families during that year, probably understates the actual number substantially. The average size of 3.0 persons per immigrant family during 1941-1944, which is small in comparison with the 5.1 persons per household in the region in 1944 (see table 2.1) and which reflects the tendency of migrants to move with few dependents, supports this interpretation. It is also possible, however, that the number of disabled persons in 1943 was extraordinarily large.

7. See Stein, *The Challenge*, pp. 36-38, and Forman, *Report*, pp. 11-19, for accounts of their visit to the Sian Labor Training Camp as well as Stein, *ibid.*, pp. 46-47, for a description of a Relief Camp for Refugees from the Communist Areas. Both accounts suggest small numbers of persons leaving the SKN border region.

8. See chapter 2, notes 46-56, and especially note 53, for indications of hidden unemployment.

9. See *Shan Kan Ning (1958)*, p. 92, for a reference to the fact that land reclamation was most promising in Suite and in the East Region (rather than in the North where the area of uncultivated arable land was largest).

10. Note that the incentives described in chapter 4, note 121, applied also to internal migrants. See *Salt Production*, p. 3.

11. See Yen-an nung-ts'un tiao-ch'a t'uan, *Mi-chih hsien*, p. 18, for a reference to the fact that several persons from Yang Chia K'ou in Michih Hsien were working in such establishments in the new manufacturing centers within the border region.

12. See *Shan Kan Ning (1958)*, p. 12.

13. See *Shan Kan Ning 1939-1941,* p. 44.

14. See Stein, *The Challenge,* p. 163.

15. For a discussion of the problem in relation to industrial employment, see *Wei kung-yeh p'in,* pp. 78-79, and *Shan Kan Ning (1958),* p. 94.

16. See Selden, *The Yenan Way,* p. 213.

17. See *ibid.,* p. 215, and *Shan Kan Ning pien ch'ü cheng-ts'e t'iao-li hui-pien,* p. 9.

18. See *Shan Kan Ning (1958),* p. 315.

19. Note that even though differences of classification are not indicated, the data are inadequately specified. The interpretation of the evidence is ambiguous because administrative personnel assigned to (part-time or full-time) material production may have been counted twice, i.e., in administration as well as in, say, industry.

20. For examples of extreme surpluses and reductions, see *Wei kung-yeh p'in,* pp. 17 ff.

21. See Selden, *The Yenan Way,* pp. 224-229, for an emphasis of this consequence.

22. For an early example see *Chieh-fang Jih Pao* (23 May 1941), p. 2: "Pien ch'ü kung-jen chan-tou ti i yüeh."

23. See *Wei kung-yeh p'in,* pp. 46-47, for a discussion of problems of labor attitudes during a protracted war.

24. See, e.g., Mao Tse-tung and others, *New Life,* chapters 3: "Declaration of the Labor Heroes Conference," and 4: "Sketches of Labor Heroes," pp. 19-41. Note that the increased efforts in farm work were to be sustained by commensurate increases in output. The yield effects, which are problematic, will be discussed in chapter 6 in the context of a review of changes in agricultural output.

25. Extreme cases are listed in Mao and others, *New Life.* Aggregate increases of substantial magnitude are implied by the data on land reclamation and on changes in cultivated land. See table 6.1.

26. See *Shan Kan Ning (1958),* p. 125, article 5, with respect to the provisions enacted by the second border region congress.

27. See Aird, "Present and Prospective Population," p. 105, for 1953 census data and Buck, *Land Utilization,* pp. 376-377, for 1929-1931 survey data on the composition of the Chinese population by age and sex.

28. See *Shan Kan Ning pien ch'ü cheng-ts'e t'iao-li hui-pien,* p. 69.

29. See Mao and others, *New Life,* p. 53, for the progress made by 1943.

30. Note that the sources refer to increased local self-sufficiency which diminished transport requirements, to increased military and administrative self-sufficiency which diminished impositions on the civilian population, and to increases in the number of pack animals which reduced the demand for carriers.

31. See table 2.1 (domestic service only, female) and table 2.3 (employed farm women) for evidence to this effect.

32. See Nym Wales, *Inside Red China,* pp. 194-195. Note also the substitution effect of female employment: "When the First Front Red Army first

came to the Northwest they were able, within a few weeks, to get about 20,000 new fighters in this sparsely populated area. Why? Because the women organized to carry on in their place in the rear. . . ." *Ibid.*

33. See *ibid.,* p. 192: "Nearly all local women had bound feet, except the Moslems and Mongols. Those in Yenshih and Tingpien near the Mongol border did not bind their feet."

34. See chapter 3, note 39, for the formulation of this objective in 1939.

35. See chapter 4 and note that resistance to the policy continued, as is evident in Mao's directives to "spread the campaigns to reduce rent, increase production and 'support the government and cherish the people' in the base areas" of 1 October 1943 (*Mao III,* p. 133): "It is wrong to consider it dishonorable and selfish either for Communists in the countryside to engage in household production in order to support their families or for Communists in government organizations and schools to engage in private spare-time production in order to improve their own living conditions, for all such activity is in the interest of the revolutionary cause. . . ."

36. See *Salt Production,* pp. 1-3.

37. See Forman, *Report,* p. 78.

38. For a review of these data, see chapter 7.

39. See *Mao III,* p. 154, and chapter 4, note 13.

40. Derived from note 39 and table 7.6.

41. See chapter 7.

42. See Forman, *Report,* p. 70.

43. See *ibid.* Note that on the basis of Buck's data, the number of persons idle or of unknown occupation is estimated as 112,000 for the area controlled in 1936. See table 2.2.

44. See Mao and others, *New Life,* p. 125.

45. See Stein, *The Challenge,* p. 46, for his description of an encounter with a "genuine vagabond" in the "Relief Camp for Refugees from the Communist Areas" in Ichuan.

46. See table 2.1 for an estimate of 254,100 households for 1941, close to 90 percent of which were peasant households according to Chinese communist reckoning.

47. See table 5.2, note b. The minority may have consisted of several thousand workers (see table 5.2, note m). Note in addition that the land reform, which was carried out in most of the SKN border region prior to 1937, may have reduced the number of farm laborers.

48. Moreover, the data of table 2.3 suggest that employment in farm work may have been abnormally low. The stagnation or decrease in employment do not preclude increases in individual efforts which cannot be measured directly.

49. Although government organs and schools engaged in agricultural production, too, it appears that their contributions were comparatively small. See chapter 7 for indications of the relative importance of various efforts.

50. Note that the extraction of all minerals required 0.0 percent of all employed persons in North China during 1929-1931 according to Buck, *Land*

Utilization, p. 372. It did not appear as a separate subsidiary occupation in Tingpien and Hsunyi.

51. See Hsü, *A Survey*, Part 2, p. 106.

52. See *ibid.*

53. See *ibid.*, and *Salt Production*, p. 9, for data on the land and animal stock of salt-producer households which suggest a substantial involvement in agricultural production in the four major locations.

54. See *ibid.*, p. 3.

55. See Nym Wales, *Inside Red China*, p. 197: "There were several state-owned factories for supplying uniforms, shoes and other necessities for the Red Army. Altogether in North Shensi, there were seven hundred men and six hundred women employed in these state, or "national," as the Soviets called them, factories." See also Snow, *Red Star*, p. 268, for a list of enterprises which suggests more numerous employment.

56. Note that the 1943 data of table 23 were derived by subtracting the handicraft employment according to table 24 (see also Hsü, *A Survey*, Part 2, p. 108) and the employment in salt production from the reported manufacturing aggregates (see Hsü, *A Survey*, Part 2, p. 109).

57. See chapter 4, note 32.

58. See *Wei kung-yeh p'in*, p. 46, for the statement that the major sources of industrial labor were: (1) factory workers from cities outside the region and (2) villagers from locations inside the region. For an early statement on recruitment of skilled labor from the outside, see Snow, *Red Star*, pp. 267, 271.

59. Note that the number of soldiers employed in coal-mining is not specified in tables 5.2 and 5.3. See Forman, *Report*, p. 78, for the assertion of such employment.

60. Note that use is made of average shop sizes from the provincial handicraft surveys of 1954 rather than of those from the data for the thirteen hsien cities in the SKN border region in 1942 and 1943 (see table 5.4). Because the latter data refer to relatively large urban centers, they can be expected to overstate the territorial averages.

61. The difference may be related to the possibility that previously shop employees were counted as occupied in trade.

62. See *Wei kung-yeh p'in*, p. 52, and note that private textile enterprises, which would have to account for a large share of the total employment, numbered fifty units with 310 employees. See *ibid.*, p. 59.

63. See *Shan Kan Ning (1958)*, p. 284, and note that the population of Yenan, which reached 12,371 persons at the end of 1944 (*ibid.*, p. 378), numbered 5,029 persons according to 1941 data (*Shan Kan Ning 1939-1941*, p. 11) and probably fewer persons during earlier years. Note in addition that the population counts excluded the institutional households of army, government organs, and schools.

64. See Ch'i Li, *Shan Kan Ning*, p. 21, for references to more than one thousand new shops and to increases in the number of handicraft establishments in Tingpien.

65. See *Shan Kan Ning pien ch'ü cheng-ts'e t'iao-li hui-pien,* p. 27, and chapter 4, note 20.

66. See Nym Wales, *Notes,* p. 59, and chapter 4, note 21.

67. The difference between the estimates of tables 2.2 and 2.3 probably reflects in particular a difference in the counting of production for own consumption. See chapter 2, note 52.

68. See notes 62 and 65.

69. See *Wei kung-yeh p'in,* p. 58, for examples of institutional efforts in spinning and for targets for such efforts. References to the final result, the degree of institutional self-sufficiency, appear in chapter 7.

70. See Ch'i Li, *Shan Kan Ning,* p. 84.

71. See note 26.

72. See notes 28 and 29.

73. See Ch'i Li, *Shan Kan Ning,* p. 83.

74. See *ibid.,* p. 84.

75. Estimate: one attendant per six pack animals. Derived from *Salt Production,* p. 6, and Mao and others, *New Life,* pp. 128-129.

76. See table 6.5 for data on total salt production which suggest such a pattern. Note also that prior to the completion of the new roads, the animal-man ratio in transportation was lower. See *Salt Production,* p. 6.

77. Note that own provision was part of the campaign to "support the government and cherish the people." For an example of transportation for own use, see *Shan Kan Ning pien ch'ü cheng-ts'e t'iao-li hui-pien,* p. 37.

78. See Ch'i Li, *Shan Kan Ning,* p. 84.

79. See *ibid.,* p. 83, for an explicit reference to household laborers.

80. Note that the total included 200 practitioners of Western medicine, 1,000 practitioners of Chinese medicine, 50 veterinarians, 400 Chinese pharmacists, and 2,000 witch doctors and sorcerers (!). See *Shan Kan Ning (1958),* p. 221.

81. While the number of Chinese and Western doctors apparently increased slowly, witch doctors and sorcerers were exposed to an active campaign of persecution and suppression which may have diminished their numbers notably.

82. See Buck, *Land Utilization,* p. 298, for a reference to teaching and medicine as the only exemplary occupations.

83. See, for example, Chang Chung-li, *The Income of the Chinese Gentry* (Seattle: University of Washington Press, 1962), p. 321. Note, however, that Chang's estimates pertain to the late nineteenth century.

84. Note in particular that the occupation "scholar" frequently was used as a euphemism for rentier-landlords. Their number must have been reduced substantially by the land reform which was carried out prior to spring 1937 in eighteen of the original twenty-three hsien.

85. See Stein, *The Challenge,* pp. 137-138, for this total which included 2,000 officials in 1,250 *hsiang;* 1,000 officials in 210 *ch'ü;* 1,200 officials in 31 *hsien* and five subregions; and 300 officials of the border region government.

86. For a description of local developments prior to the formation of the SKN border region, see Mark Selden, "The Guerrilla Movement in Northwest China." Note that until the arrival of the main force of the Red Army, the numbers of troops involved in local conflicts apparently remained rather small.

87. See Buck, *Land Utilization*, p. 372.

88. See notes 63 and 64. Note the difficulties involved in distinguishing between handicrafts and trade establishments in these instances.

89. See especially *Salt Production*, p. 5, for a reference to the fact that the formation of salt-production cooperatives involved specialization in marketing activities and reductions in the number of persons going to market.

90. Note, however, that all members of the school staff, teachers, and students above the age of 12 were held to participate in production (spinning, gardening, wood-cutting, sewing, etc.). See *General Survey of National Education in the Shensi-Kansu-Ninghsia Border Region*, p. 9

Notes to Chapter 6

1. Note that the Chinese communists had pursued such measures at the latest since their economic construction campaign of 1933 (see chapter 3, notes 22 and 23). Note also that most of the proposed improvements were similar to those which "bourgeois" farm economists recommended at that time. (See Peter Schran, *The Development of Chinese Agriculture, 1950-1959*, p. 103, for the observation that the agricultural development program of 1956, which restated the policies practiced in the SKN border region and in other base areas, was practically identical with the proposals of John Lossing Buck). The SKN program is outlined in Chung kung hsi-pei chung-yang chü, tiao-ch'a yen-chiu shih, *Pien ch'ü kai-liang nung tso wen-t'i* (Problems of improving agricultural work in the Border Region) (Shan Kan Ning pien ch'ü sheng-ch'an yün-tung ts'ung-shu; no location: same as author, 1944).

2. Note that this advocacy of cooperation may well have antedated many of the technical recommendations. Cooperatives are referred to in the 1928 resolution on the agrarian question (see chapter 3, note 3), and they appear generally as organizational alternatives to capitalist transformation in soviet socialist thinking.

3. See chapter 2, notes 57 and 58.

4. See *ibid.* and *Shan Kan Ning (1958)*, p. 92.

5. See chapter 2, notes 54 to 56, for estimates of the initial underutilization of farm labor.

6. See *Shan Kan Ning 1939-1941*, p. 43. See also *Brief Account*, p. 11, for a reference to high death rates among cattle as a cause of this shortage.

7. See Stein, *The Challenge*, p. 166, for the statement: "It is all marginal land, bound to become useless from erosion in the course of years. . . ."

8. See Buck, *Land Utilization*, pp. 116-121, for a description of the climate, which is characterized by little rainfall, large temperature variations, and a short growing season.

9. See Stein, *The Challenge*, p. 166.

10. See table 7.6 for information on the reclamation and cultivation of land by the SKN border region garrison.

11. Note that if the number of cilivians occupied in agriculture did not change from 1940 to 1944, the cultivated land per civilian increased by at least 30 and at most 40 percent. Buck's data for the *spring wheat region* and the *winter wheat-millet region* depict much larger differentials between the land-labor ratios of small and large farms (in combination with similar differentials between the land-animal ratios and under conditions of constant returns to land by farm size class). See Buck, *Land Utilization*, pp. 273, 276, 277. Buck stresses the close correspondence between land and product per laborer. Moreover, in an earlier study he found that the man-work units (ten-hour days) per man equivalent (adult male) were almost twice as high on large farms as on small farms. See Buck, *Chinese Farm Economy*, p. 448. The SKN garrison in 1943-44 cultivated eighteen *mou* per soldier (see *Mao III*, p. 154), i.e., about half the area of the average farm in the region.

12. See *Shan Kan Ning 1939-1941*, p. 50, and *Shan Kan Ning (1958)*, p. 21, for the early data and comments on early successes and failures.

13. See chapter 2, table 2.6 and note 70. Note that the goal of ten million sheep was not reached by 1945. See *Shan Kan Ning 1939-1941*, pp. 43, 51, and table 6.2. See in addition *Shan Kan Ning pien ch'ü cheng-ts'e t'iao-li hui-pien*, p. 44, for the challenge to increase the production of grazing grass in 1944.

14. See Buck, *Land Utilization*, p. 233, for survey data on the effects of irrigation on wheat yields and millet yields. These effects were particularly great in the *spring wheat* and *winter wheat-millet* regions. See also Mao and others, *New Life*, p. 86, for a reference to similarly large gains in Chingpien.

15. Note in addition that irrigation facilitated the introduction of rice cultivation on a very small scale. The small share of irrigated land may be attributable to technical difficulties, shortages of equipment, the danger of alkalization, etc. See also chapter 2, note 74.

16. See *Shan Kan Ning (1958)*, p. 285.

17. Note that the climate must have imposed severe limitations on the expansion of double cropping. See note 8 and chapter 2, note 71.

18. See chapter 2, note 75, plus table 2.9, and Forman, *Report*, p. 83.

19. See *Shan Kan Ning pien ch'ü cheng-ts'e t'iao-li hui-pien*, p. 44. Potato crops were expected to yield 800 to 1,000 catties per *mou*. At the conversion rate of 4:1, this amounted to 200 to 250 catties of grain equivalent. In comparison, the actual yields of grain apparently did not exceed 50 catties per *mou* on the average.

20. Note that the production of cotton was promoted by exempting cotton fields from taxation and by lending to cotton growers at low rates of interest. See Van Slyke, *The Chinese Communist Movement*, p. 160.

21. See chapter 2, note 85, for specific shortcomings of Buck's survey data.

22. See Van Slyke, *The Chinese Communist Movement,* p. 159. For examples of instructional materials, see Shan Kan Ning pien ch'ü cheng-fu chien-she t'ing, *Tsen-yang chung mien-hua* (How to grow cotton) (1944), 24 pp., ill., and idem, *Hsiao-mieh ch'ung hai* (Exterminate insect pests) (1946), 2 + 47 pp., ill.

23. See *Shan Kan Ning pien ch'ü cheng-ts'e t'iao-li hui-pien, p. 34.* See *ibid.,* p. 44, for the proposed changes in 1944: ". . . Thirdly, we must promote the improvement of agricultural methods, deep furrowing and careful management, increase the amount of manure, increase times of hoeing, turn more lowland into irrigated fields, exterminate insects, select seeds. . . ." Note also that deep furrowing and frequent hoeing were problematic because of the consequent increase in the evaporation of moisture.

24. See Mao and others, *New Life,* pp. 52, 126.

25. See *ibid.,* p. 47, on this use of cotton seeds.

26. See Van Slyke, *The Chinese Communist Movement,* p. 166, and Chao Kuo-chun, *Agrarian Policy,* pp. 44-45, 51-52.

27. Derived from table 7.3 and *Shan Kan Ning (1958),* p. 285. The latter source lists the following agricultural loans: 1942—3,600,000 yuan; 1943—27,800,000 yuan; 1944—100,000,000 yuan; 1945—599,000,000 yuan. Most of the loans apparently were made for the purpose of purchasing work animals. Systematic information on the prices of work animals is lacking.

28. See Van Slyke, *The Chinese Communist Movement,* p. 166, for a reference to loans given to poor peasants. See also note 20 with respect to loans granted to cotton growers. Note in addition that the government had to supply the army units which engaged in agricultural production with some implements and loans.

29. See note 11 for evidence in support of this possibility.

30. See chapter 5, notes 24 and 25.

31. See chapter 2, notes 79 and 80.

32. Note the continuing use of Hsunyi data in the derivation of SKN border region averages. Hsunyi, which may have had unusually high yields in comparison with the rest of the *winter wheat-millet region* within the SKN territory, was lost during 1939/1940.

33. See chapter 2, note 116, for a grain requirement of 1.82 million piculs in 1940. The corresponding requirement for 1944/1945 approximates two million piculs (or 300,000 tons).

34. Note that the official consumption estimates for 1943 imply an even lower standard which the revised data cannot meet either. See Mao and others, *New Life,* p. 123, for a total consumption estimate of 1.62 million piculs which entails average rations of about one picul, i.e., 300 catties, per person per annum in 1943.

35. See Buck, *Land Utilization,* p. 238, for information on the use of by-products.

36. Such averages are implicit in the totals listed in *Brief Account,* p.

11, and *Shan Kan Ning pien ch'ü cheng-ts'e t'iao-li hui-pien.* See also Mao and others, *New Life,* p. 47. See in addition T. H. Shen, *Agricultural Resources,* p. 309, for implicit yield estimates of twenty-three catties per *mou* in Shensi and twenty catties per *mou* in Kansu.

37. See *Brief Account,* p. 11.

38. See *ibid.*

39. See *ibid.* and *Wei kung-yeh p'in,* p. 58.

40. See Mao and others, *New Life,* p. 47, and T. H. Shen, *Agricultural Resources,* p. 263.

41. See *ibid.,* p. 245. Note also that Mao operated with an extraction rate of 12 percent. See his "Ching-chi wen-t'i," p. 31.

42. See Chao Kuo-chun, *Agrarian Policy,* p. 60. For an earlier estimate of 360,000 catties, see Mao Tse-tung, "Ching-chi wen-t'i, " p. 48.

43. See chapter 2, note 86.

44. See T. H. Shen, *Agricultural Resources,* pp. 380-383, and note that we use the lower of the two estimates.

45. See *ibid.* for estimates of the weight of cattle. See Buck, *Land Utilization,* p. 473, for the estimate that one oxen was equivalent to two donkeys. See Phillips et al., *The Livestock of China,* pp. 33, 47, for the indication that considerable numbers of cattle and donkeys in the area were of the large type. The estimate therefore may understate the actual average carcass weight.

46. See table 2.9 for an estimate of 175 grams per month.

47. See Van Slyke, *The Chinese Communist Movement,* p. 148, for referances to four or more pounds per month.

48. See *ibid.,* p. 147, as well as chapter 8.

49. See Phillips et al., *The Livestock of China,* pp. 78-79.

50. See *ibid.,* p. 80, and T. H. Shen, *Agricultural Resources,* p. 327.

51. Because land as well as labor were underutilized and because the efforts involved in reclamation work are not known, it is impossible to attach meaningful values to the additions to cultivated land. However, if an incremental capital-output ratio near two were to be used, it could be inferred that reclaimed land added about 10 percent per annum to the farm product during 1940-1944, the share rising to 15 percent on the average during 1943-1944.

52. See *Salt Production,* p. 2, for a statement to this effect.

53. See table 6.5, notes d and h, which suggest a growth from perhaps 200 *mou* to more than 2,200 *mou.*

54. See *Salt Production,* p. 1, for the information that the soldiers built 282 salt fields in Kaochih and 801 salt fields in Laochih, Whether they participated in construction activities in the other locations is not made clear in the text.

55. See *ibid.,* pp. 4-6, and note the importance attributed to labor cooperation in this connection.

56. Note in particular the possibility of accelerating evaporation by means of heating. Note also, however, that improved tools (new rakes, new methods of transport) were introduced. See *ibid.,* p. 6.

57. In 1942 the labor force in salt extraction apparently consisted of 3,000 to 4,000 soldiers and of about 2,000 salt farmers (see table 5.2). It seems unlikely that the initial civilian labor force exceeded 500 persons. The degree of part-time participation in salt production cannot be determined.

58. See table 6.5, note n, for a reference to the transit of 20,000 loads of salt from Inner Mongolia during 1943.

59. The observation of a constant average yield per salt field is consistent with the attribution of positive returns to water works if the newly added salt fields were naturally inferior.

60. See Mao, "Ching-chi wen-t'i," p. 72, and *Salt Production*, p. 2.

61. See *Salt Production*, p. 8.

62. For a reference to the dependence of salt production on external demand, see Mao Tse-tung, "Ching-chi wen-t'i," p. 72.

63. See *Wei kung-yeh p'in*, pp. 56-57, and *Chieh-fang jih pao*, No. 1295 (7 December 1944), p. 1.

64. See table 7.3.

65. Note that such additions increased salt production by perhaps 50 percent. It therefore seems reasonable to assume that they accounted for at least one-third of the total capital stock in salt extraction. On the assumption of an incremental capital-output ratio near two, capital construction in 1941 probably added nearly as much as the value of salt production in that year.

66. Note that there remained the problem of replacing the members of institutional households who engaged in salt production.

67. See Snow, *Red Star*, p. 269, for a contemporaneous reference to this venture. See also Forman, *Report*, p. 82, for its history.

68. See Snow, *Red Star*, pp. 266-267.

69. See Hsü, *A Survey*, Part 2, pp. 103-104.

70. See Stein, *The Challenge*, p. 171.

71. See *ibid.*

72. See Forman, *Report*, pp. 82-83.

73. See *ibid.*, p. 82, and note that Forman observed this condition in 1944.

74. See Snow, *Red Star*, p. 267, and note that he also mentions the importation of gold and silver as well as of printing equipment in this context.

75. See Nym Wales, *Inside Red China*, p. 197.

76. See Snow, *Red Star*, p. 267.

77. See Forman, *Report*, pp. 77, 79, and Stein, *The Challenge*, pp. 174-175. Stein also reports the capture of machinery in this context.

78. See Stein, *The Challenge*, p. 174, and note that the equipment which he mentioned may have included imports from the Long March and the Shansi expedition.

79. See Forman, *Report*, p. 79.

80. See Stein, *The Challenge*, pp. 181, 184-185, for comments on the difficulty of blockade-running and the cost of smuggling. See also Snow, *Red Star*, pp. 244 and 266, for comments on smuggling in Kiangsi as well as in North Shensi prior to the Sian incident.

81. See chapter 7 for a discussion of Kuomintang trade restrictions by means of import and export tariffs.

82. Note that a number of experts immigrated in the train of the Red Army. Note also that refugee workers, e.g., those who staffed the refugee factory, apparently came without capital. Persons doubtlessly slipped more easily through the blockade than goods, esp. bulky ones. In general, of course, it is characteristic of backwardness that the former move more easily than the latter.

83. For a specific assertion of this relation, see Snow, *Red Star,* p. 267. Note that Snow's report refers to the situation in 1936.

84. See chapter 5, note 58, for a reference to villagers from the SKN border region as a second major component of industrial employment.

85. See chapter 4 for a discussion of this aspect.

86. See Snow, *Red Star,* p. 269. See *ibid.* for this quotation of the official anticipation: ". . . It is expected that in two years North Shensi will be able to produce its entire supply of cloth." Of course, this expectation did not materialize.

87. See Stein, *The Challenge,* p. 173.

88. See *ibid.,* p. 176.

89. See Forman, *Report,* p. 80.

90. See *ibid.* ". . . For lack of long leather belts to run the bobbin machines, the workers had devised a belt of tightly woven wool, hardened and strenghtened with pine resin and beeswax; it served the purpose well. The inventor had got the idea for this by observing that the peasants used waxed wool belts on their hand-operated spinning-wheels. When applied on a larger scale to the factory's motor-run machines, the wax melted in the heat generated by the speed; so they added pine resin for hardening.

Essential springs were made of coiled telephone wire looted from the Japanese. This was hardened and tempered by heating in a crucible with charcoal and old bones to a temperature of $700\text{-}800^\circ$ Centigrade. The shop foreman who had improvised this was justly proud. He demonstrated the superiority of his telephone-wire spring which, dropped from the same height, bounced higher than did an imported sample."

91. See Band, *Two Years,* pp. 253-254. Note that the wool was imported from Inner Mongolia according to the information which they received. For the propagation of similar relations in cotton-spinning in Yenan Hsien, see Mao and others, *New Life,* p. 80.

92. See *Chieh-fang jih pao* (12 November 1941), p. 3. Note that the twelve state enterprises included eight units operated by institutional households.

93. See Stein, *The Challenge,* p. 176.

94. See *ibid.,* p. 228.

95. See *ibid.,* p. 173.

96. See Forman, *Report,* p. 78. Note that this iron foundry, which was founded in 1943, was the first enterprise of its kind according to Forman. A reference to iron production in *Chieh-fang jih pao* (12 November 1941), p. 3, indicates, however, that iron was produced previously in the SKN border region.

97. See Stein, *The Challenge*, p. 175.

98. See *ibid.* Forman, *Report*, p. 79, describes the power unit more specifically as follows: ". . . Power is supplied by a 1933 Soviet Zis truck engine and a 1929 Chevrolet truck motor. These units, fueled with charcoal gas, are coupled to nineteen overhead pulleys on a single overhead shaft."

99. See Stein, *The Challenge*, p. 175. Note in addition that such solutions were not limited to manufacturing and mining. For extraordinary examples of improvisation in medical care, see Forman, *Report*, pp. 50-51.

100. See Mao, "Ching-chi wen-t'i," p. 94.

101. See, e.g., Mao and others, *New Life*, p. 52. Note also that many of the travellers' reports contain references to specific factories which cannot be aggregated. So far as iron-making is concerned, note Forman's report that the first (state-operated) iron foundry operated with three comparatively large and two small furnaces. See Forman, *Report*, p. 78. Private iron-making cannot be accounted for.

102. See Mao and others, *New Life*, pp. 48-50.

103. See *Wei kung-yeh p'in*, p. 59.

104. As noted previously, wage quotations are extraordinarily rare. See chapter 4, notes 101 ff. The scale for communications workers (see *ibid.*, note 116) appears to have been based on an unusually high minimum wage. Teachers on salaries are said to have earned five to six piculs of millet per annum. See *General Survey of National Education*, p. 6. The millet equivalent of the average food plus clothing rations of public service employees and students also was reported as six piculs. See *Shan Kan Ning (1958)*, p. 214. Skilled workers probably earned somewhat more and soldiers as well as students received somewhat less than this average.

105. See Stein, *The Challenge*, p. 198.

106. Note that the latter in 1941 apparently included loans to CIC enterprises. See Nym Wales, *Notes*, p. 64.

107. See table 5.2 for membership data. Note the continuing assumption of an annual wage of six piculs of millet.

108. See Nym Wales, *Notes*, pp. 64, 66ff. for an account and a description of CIC solicitations among overseas Chinese especially in Southeast Asia.

109. Note, however, that part of these funds may have served to subsidize CIC operations.

110. See Nym Wales, *Notes*, p. 63, for the possibility that these funds served to finance home industry on a much larger scale.

111. See Nym Wales, *Notes*, pp. 59, 64. In 1944 the share capital of all other producer cooperatives reached only 25 percent of the share capital of all CIC cooperatives. The difference reflects primarily the inexpensiveness of the spinning equipment relative to the weaving equipment. Much of the working capital of the other producer cooperatives was provided by state enterprises under the previously mentioned putting-out arrangements. See note 92.

112. See Stein, *The Challenge*, p. 177.

113. See Mao and others, *New Life*, p. 51. See also Van Slyke, ed., *The Chinese Communist Movement*, p. 163, for a listing of various pharmaceutical products.

114. See *ibid.*

115. See Band, *Two Years*, p. 253.

116. See Stein, *The Challenge*, pp. 174-175. See also *ibid.*, pp. 173-174: "It seems that wherever some ore or scrap is available in the war areas, the two main weapons of the Communist-controlled armies and militia were being produced on the spot. One is the hand grenade and the other the land mine. Both are charged either with a fairly effective 'yellow powder,' which is also said to be made in most areas now, or with the old fashioned 'black powder,' in the production of which the Chinese once were far ahead of a bow and arrow using world."

117. See *Chieh-fang jih pao* (12 November 1941), p. 3, for a conversion ratio of 4:1 between homespun (t'u pu) and machine-made cloth (yang pu).

118. See *Wei kung-yeh p'in*, p. 60, and Mao, "Ching-chi wen-t'i," pp. 90-91, on the protection especially of weaving. See *Mao*, "Ching-chi, wen-t'i," p. 93, for the promotion of local products by the requirement that the army, government organs, and schools use local cloth.

119. See Snow, *Red Star*, p. 271.

120. See Stein, *The Challenge*, p. 175, and Van Slyke, *The Chinese Communist Movement*, p. 164, for statements to this effect.

121. See *Wei kung-yeh p'in*, p. 61.

122. See chapter 4 and Mao, "Ching-chi wen-t'i," pp. 140-142.

123. See Band, *Two Years*, pp. 58, 67, 254, and 268. Note that the first two quotations refer to the Shansi-Chahar-Hopei border region war base.

124. See Forman, *Report*, p. 83. See also note 90 for an observation of the quality of coiled springs made from telephone wire.

125. See Stein, *The Challenge*, p. 174.

126. See Van Slyke, *The Chinese Communist Movement*, p. 163. Note the absence of comments on the quality of military products, *ibid.*, p. 164.

127. See *Wei kung-yeh p'in*, p. 58.

128. *Ibid.*

129. Derived from Hsü, *A Survey*, Part 2, p. 122, and table 7.3.

130. See table 6.3 and note 50. The wool production estimates have to be multiplied by 0.6 or 0.7 in order to eliminate the weight of dirt and grease.

131. See Stein, *The Challenge*, pp. 184-186. Note that it is impossible to separate the imports of fibers, yarn, and cloth from each other.

132. See Mao, "Ching-chi wen-t'i," p. 45, and *Wei kung-yeh p'in*, p. 58, for such a goal.

133. See table 6.6 for such a relation in weaving. Note in addition that the government planned to purchase in 1943 only 750,000 catties of cotton, i.e., about 43 percent of the estimated output of cotton. See Mao, "Ching-chi wen-t'i," pp. 90-91.

134. Note that the discrepancies are attributable primarily to differences of opinion about the output of home industry. In 1942, however, they are

substantial for all sectors. See table 6.6 and Nym Wales, *Notes,* p. 61 plus Mao and others, *New Life,* pp. 49-50.

135. See Mao, "Ching-chi wen-t'i," pp. 44-45, and *Wei kung-yeh p'in,* p. 58. The US government reported Mao as placing the demand for cloth at 360,000 bolts. See Van Slyke, *The Chinese Communist Movement,* p. 162. Note that one bolt *(p'i)* as a rule measured two *ch'ih* four *ts'un* in width and ten *ch'ih* in length. The metric equivalents were 0.86 m x 35.8 m according to the customs norm and 0.78 m x 32.3 m according to the SKN border region norm.

136. See Mao, "Ching-chi wen-t'i," p. 45, and *Wei kung-yeh p'in,* p. 58. Both required three million catties of homespun, the former for the weaving of 250,000 bolts, the latter for the weaving of 310,000 bolts. The yarn inputs were 12 catties per bolt in the former and 9.7 catties per bolt in the latter case. An earlier source, *Chieh-fang jih pao* (12 November 1941), p. 3, operated with a norm of 14 catties of cotton per bolt of cloth.

137. In support of this argument, see *Chieh-fang jih pao* (12 November 1941), p. 3, for estimates of textile production which show the uncertainty of the government:

Sector of production	Estimated Output, 1941 Minimum bolts	Maximum bolts	Planned Output 1942 bolts
State	18,839	21,840	36,752
Cooperative (CIC)	4,356	5,614	31,116
Private	5,008	87,250	87,250
Home Industry	33,036		
Total	61,239	114,704	155,118

The government evidently envisaged a wide range of possible outcomes, but it tended to claim the less extreme ones as having been achieved (see table 6.10). By implication, much of what was considered feasible in 1941 and 1942 did not appear as a claim until 1943 or even 1945. The extraordinary fluctation in the output claims for CIC enterprises and private enterprises, which is evident in table 6.10, suggests that this uncertainty may have remained.

138. See *Chieh-fang jih pao* (12 November 1941), p. 3, and *Wei kung-yeh p'in,* pp. 49, 57. Note, however, that *Shan Kan Ning (1958),* p. 325, reported annual imports of 40,000 reams of paper during 1942-1945. Note also that a Chinese ream *(ling)* had 1,000 sheets.

139. See *Chieh-fang jih pao* (12 November 1941), p. 3, and *Wei kung-yeh p'in,* pp. 49, 57. Note, however, that *Shan Kan Ning (1958),* p. 325, reported annual imports of 40,000 reams of paper during 1942-1945. Note also that a Chinese ream *(ling)* had 1,000 sheets.

139. See Van Slyke, *The Chinese Communist Movement,* p. 163.

140. See *ibid.* plus Mao and others, *New Life,* p. 52.

141. See table 6.6 and notes 102, 103.

142. See Mao, "Ching-chi wen-t'i," p. 93. In 1943 the number was to increase 5.1 percent to 53,600,000 characters.

143. See Van Slyke, *The Chinese Communist Movement,* p. 164.

144. See *ibid.*

145. See Mao and others, *New Life,* pp. 53-55, for a more detailed description of the road system. See also *Salt Production,* p. 7, for the pattern of salt flows in 1943. Of the 329,893 loads of salt, 181,482 loads were carried along the western route and 114,277 loads along the southern route (via Yenan to Fuhsien).

146. See *Salt Production,* p. 54. Note that two-thirds of the total outlay were spent on repairing Yungting bridge in Suiteh. Note in addition that the periodization of this outlay is vague and that table 6.11 therefore may exaggerate its millet equivalent.

147. For a description of a road scene outside Yenan, see Band, *Two Years,* pp. 234-235. The outlay for improvements of the major salt roads in 1943 amounted to two million yuan; see Mao, "Ching-chi wen-t'i," p. 74. At June 1943 prices, this would be equivalent to 446 piculs of millet and thus to about 74 man-years of work; see table 7.3.

148. See Mao and others, *New Life,* p. 53, and *Shan Kan Ning (1958),* pp. 125-126.

149. See *ibid.*

150. See chapter 7, note 79. The millet equivalents of these contributions may be placed at 2,040 piculs and 450 piculs, respectively. The maximum of 4,500 man-years would be equivalent to 27,000 piculs at prevailing wages in the public sector, but it would be worth less at prevailing farm earnings.

151. See Mao and others, *New Life,* p. 55, for the observation that the transport potential of the Chingchien-Chingpien highway could not be fully realized.

152. See Forman, *Report,* p. 83. Note that at least one truck was the "Gift of the Chinese Laundrymen's National Salvation Association, New York" according to Band, *Two Years,* p. 252.

153. Recall the use of truck engines as energy sources in manufacturing establishments; see note 98. Note also the cessation of bus service between Michih and Yenan; see Band, *Two Years,* p. 230.

154. Note that the region produced gasoline and apparently kept most of it for its trucks; see Forman, *Report,* p. 83. Note also, however, that the use of charcoal-burning attachments on stationary truck engines points to gasoline shortage; see note 98.

155. See Mao and others, *New Life,* p. 52.

156. See *ibid.* as well as Nym Wales, *Notes,* p. 62, for a reference to "nine public wagon plants" which probably appear among the wood manufacturing enterprises in table 4.4.

157. See Forman, *Report,* pp. 78, 83. More general impressions of the composition of traffic on the road from Michih via Suite to Yenan can be found in Band, *Two Years,* pp. 230, 232, 234.

158. See chapter 2, note 86. Mules as well as oxen also were used as draft animals for carts.

159. See Mao and others, *New Life,* p. 55. See also *Shan Kan Ning pien ch'ü cheng-ts'e t'iao-li hui-pien,* pp. 36-37, for an emphasis on military self-sufficiency in transportation as a measure of relief for the civilian population. Work animals, with few exceptions, were required to render at most thirty-six days of corvée per annum; see *Shan Kan Ning (1958),* p. 126.

160. See *Brief Account,* p. 11. Note that a pack animal was expected to make thirteen journeys per annum.

161. See *ibid.* Note that full-time animals in salt transportation were exempted from rendering corvée. In addition, the income earned in salt transportation was exempted from taxation.

162. See Band, *Two Years,* pp. 225-236, for brief descriptions of various rest houses along the road from Paoteh to Yenan.

163. See Mao, "Ching-chi wen-t'i," pp. 75-80.

164. See *Salt Production,* p. 6.

165. See chapter 4, note 22, and *Salt Production,* p. 7. According to the latter source, the South Ch'ü cooperative by 1943 had more than 1,000 pack animals assigned to salt transportation. For changes in the number of transport cooperatives, see table 4.2.

166. See Mao, 'Ching-chi wen-t'i," p. 73. Note that the emphasis on military self-sufficiency in transportation appeared at this time rather than during the preceding years; see note 159.

Notes to Chapter 7

1. Snow, *Red Star,* p. 247.

2. See *ibid.,* p. 246.

3. See *ibid.,* pp. 248-249. Note that not only cash but also goods were subject to confiscation. Note also Snow's insistence that the Chinese communists did not receive aid from the Soviet Union. See *ibid.,* pp. 283-284.

4. See *ibid.,* p. 245. After the national currency reform of November 1935, the soviet held silver as a reserve against note issue.

5. See Stein, *The Challenge,* p. 197.

6. Note that data on the local money supply in 1937 are lacking. The issue of five million yuan in February 1941, when the support payments had stopped, plus the assumption that notes in circulation increased porportionately to the price index for all commodities imply an estimate of about 500,000 yuan for 1937. The substitution of the price index for millet raises the estimate to about one million yuan (Hsü, *A Survey,* Part 2, p. 9, and Tables 7.3, 7.7). These totals were about equal to one or two monthly support payments by the national government to the Eighth Route Army.

7. Hsü, *A Survey,* Part 2, p. 18.

8. Note that Hsü reports for 1937 a monthly civilian expenditure of 150,000 yuan, monthly civilian revenue of 30,000-40,000 yuan transfers from the army plus 10,000 yuan from taxes etc., and a monthly deficit of 100,000 yuan which was met temporarily by borrowing. See *ibid.,* pp. 18-20.

9. See Snow, *Red Star*, pp. 476-477. Among the equipment purchased was "a fleet of American lorries." *Ibid.*, p. 474. Its remnants were observed by visitors such as the Bands, Forman, and Stein.

10. Table 4.8 implies that the price index ratio for fine cloth and salt averaged 216 during 1938-1940. The prices index ratio for cotton fiber and salt averaged only 80 during the same years. Imports of cloth are likely to have been more substantial than imports of fiber, since internal textile production was insignificant in the beginning. See tables 6.6, 6.10.

11. See Yu-kwei Cheng, *Foreign Trade and Industrial Development of China* (Washington, D.C.: The University Press of Washington, D.C., 1956), p. 121, note 20, for the information that in Chungking the price of manufactured goods increased almost three times as much from 1937 to 1940 as the price of raw materials did.

12. In Yenan, the price index for all commodities rose to seven times its June 1937 level by December 1940, while the price index for fine cloth increased three times as much. See table 7.3.

13. See Stewart, *War-time China*, p. 47.

14. See *Shan Kan Ning (1958)*, p. 94. The amount of the surplus is not known. Since the carrying of cash balances is disadvantageous in an inflationary situation, it seems likely that the surplus was quite small.

15. See Forman, *Report*, p. 74.

16. See *Mao III*, pp. 328-329. Italics added.

17. See Nym Wales, *Notes*, p. 64, for references to payments earmarked for but not received by the Yenan depot of the CIC. The reason for the decline in contributions generally was the extension of the war to the contributing areas.

18. Note that the SKN border region government issued small amounts of token notes in small denominations prior to the break of relations, beginning in 1938 with 90,000 yuan which probably accounted for 10 to 20 percent of the money in circulation (see note 6). The alleged reason for this issue was that the border region government could not obtain coins and subsidiary notes from the national government. See Stein, *The Challenge*, p. 197.

19. See *Brief Account*, pp. 13-14.

20. See Van Slyke, *The Chinese Communist Movement*, p. 165. Note that the import prohibitions according to Stein dated from 1944. See Stein, *The Challenge*, p. 185.

21. See Stein, *The Challenge*, pp. 185-186, and note the importation of relatively large quantities of paper according to *Shan Kan Ning (1958)*, p. 325.

22. See *Shan Kan Ning (1958)*, p. 92.

23. See *Brief Account*, p. 13.

24. See Van Slyke, *The Chinese Communist Movement*, p. 165, for such an assertion which conflicts with *Brief Account*, p. 13.

25. See chapter 3, note 39, and *Shan Kan Ning (1958)*, p. 32, for the prohibition in 1939 to export ewes. Because of the monopolization of external trade in response to the blockade, it may not have been necessary to issue prohibitions any longer.

26. See *Brief Account,* pp. 13-14, and *Wei kung-yeh p'in,* pp. 56-57.

27. See *Chieh-fang jih pao* (7 December 1944), p. 1.

28. Note that the price of salt increased internally during the same interval, but at lower rates than all other products. See table 4.8 and 7.3.

29. See *Wei kung-yeh p'in,* pp. 56-57. Note that the price level in the SKN border region appears to have increased much more rapidly than that in Chungking. See Yu-kwei Cheng, *Foreign Trade,* p. 121, and table 7.3.

30. See table 4.8.

31. See *Brief Account,* p. 11, and chapter 4, note 122.

32. See *Wei kung-yeh p'in,* p. 45, and chapter 4, note 123.

33. See *Chieh-fang jih pao* (22 May 1941), p. 2. Note that the border region in 1941 imported a large quantity of paper. See *ibid.* (12 November 1941), p. 3. In addition, it imported a large number of shovels (hua). See Mao, *New Life,* p. 45. *Wei kung-yeh p'in,* p. 60, in 1944 called for increases in the import duties on nonessentials and for decreases in the export duties on local products.

34. See *Wei kung-yeh p'in,* p. 60.

35. See Stein, *The Challenge,* p. 207. Note that salt tax used to be paid (and in KMT territory continued to be paid) at the city gate. The SKN border region government changed this practice to collecting the tax when the salt left the salt field area. It also lowered the tax rate substantially. See *Shan Kan Ning 1939-1941,* p. 56. In 1942, salt became a government monopoly according to Hsü, *A Survey,* Part 2, p. 20.

36. Estimate: 70,000 loads at 150 catties times 18 yuan per catty (price in 1943), divided by 411 (increase in export price, 1937-1943). See table 6.5 and *Wei kung-yeh p'in,* pp. 56-57.

37. See note 7.

38. See Stein, *The Challenge,* p. 184, and *Brief Account,* p. 14.

39. See *Shan Kan Ning (1958),* p. 93, for the statement that in 1941 public salt was used to "balance trade, make up the import surplus, and subsidize military expenditures."

40. See Forman, *Report,* pp. 9-10, and Stein, *The Challenge,* pp. 33-34, 47-48. Both Stein and Forman heard the charge made by the governor of Shensi Province.

41. See Van Slyke, *The Chinese Communist Movement,* p. 165.

42. See Stein, *The Challenge,* p. 183.

43. See Band, *Two Years,* pp. 141, 200.

44. See Stein, *The Challenge,* pp. 75-76.

45. See Forman, *Report,* p. 192.

46. See Mao, "Ching-chi wen-t'i," p. 75. Mao noted as late as in December 1942 that if the production of cotton were to grow as planned, decreases in cotton imports would be possible, and the export of 300,000 to 360,000 loads of salt would suffice to balance imports. In addition, Mao encouraged increases in the exports of woolens (p. 97) and of kerosene (p. 98). Note that Mao expected a salt price of ten yuan per catty.

47. See Stein, *The Challenge,* p. 185. Stein was told that the primary

cause for the import surplus was the distortion of prices due to the KMT restrictions.

48. See note 4. The indications are that the border region bank in 1941 held four to five million yuan in silver. See *Chieh-fang jih pao* (9 November 1941), p. 4, for a reported note issue of twelve million yuan, eight million of which were secured by construction loans and 40 percent by silver.

49. See Yu-kwei Cheng, *Foreign Trade*, p. 121, and table 7.3. See also Stein, *The Challenge*, p. 199, for the observation of such a difference.

50. See *ibid*.

51. See *ibid*.

52. See table 7.3 and Hsü, *A Survey*, Part 2, p. 10, for evidence to this effect. See also table 4.8 for the tendency of a return to the precrisis price structure.

53. See Snow, *Red Star*, pp. 248-249.

54. See *Shan Kan Ning (1958)*, p. 25.

55. See chapter 2, note 109.

56. See note 6 for an estimated circulation of at most one million yuan in 1937. Note also that deficit-financing apparently required about 1.3 million yuan in 1936 according to table 7.2.

57. See Snow, *Red Star*, p. 246.

58. See Yenan Nung-ts'un tiao-ch'a t'uan, *Mi-chih hsien*, p. 149, for a doubling or tripling of farm prices.

59. See chapter 3, note 34.

60. See table 7.2, note c.

61. Note that the grain equivalent of the public expenditures in 1936 may be exaggerated due to our use of farm prices.

62. See note 53.

63. See Mao, "Ching-chi wen-t'i," pp. 167-168, and Stein, *The Challenge*, p. 205.

64. See table 7.2.

65. See Mao, "Ching-chi wen-t'i," p. 166.

66. See Hsü, *A Survey*, Part 2, p. 26.

67. See *Brief Account*, p. 13.

68. See table 6.3 in regard to grain production and table 5.2 with respect to changes in the number of troops in the area.

69. See chapter 6, notes 33-36.

70. See chapter 2, notes 107-110.

71. See table 8.10. Note in addition the elimination of payments of land rent in much of the area and their reduction in the remainder of the territory. Payments of land rent in 1930/1931 have been estimated as 111,000 piculs in the territory until 1939/1940 and as 128,000 piculs in the territory after 1939/1940 (see chapter 2, note 112). In contrast, payments during the 1940s probably did not exceed 50,000 piculs (7,500 tons) per annum.

72. Note that the 1942 plans called for 26,000,000 catties of public straw. See *Chieh-fang jih pao* (11 November 1941).

73. See *Shan Kan Ning (1958)*, p. 282, for a reference, which appears to be mistaken, to 21,000,000 catties of straw produced by the army.

74. See *Shan Kan Ning 1939-1941*, p. 55.

75. Note that the tax was supposed to be incorporated into the agricultural income tax. See Hsü, *A Survey*, Part 2, p. 30.

76. See Mao, "Ching-chi wen-t'i," p. 149, for a price ratio of millet to straw near 4:1. Estimates of millet equivalents have been formed on this assumption with the straw collection data listed in table 7.5.

77. Estimate derived from note 74 and table 7.3.

78. Note in particular the coincidence of the reintroduction of the wool tax with the wool spinning and weaving campaign which aimed at providing the Eighth Route Army with winter cloth.

79. See Hsü, *A Survey*, Part 2, p. 32, and note that the conversion assumes 365 days and six piculs of millet per annum.

80. See *ibid.* and note that transportation cooperatives could conceivably make profit under this arrangement, which enabled them to refund the cash substitute of corvée to their members.

81. See *Shan Kan Ning 1958*, p. 24.

82. See *ibid.* Note that the salt tax previously had been fourteen yuan per camel load and that it had been collected at the city gate rather than upon leaving the salt field area. See *Shan Kan Ning 1939-1941*, p. 56.

83. See *ibid.* Hsü, *A Survey*, Part 2, pp. 19, 31, reports the following salt tax rates:

	1937	1938
Donkey load	1.00 yuan	1.00 yuan ?
Mule or ox load	1.50 yuan	2.50 yuan
Camel load	?	3.20 yuan

84. See Stein, *The Challenge*, p. 207. Note Hsü's intimation that the sales tax was actually eliminated in favor of the cash substitute for corvée.

85. See notes 32 to 35.

86. See *Shan Kan Ning 1939-1941*, p. 55.

87. See Stein. *The Challenge*, p. 205-207, for a description of the assessment procedure and these results. Note that the tax applied also to all non-agricultural enterprises of the institutional households of rear army, organs, and schools.

88. See *Brief Account*, p. 13.

89. Estimate: loads of salt sold (table 6.5) times price index of salt (table 7.3) times 1.2 yuan (note 83), divided by price per picul of millet (table 7.3).

90. Estimate: 330,000 x .06 x 4,050/4488. See tables 6.5 and 7.6, note i.

91. Note the divergence of salt prices and millet prices in 1944. See table 4.8.

92. Estimate: 400,000/76. See table 7.3.

93. See Hsü, *A Survey*, Part 2, p. 20, for such an indication.

94. See Mao, "Ching-chi wen-t'i," p. 138. Note that the claims refer to the government organs and schools which were said to produce one-fourth of their grain, one-half of their grass, and part of their vegetables and pork. The value of this output was listed as 368,000 yuan in silver or 10,179,000 yuan at 1942 prices.

95. See *K'ang Jih chan-cheng shih-ch'i chieh-fang ch'ü kai-k'uang,* p. 16. Note that the claim refers to the army, which was also said to provide its own grain for one-and-one-half months of 1939.

96. See *Shan Kan Ning 1939-1941,* pp. 56-57.

97. See Mao, "Ching-chi wen-t'i," p. 139, for a reference to 3,000 piculs of fine grain and 900,000 catties of vegetables.

98. See table 7.6.

99. See Mao, "Ching-chi wen-t'i," p. 98-158, for a discussion of various projects with emphasis on these two years.

100. See *ibid.* and note in addition the importance of commercial profit as a source of earnings for the organs and schools (Mao, "Ching-chi wen-t'i," pp. 147, 154). Commerce and profit were strongly deemphasized during 1943-1945 in favor of material production.

101. See *Chieh-fang jih pao* (1 June 1942), p. 1.

102. See Mao, "Ching-chi wen-t'i," p. 75.

103. See table 6.4. One kg equals two catties.

104. See tables 6.3 and 7.5.

105. See table 7.6.

106. Note that *Brief Account,* p. 13, may fail to account for the tax burden of the urban population and thereby omit perhaps 10 to 15 percent of the revenue from other taxes. By implication, public production may be understated proportionately, so that it actually reached the equivalent of 100,000 to 110,000 piculs of grain.

107. Note that the reference to "not less than in excess of 200,000 piculs," which was made in April 1946 by Lin Pai-ch'ü, concerns handicrafts, animal husbandry, and other earnings of the army.

108. Note that the government planned to reduce the levy of public grain in 1944 in response to increased self-sufficiency. See *Shan Kan Ning pien ch'ü cheng-ts'e t'iao-li hui-pien,* p. 9.

109. Note that *Shan Kan Ning (1958),* p. 281-282, does not provide information on public production in 1945.

110. See chapter 3, notes 3, 14, for references to such provisions in the resolutions of the sixth CCP congress and of the first soviet congress.

111. See Hsü, *A Survey,* Part 2, p. 34.

112. See chapter 4, note 14, on recruitment and chapter 5, note 3, on the settlement of veterans in the region.

113. See Hsü, *A Survey,* Part 2, p. 33, for a listing of the gifts and *ibid.,* p. 35, for the statement of its total value.

114. See *Mao III,* pp. 134-135.

115. See Stein, *The Challenge,* p. 207, for the statement that ". . . since 1944 all borrowing has been stopped. . . ." In contrast, see Van Slyke, *The*

Chinese Communist Movement, p. 167, for the statement that "in 1944, 70 per cent of the government revenue was said to be derived from government and army production, and the deficit was said to be considerably less than in 1943. . . ." Note also that the 1943 estimate of notes outstanding was made by the national government and may be inaccurate. See Van Slyke, *The Chinese Communist Movement,* p. 155. Note further the possibility of a lag between government borrowing and bank note issue which might account for a residual discrepancy.

116. See Stein. *The Challenge,* p. 198.

117. See note 50.

118. See *Wei-kung-yeh p'in,* pp. 56-57, and note 29. Note that the data of tables 4.8 and 7.3 indicate less extreme changes in the ratio of domestic retail prices.

119. See *Brief Account,* p. 13.

120. See Stein. *The Challenge,* pp. 207-208.

121. For conflicting information, see Hsü, *A Survey,* Part 2, p. 35. Hsü mentions that the deficit in 1943 reached 1,080 million yuan, which according to table 7.3 would have been equivalent to much more than 10 percent of total expenditure.

122. See Mao, "Ching-chi wen-t'i," p. 159, for the statement that public enterprises produced 60 percent of the revenue in 1942, exclusive of taxes in kind. Other taxes probably yielded amounts similar to 1943.

123. See note 115.

124. See Chang Chia-ao, *The Inflationary Spiral* (New York: John Wiley, (1958), p. 45, for deficits of 77.0 percent in 1942, 65.3 percent in 1943, and 77.6 percent in 1944.

125. See *ibid.,* pp. 52, 57, and Cheng-Yu-kwei, *Foreign Trade and Industrial Development of China,* pp. 104, 121, for relevant information on price changes.

126. See Mao, "Ching-chi wen-t'i," p. 166, for a reference to buying problems in the spring of 1941 which led the government to increase the taxes in kind on agriculture.

127. See table 8.2 for this approximate relation between other taxes and bank loans in 1943.

128. See note 115.

129. See note 50.

130. See Stein, *The Challenge,* pp. 200, 207. The steadying of prices in the summer of 1944, to which he referred, was followed by a new price rise in the fall. See Hsü, *A Survey,* Part 2, p. 9.

Notes to Chapter 8

1. Note that the information on public expenditures generally is rather sketchy. See table 7.2 for the available quantitative information. See also *Ching-chi yen-chiu,* No. 2 (1956), p. 101, for the statement that military ex-

penditures accounted for 70 to 80 percent of total expenditures. The civilian expenditures included outlays for the development of agriculture, handicraft production, culture, education, public health, disaster relief, and refugee settlement. *Chieh-fang jih pao* (19 November 1941), p. 3, ranked military expenditures first, construction expenditures second, and education expenditures third. *Shan Kan Ning* (1958), p. 95, reported relief grant totals of 3,000 piculs of millet in 1941 and of 11,000 piculs of millet for all preceding years.

2. See *Shan Kan Ning 1939-1941*, p. 57.

3. See *Chieh-fang jih pao* (12 November 1941), p. 3. The difference is attributable to different methods of estimation.

4. See note 2 and table 7.3. Note that the source refers to current prices without specifying the period.

5. See *Mao III*, p. 242.

6. See Mao, "Ching-chi wen-t'i," p. 166.

7. Note that because agricultural output was consumed during the year following its production, the revenue problems of 1940 and 1941 affected public consumption during 1941 and 1942.

8. See *Shan Kan Ning (1958)*, p. 214.

9. See *ibid.* for a reference to 1939 generally. *Ibid.*, p. 282 mentions the period when the national government stopped the supply of medicine as the base. And Forman, *Report*, p. 74, lists December 1939 as 100.0.

10. See *Shan Kan Ning (1958)*, p. 213, for the assertion that the real wages of workers in public enterprises had increased 58.7 to 84 percent from the (unspecified) prewar period until 1944, not counting changes in medical and educational expenses nor changes in labor and social insurance.

11. See Mao, "Ching-chi wen-t'i," pp. 149, 151-153, for a few price quotations which suggest the following approximate relations for 1942: one catty of pork = one catty of oil = six catties of millet = 10 catties of vegetables = 25 catties of charcoal.

12. Note, that the assumption of proportionality, which accounts for estimated changes of such magnitudes, may be uncalled for.

13. Note that the latter activities were undertaken as part of the campaign to "support the government and cherish the people." See *Shan Kan Ning pien ch'ü cheng-ts'e t'iao-li hui-pien*, pp. 35-37.

14. All visitors to the SKN border region commented on this problem. See, e.g., Forman, *Report*, pp. 43-44.

15. See *Mao III*, p. 242.

16. See chapter 7, notes 23 and 24.

17. See *ibid.*, note 119.

18. See *Shan Kan Ning pien ch'ü cheng-ts'e t'iao-li hui-pien*, p. 26.

19. Note that the visitors to the SKN border region did not comment precisely on the living of the private population. However, they all provide the impression that the people lived comparatively well.

20. See chapter 7, note 21.

21. See table 6.4.

22. See chapter 6, notes 40-42.

23. To meet a normal ration of 80 percent of 5.6 kg per person per annum for about 100,000 persons, the government had to supply about 450,000 kg of oil, i.e., as much as the estimated output of cotton oil in 1944. See note 22. Note, of course, that it is not certain that cotton oil was used for this purpose.

24. See chapter 6, notes 44 and 45.

25. It is assumed that 100,000 persons in the public sector consumed 12 kg of meat per capita per annum.

26. Note that no allowance has been made for inedible diseased meat.

27. Derived from chapter 6, notes 44-45, table 6.3, and table 8.5.

28. See *Chieh-fang jih pao* (12 November 1941), p. 3.

29. See *ibid.* and *Wei kung-yeh p'in,* p. 57. The former source lists public requirements as 44,000 to 49,000 bolts. The latter states an autarky goal of 310,000 bolts.

30. The 1941 estimate was based on a population of 1.342 million persons rather than the 1.524 million persons of table 8.5. For a rejection of the 1941 census estimate, see the discussion of table 2.1.

31. See chapter 6, notes 127 and 137.

32. See *Shan Kan Ning (1958),* p. 214, for a statement of December 1944 which stresses the continuing backwardness of the region in this perspective. Death rates remained at 60 percent for infants and at 3 percent for adults, death rates for animals remained very high, illiteracy remained at 90 percent, feudal literary remnants predominated in the minds of the people, etc.

33. Note the use of June rather than of annual average prices.

34. See chapter 3, note 33, in regard to the termination of land redistribution. Note that table 8.11 implies that land reform had not been carried out fully in Chingyang Hsien.

35. See chapter 2, note 7, for the areas added.

36. See Mao, "Ching-chi wen-t'i," p. 160, for the statement that more than half of the peasantry had been affected by land reform.

37. Estimate: 0.5 x (11.4 x .315 + 19.1 x .685). Derived from *ibid.* plus table 2.5 and chapter 2, note 14.

38. Estimate: unweighted average of four rates. See *Shan Kan Ning (1958),* p. 242. Note that the rent law dates from December 1944.

39. Estimate: highest rate of table 7.4. For the realism of this assumption, see table 8.11.

40. The rent reductions listed in *Shan Kan Ning (1958),* p. 242, ranged from 10 to 40 percent, depending on the type of rental. The tax rate revision of 1943, according to table 7.4, increased the tax rates by 10 to 20 percent for the highest income classes.

41. Note that whereas 1930-1931 was clearly a "poor" period, 1938 and 1939 were "good" years according to the evidence of table 6.4. The improvement in natural fortunes should have reflected itself in superior yields, greater average products, and higher average incomes.

42. For references to exemplary improvements, see *Shan Kan Ning (1958),* pp. 22-23, 94-95, and 213. Pp. 22-23 list the population, assets, and

product of nine households in 1938 and in 1939. The per capita output of grain reached 364 kg in the former and 653 kg in the latter year. Pp. 94-95 describe improvements in the class structure of several villages from pre-revolutionary times to 1941. Middle peasants, who had become the majority or at least a strong plurality, typically were said to have a crop of 6,000 kg of grain per household and thus of perhaps 1,000 kg per capita. P. 213 presents data on the production, consumption, taxation, and surplus of grain for a village of twenty-six households. The implicit per capita consumption was 164 kg in 1941 and 213 kg in 1943.

43. Note that the only reference to wages in subsidiary production that could be found concerns home spinning under cooperative putting-out arrangements. See Mao, *New Life,* p. 80, for a regulation of Yenan Hsien that ". . . the wage for one catty of thread is equal to one catty of cotton, spinning women are freed from taxation, . . ." In 1943 one catty of cotton exchanged for 4.74 catties of millet in external trade (see *Wei kung-yeh p'in,* pp. 56-57, for the price quotations). Spinning the average of six catties of yarn per annum thus added 28.44 catties of millet to one's income. The potential output of about three million catties of yarn (see chapter 6, note 132) would account for earnings equivalent to 7.11 million kg of millet in toto and of 5.28 kg of millet per capita of the farm population. The latter quantity was equal to 2 to 3 percent of the likely average farm income as well as to 7 to 10 percent of the likely average subsidiary income. Weaving may have added similarly to the income of farm households, so that the total income effect of increasing textile production appears to have been relatively small.

44. Note also that marketing may have been a form of hiding unemployment, so that the shift to production activities need not have affected the income from merchant activities.

45. Note that Ma Wei-hsin, whose records are being discussed, had his lands cultivated by tenants and sharecroppers but not by farm laborers proper. Ma switched from tenancy proper to sharecropping in response to the rent reduction regulations. See Yenan nung-ts'un tiao-ch'a t'uan, *Mi-chih hsien,* pp. 117-119.

46. Note that the decline also reflects a shift to marginal labor force members. See *ibid.,* p. 125.

47. Derived from *ibid.,* p. 129.

48. See *ibid.,* p. 127, for a contrast of the situations in 1936 and in 1941 which reveals these changes.

49. See table 8.10.

50. See chapter 2, note 119.

51. See *Salt Production,* p. 9. Note that Kaochih's income from salt sales accounted for 110,000 loads, i.e., about one-third of the total salt sales in 1943 according to table 6.5.

52. See *ibid.,* p. 8.

53. Note in particular the low rate of taxation, which contrasted sharply with presoviet practices. See chapter 7, note 82.

54. See *Shan Kan Ning (1958),* pp. 23-24.

55. See tables 2.11, 7.3, and Yenan nung-ts'un tiao-ch'a t'uan, *Mi-chih hsien*, p. 149.

56. Note that Yenan was included among the locations. Earnings levels there of 0.20 yuan prior to the revolution and of 0.30 yuan in 1938 also were low in comparison with the data of table 8.8.A.

57. See Stein, *The Challenge*, pp. 189-195.

58. See *Shan Kan Ning (1958)*, p. 213. Note that an increase in the number of workdays could have increased craftsmen's earnings considerably. The annual earnings of table 8.10 seem to imply totals of at most 200 days per annum.

59. See chapter 4, notes 86 ff.

60. See Evans F. Carlson, *Twin Stars of China* (New York: Dodd, Meade and Company, 1940), p. 281.

61. See Ch'i Li, *Shan Kan Ning pien ch'ü shih-lu,* p. 169, as well as chapter 4, note 96.

62. Not that it is not clear whether Forman, *Report* p. 76, refers to total earnings or merely to the cash portion thereof.

63. Note that the earnings of communications workers may have been relatively high because these workers lived outside the institutional households and probably had larger shares of dependents than the teachers did, who often were single teenagers.

64. Estimate: 11.4 x .354 + 19.1 x .646. Derived from table 2.5 and chapter 2, note 14.

65. See chapter 2, note 63. Note that the estimate of rural population includes 5-10 percent nonagricultural population.

66. See *Shan Kan Ning (1958)*, pp. 94-95, for references to extreme changes in four villages of Anting Hsien as well as in four villages of the western *ch'ü* and in five villages of the central *ch'ü* of Yenan Hsien. The share of rich and middle peasant households in Anting increased from 7 percent before the revolution to 61 percent in 1941. During the same interval, the number of middle peasant households in the western *ch'ü* of Yenan increased from 10 to 64. In the central *ch'ü* in 1941, rich peasants accounted for 10.6 percent, middle peasants for 49.4 percent, poor peasants for 19.0 percent, and farm laborers for 12.5 percent of the households. In comparison, see table 2.5 and chapter 2, note 63.

67. See notes 36-38.

68. Note in table 2.5 that the share of tenant farmers in all farmers was substantially less than the share of rental land in the total farm area.

69. Note that table 7.4 does not contain a tax rate schedule for Ching-pien Hsien.

70. See table 2.8 for such a relative share in 1930-1931.

71. Note that implicit allowance is being made for the likelihood that the SKN border region government underestimated incomes in the farm sector.

72. Note the implicit inclusion of payments in kind for board.

73. See note 58.

74. For the inherence of this objective in Marxist theory, see Peter Schran, "On the Marxism-Leninism of Chinese Communist Development Strategy," *Mainland China in the World Economy,* Hearings before the Joint Economic Committee, Congress of the United States, Nineteenth Congress, First Session, U.S. Government Printing Office, Washington, D.C., 1967, pp. 215 ff.

75. Derived from tables 6.1 and 6.2.

76. See table 6.1 for extraordinarily small shares of irrigated land.

77. See chapter 6, note 51. Note that the value added in basic construction by peasant labor is included in the capital formation estimates.

78. See chapter 6, note 65.

79. Note that the estimate is based on the sales data of table 6.5.

80. Derived from table 6.5 and table 7.6, note i. Estimate: one-fourth of 2 x 140,000 loads x 4,050 yuan per load/4,488 yuan per picul of millet.

81. See chapter 6, note 146.

82. See chapter 6, note 150. The estimate of 15,000 piculs relates to a per capita income of 500 kg of grain per annum.

83. See Yenan nung-ts'un tiao-ch'a t'uan, *Mi-chih hsien,* for information which suggests that landlords typically invested in land by mortgaging or buying the land of others. Since the loans or sales receipts tended to be consumed rather than invested, capital formation in the aggregate did not result.

84. See *Shan Kan Ning (1958),* p. 287.

85. See table 2.2.

86. See Stein, *The Challenge,* pp. 193-195, for the expression of this acceptance by one progressive landlord.

Notes to Chapter 9

1. See Huang T'ao, *Chung-kuo jen-min chieh-fang chün ti san-shih nien* (Peking: Jen-min Press, 1958), p. 32. See *ibid.,* pp. 18 ff. for a description of the expansion and temporary contraction of the base areas. See in addition Van Slyke, *The Chinese Communist Movement,* pp. 140-141, for more conservative estimates made by the US Military Intelligence Service.

2. See Carlson, *Twin Stars.*

3. See Band, *Two Years.*

4. See Forman, *Report,* esp. pp. 131 ff.

5. See Michael Lindsay, "The North China Front," *Amerasia,* No. 7 and 8 (1944), pp. 100-125. See also his recent article on "The Taxation System of the Shansi-Chahar-Hopei Border Region, 1938-1945," *The China Quarterly,* No. 42 (April-June 1970): 1-15. Note in addition that Lindsay was interviewed in Yenan by Gunther Stein. See Stein, *The Challenge,* pp. 366-378, for an account of this interview.

6. See Van Slyke, *The Chinese Communist Movement,* chapter 6, esp. pp. 167-176.

7. See in particular the following sources in English: Ke Han, *The Shansi-*

Hopei-Honan Border Region (Chungking: New China Information Committee, 1940) and Mao, *New Life,* chapters 8, 9, 10, and 12.

8. See Band, *Two Years,* pp. 141-142, for a reference to assertedly successful efforts of the border region governments to curb cotton and opium growing in many parts of North China.

9. See *ibid.,* esp. p. 170, for the description of an incident of surprise which concerned an army propaganda unit and its equipment.

10. Note that whereas the SKN garrison constituted about 3 percent of the population of this region, all the troops accounted for less than 1 percent of the population of all the base areas early in 1945. See note 1.

11. See *Ching-chi yen-chiu,* No. 2 (1956), p. 109, for information on differential taxation in the Shansi-Chahar-Hopei Border Region. Note in this connection that the peripheral regions in the plains were usually more fertile than the core areas in the mountains. For this reason, the rates of taxation were normally much more highly differentiated than the absolute tax burdens.

12. See *Mao III,* p. 132.

13. See *ibid.,* p. 299. Note that at about the same time, the US government appraised the communist achievements in the economic sphere as follows, according to Van Slyke, *The Chinese Communist Movement,* pp. 175-176:

> The Communists have endeavored, rather successfully, to revitalize the spirit of the peasantry, to increase agricultural production, and to develop handicraft industries to meet civilian and military needs. As a result of their efforts most of the resistance bases may be said to be practically self-sufficient in terms of their relatively simple requirements.

Bibliography

Note that the following listing is limited to items referred to in the text.

Aird, John S. "Present and Prospective population of Mainland China," Milbank Memorial Fund. *Population Trends in Eastern Europe, the USSR and Mainland China.* New York: Milbank Memorial Fund, 1960.

Band, Claire and William. *Two Years with the Chinese Communists.* New Haven: Yale University Press, 1948.

Bisson, Thomas Arthur. *Yenan in June 1937: Talks with the Communist Leaders.* Berkeley: Center for Chinese Studies, University of California, 1973.

Buck, John Lossing. *Chinese Farm Economy.* Chicago: University of Chicago Press, 1930.

———. *Land Utilization in China.* Nanking: Nanking University, 1937.

———. *Land Utilization in China, Atlas.* Nanking: Nanking University, 1937.

———. *Land Utilization in China. Statistics.* Nanking: Nanking University, 1937.

Carlson, Evans Fordyce. *The Chinese Army. Its Organization and Military Efficiency.* I.P.R. Inquiry Series; New York: International Secretariat, Institute of Pacific Relations, 1940.

———. *Twin Stars of China.* New York: Dodd, Mead & Co., 1940.

Chang, Chung-li. *The Income of the Chinese Gentry.* Seattle: University of Washington Press, 1962.

Chang, Chia-ao. *The Inflationary Spiral.* New York: John Wiley & Sons, 1958.

Chao, Kuo-chun. *Agrarian Policy of the Chinese Communist Party, 1921-1959.* Bombay: Asia Publishing House, 1960.

Cheng, Yu-k'uei. *Foreign Trade and Industrial Development of China.* Washington, D.C.: The University Press of Washington, D.C., 1956.

Ch'i, Li. *Shan Kan Ning pien ch'ü shih-lu* (True Accounts of the Shensi-Kansu-Ninghsia Border Region). Yenan?: Chieh-fang she, 1939; reproduced by Center for Chinese Research Materials, Association of Research Libraries, Washington, D.C., 1969.

Chieh-fang jih pao (Liberation Daily). Yenan, 1941-1945.

Chieh-shao nan ch'ü ho-tso she (Introducing the South Ch'ü Cooperative). Hong Kong: Hsin Min Chu Press, 1949.

China. Nung ts'un fu hsing wei yüan hui. *Shan-hsi sheng nung ts'un tiao ch'a* (Shensi Province Rural Survey). Shanghai, 1934.

Chung kung hsi-pei chung-yang chü, tiao-ch'a yen-chiu shih. No place, 1944. *Pien ch'ü kai-liang nung tso wen-t'i* (Problems of improving agricultural work in the border region), 18pp. *Pien ch'ü ti shu-li shih-yeh* (Water conservancy activities in the border region), 33pp. *Pien ch'ü ti lao-tung hu-tsu* (Mutual labor aid in the border region), 94pp.

Chung-kuo kung yeh ho tso hsieh hui. *A Nation Rebuilds*. New York: Indusco, Inc. 1943?

Compton, Boyd. *Mao's China. Party Reform Documents, 1942-44*. Seattle: University of Washington Press, 1952.

Forman, Harrison. *Report from Red China*. New York: Henry Holt, 1945.

Fundamental Laws of the Chinese Soviet Republic. New York: International Publishers, 1934.

Giga, Soichiro. *Chugoku no shakaishugi kigyo* (Socialist Enterprises in China), Kyoto: Minerva Shobo, 1965.

Gillin, Donald G. " 'Peasant Nationalism' in the History of Chinese Communism," *Journal of Asian Studies* 23, 2 (1964): 269-289.

Griffith, Samuel B. *The Chinese People's Liberation Army*. New York: McGraw-Hill, 1967.

Hsiao, Tso-liang. *Power Relations Within the Chinese Communist Movement, 1930-1934*. Seattle: University of Washington Press, 1961-1967.

Hsiao, Tso-liang. *The Land Revolution in China 1930-1934*. Seattle: University of Washington Press, 1969.

Hsü, Yung-ying. *A Survey of the Shensi-Kansu-Ninghsia Border Region*. 2 volumes. New York: International Secretariat, Institute of Pacific Relations, 1945.

Huang, T'ao. *Chung-kuo jen-min chieh-fang chün ti 'san-shih nien* (Thirty Years of the Chinese People's Liberation Army). Peking: Jen-min Press, 1958.

Jen min ch'u pan she, *K'ang Jih chan-cheng shih-ch'i chieh-fang ch'ü kai-k'uang,* (The situation in the liberated regions during the period of the anti-Japanese war). Peking: Jen-min Press, 1953.

Ke, Han. *The Shansi-Hopei-Honan Border Region*. Chungking: New China Information Committee, 1940.

Kim, Ilpyong J. *The Politics of Chinese Communism*. Berkeley: University of California Press, 1973.

Li, Ch'eng-shui, "K'ang Jih chan-cheng shih-ch'i chi-ko jen-min ke-ming ken-chü-ti ti nung-yeh shui-shou chih-tu yü nung-min fu-tan" (The Agricultural taxation system and the peasantry's burden in several people's revolutionary base areas during the period of the anti-Japanese war). *Ching-chi yen-chiu* (Economic Research) 2 (1956): 100-115.

Lindsay, Michael. "The North China Front," *Amerasia,* 7 and 8 (1944): 100-125.

———. "The Taxation System of the Shansi-Chahar-Hopei Border Region," *The China Quarterly* 42 (April-June 1970): 1-15.

Liu, Ta-chung, and Yeh, Kung-chia. *The Economy of the Chinese Mainland, 1933-1959.* Princeton, N.J.: Princeton University Press, 1965.

Mao Tse-tung. *Hsüan-chi, Volumes 1 to 6.* 1947 edition; reprinted by Center for Chinese Research Materials, Association of Research Libraries, Washington, D.C., 1970.

———. *Selected Works, Volumes 1 to 4.* Peking: Foreign Languages Press, 1965.

Mao Tse-tung and others. *New Life in New China.* Calcutta: Purabi Publishers, no date.

Phillips, Ralph W., Johnson, Ray G., and Moyer, Raymond T. *The Livestock of China.* Washington, D.C.: United States Government Printing Office, 1945.

Rue, John E. *Mao Tse-tung in Opposition 1927-1935.* Stanford: Stanford University Press, 1966.

Schran, Peter. *The Development of Chinese Agriculture, 1950-1959.* Urbana, Illinois: University of Illinois Press, 1969.

———. "Unity and Diversity of Russian and Chinese Industrial Wage Policies," *Journal of Asian Studies* 23, 2 (1964): 245-251.

———. "Handicrafts in Communist China," *The China Quarterly* 17 (1964): 151-173.

———. "On the Marxism-Leninism of Chinese Communist Development Strategy," *Mainland China in the World Economy,* Hearings Before the Joint Economic Committee, Congress of the United States, Ninetieth Congress, First Session. Washington, D.C.: U.S. Government Printing Office, 1967, pp. 215-223.

Schwartz, Benjamin. *Chinese Communism and the Rise of Mao.* Cambridge: Harvard University Press, 1951.

———. "The Legend of the "Legend of 'Maoism' "," *The China Quarterly* 2 (1960): 35-42.

Selden, Mark. "The Guerrilla Movement in Northwest China: The Origins of the Shensi-Kansu-Ninghsia Border Region, Parts I and II," *The China Quarterly* 28 (1966): pp. 63-81, and 29 (1967): 61-81.

———. "The Yenan Legacy: The Mass Line," in A. Doak Barnett, ed. *Chinese Communist Politics in Action.* Seattle: University of Washington Press, 1969.

———. *The Yenan Way in Revolutionary China.* Cambridge: Harvard University Press, 1971.

Shan Kan Ning pien ch'ü cheng-fu wei-yuan hui. *Shan Kan Ning pien ch'ü cheng-fu kung-tso pao-kao* (28 nien — 30 nien) (Shensi-Kansu-Ninghsia Border Region Government Work Report, 1939-1941). Yenan?: Border Region Government Secretariat, July 1941.

Shan Kan Ning pien ch'ü cheng-ts'e t'iao-li hui-pien (Compilation of administrative policies and regulations of the Shensi-Kansu-Ninghsia Border Region). Yenan?: Shan Kan Ning pien ch'ü cheng-fu pan kung t'ing pien, May 1944.

Shan Kan Ning pien ch'ü ts'an i hui. *Shan Kan Ning Pien ch'ü ts'an-i hui wen-hsien hui-chi* (Collection of records of the Association of Representatives of the Shensi-Kansu-Ninghsia Border Region). Chung-kuo k'o-hsueh yüan. Li-shih yen-chiu so, Peking. Ti-3 so. Peking: K'o-hsueh Press, 1958.

Shensi-Kansu-Ninghsia Border Region Government.

Brief Account of the Reconstruction in the Shensi-Kansu-Ninghsia Border Region. Unpublished translation, no author, no place, no date.

General Survey of National Education in the Shensi-Kansu-Ninghsia Border Region. Unpublished translation, no author, no place, no date.

Salt Production. Unpublished translation, no author, no place, no date.

Shen, Tsung-han. *Agricultural Resources of China.* Ithaca, N.Y.: Cornell University Press, 1951.

Snow, Edgar. *Red Star Over China.* New York: Grove Press, 1938.

———. *Random Notes on Red China 1936-1945.* Harvard East Asian Monographs 5; Cambridge: Harvard University, 1957.

Snow, Helen (Foster). *Inside Red China.* New York: Doubleday, Doran & company, Inc., 1939.

———. *Notes on the Beginning of the Industrial Cooperatives in China.* Madison? 195-

Stein, Guenther. *The Challenge of Red China.* New York: McGraw-Hill, 1945.

Stewart, Maxwell Slutz. *War-time China.* IPR Pamphlets No. 10; New York: American Council, Institute of Pacific Relations, 1944.

Thornton, Richard C. *The Comintern and the Chinese Communists 1928-1931.* Seattle: University of Washington Press, 1969.

U.S. Senate, Committee on the Judiciary, Subcommittee to Investigate the Administration of the Internal Security Act and Other Internal Security Laws. *The Amerasia Papers: A Clue to the Catastrophe of China.* Washington: U.S. Government Printing Office, 1970. 2 volumes, 1819 pp.

U.S. War Dept. *The Chinese Communist Movement.* Edited by Lyman P. Van Slyke. Stanford: Stanford University Press, 1968.

Van Slyke, Lyman P.: See U.S. War Dept.

Wales, Nym: See Snow, Helen (Foster).

Wei kung-yeh p'in ti ch'üan-mien tzu-chi erh fen-tou (Struggle for complete self-sufficiency in industrial commodities) Yenan: Shan Kan Ning pien ch'ü cheng-fu pan kung t'ing pien, October 1944.

Wittfogel, Karl August. "The Legend of 'Maoism'," Parts 1 and 2, *The China Quarterly* 1 and 2 (1960).

Yakhontoff, Victor. *The Chinese Soviets.* New York: Coward-McCann, 1934.

Yen-an nung-ts'un tiao-ch'a t'uan. *Mi-chih hsien Yang Chia K'ou tiao-ch'a* (Survey of Yang Chia K'ou in Mi-chih Hsien). Peking: San Lien Bookstore, 1957.

Subject Index

Accumulation: 9, inventory, 246; material, 244-246; non-material, 246

Activism: cadre norm, 82; in administration, 86; and incentives, 8, 65-66; and rectification, 84

Administration: 18; improvements, 54, 58-59; methods, 7; rationalization, 100; simplification, 85-86

Administrative organs: employment, 69, 107, 115; production, 63-64, 167, 192-196, 198; rationalization, 100-101

Afforestation, 56, 101, 121

Agrarian revolution: 1, 2, 66; resolution, 49-50; termination, 3, 62; and mobile warfare, 60

Agriculture: 11, 118ff.; development program, 101, 118; employment, 19-21, 104-106, 117, 126; extension, 123; implements, 125, 245; methods of development, 56, 62, 64, 118; migration; 98-99; output, 126-132; quality of season, 126, state assistance, 50

Aid, 168-172, 180, 182-183, 185, 197-198, 205

Animal: husbandry, 63-64, 121-124; manure, 122; pack, 164; product, 33-34, 128, 131-132; stock, 31-32, 119, 123, 161, 226, 244

Anti-Japanese Military Academy, 69, 84, 89

Area: agricultural, 26-30; gross, 15-16; irrigated, 120-121

Armaments: aid, 170-171, 185; employment, 109; enterprises, 76; quality, 153-154; quantity, 160; technology, 144; trade restrictions, 172; variety, 152

Army: 4, 61; income structure, 237-238; nationalist support, 170-171; participation in production, 63-66, 75, 167, 192-196, 198, 251-252; reclamation, 119-120; size, 70; standard of living, 207-209

Autarky: 7-8, 11, 118, 122, 166-168; campaign, 75, 154; in clothing, 123, 155-156; promotion, 172, 251; public sector, 8; scale, 96

Autumn harvest uprising, 2

Banditry, 14, 17

Base areas: anti-Japanese, 4, 5, 10, 12, 15, 249-252; Central-South, 2, 3, 48, 50, 67; Northwest, 3; security, 61-62. See also Border Region, Soviet

Blockade: 4, 6, 11, 49-50, 54, 140, 156, 169-170, 172; effect, 127, 171; running, 8, 57, 169

Bonds, 58. See also credit, loans

Border Region (SKN): 5, 67; bank, 170, 177, 198, 204; first congress, 62, 64; formation 61. See also base area, Soviet

Budget: balanced, 171; deficit, 8, 11,

DATE DUE	
CT DEC 1 0 1981	SEP 1 7 1990
AUG 30 1990	
JUL 1 6 1990	
AUG 1990	
	MP 728